Windows 3.0 By Example

Windows 3.0 By Example

The complete

hands-on-guide

to using

Windows 3.0.

Michael Hearst

M&T Books
A Division of M&T Publishing, Inc.
501 Galveston Drive
Redwood City, CA 94063

Limits of Liability and Disclaimer of Warranty
The Author and Publisher of this book have used their best efforts in preparing the book and the programs contained in it. These efforts include the development, research, and testing of the theories and programs to determine their effectiveness.

The Author and Publisher make no warranty of any kind, expressed or implied, with regard to these programs or the documentation contained in this book. The Author and Publisher shall not be liable in any event for incidental or consequential damages in connection with, or arising out of, the furnishing, performance, or use of these programs.

Library of Congress Cataloging-in-Publication Data

Hearst, Michael

Windows 3.0 By Example / Michael Hearst.
p.   cm.
Includes index.
ISBN 1-55851-180-6
1. Microsoft Windows (Computer programs) I. Title.
QA76.76.W56H43 1990
005.369--dc20   90-21530

Trademarks:
All products, names, and services are trademarks or registered trademarks of their respective companies. This book was produced with files converted with the DATAVIZ® MacLinkPlus®/PC software.
Microsoft, MS-DOS, Excel, and the Microsoft logo are registered trademarks of Microsoft Corporation. Windows, Windows/286 and Windows/386 are trademarks of Microsoft Corporation. 8086, 8088, 80186, 80188, 80286, 80386SX, 80386, 80486 and Intel are trademarks of Intel Corporation. Apple, LaserWriter and LaserWriter NTX are registered trademarks of Apple Computer, Inc. Corel Draw is a registered trademark of Corel Systems Corporation. Hayes is a registered trademark of Hayes Microcomputer Products, Inc. HP, LaserJet and PCL are registered trademarks of Hewlett-Packard Company. IBM and IBM PC are registered trademarks of International Business Machines Corporation. IBM PC-AT and IBM PC-XT are trademarks of International Business Machines Corporation. ITC and ITC Zapf Dingbats are registered trademarks of International Typeface Corporation. Laser 386 and Vtec are trademarks of Video Technology Computers Corporation. The Norton Utilities and Speed Disk are trademarks of Peter Norton Computing, Inc. PageMaker is a registered trademark of Aldus Corporation. Paintbrush is a trademark of ZSoft Corporation. Ami Professional is a registered trademark of Samna Corporation. PC Tools is a trademark of Central Point Software. PostScript is a registered trademark of Adobe Systems, Inc. WordStar is a registered trademark of WordStar International Corporation.

Cover Design: Lauren Smith Design

93 92 91 90   4   3   2   1

Dedication

For Pat Bitten,
Who has always had the Write Idea
and is the current Solitaire Champion.

Contents

WHY THIS BOOK IS FOR YOU

INTRODUCTION

A Brief History of Windows 4

What's the Point? 5

NOTATIONAL CONVENTIONS

Key Names and Labels 9

Key Combinations and Sequences 9

Entering Commands 10

Keyboard Actions 10

Mouse Actions 10

Terminology 11

CHAPTER 1: INSTALLING WINDOWS 3

Open the Box 15

Before You Begin 16

A Word of Warning 16

Running Setup 17

Allocating Memory 20

Some Conclusions about Memory 22

Installing a Printer 22

Setting Up Existing Applications 23

Summary 25

CHAPTER 2: INSIDE WINDOWS

What's a Window? 27

Dialog Boxes 31

System Messages 33

The Icons Have It 34

Of Mice and Menus 34

Moving and Editing 35

Summary 37

Keyboard Summary 37

CHAPTER 3: STARTING WINDOWS

Select a Mode 39

Swap Files 40

Creating a Swap File 41

Windows Layout 44

Exercise 3.1

   The Window Dance 46

Exercise 3.2

   Imagine That 47

Exercise 3.3

   A Whole Lot of Window 48

Exercise 3.4

   All Sizes and Shapes 49

Exercise 3.5

   Ending It All 51

Summary 52

Keyboard Summary 53

CHAPTER 4: PROGRAM MANAGER

Windows in Use 55

Exercise 4.1

   Windows and Icons 57

Exercise 4.2

   Size is Everything 58

Exercise 4.3

   A Cascade of Windows 59

Exercise 4.4
  On the Tiles 61
Groups 63
Rearranging Group Contents 67
Exercise 4.5
  Moving Files 68
Adding Items to Groups 72
Exercise 4.6
  Adding Programs Using File 72
Exercise 4.7
  Adding Programs Using Setup 76
Deleting Items from Groups 79
Exercise 4.8
  Deleting Items 80
Creating a New Group 80
Exercise 4.9
  A New Group 81
Exercise 4.10
  Deleting Groups 85
Menus 85
Exercise 4.11
  Tidy Icons 90
Help 91
Program Manager Summary 93
Keyboard Summary 94

CHAPTER 5: CONTROL PANEL
Running the Program 97
Color 100
Exercise 5.1
  Color Schemes 103

Exercise 5.2
    Design a Scheme 105
Exercise 5.3
    Create a Color 106
Exercise 5.4
    Save the Scheme 110
Fonts 111
        Typefaces and Fonts 111
        Pitch and Point 111
        Screen Fonts 112
        Fonts in Windows 113
Exercise 5.5
    Adding and Removing Fonts 114
Ports 116
Exercise 5.6
    Changing Port Settings 116
Mouse 118
Exercise 5.7
    Mouse Work 118
Desktop 120
Exercise 5.8
    Choose a Pattern 121
Exercise 5.9
    Design a Pattern 122
Exercise 5.10
    Internal Decoration 124
        Cursor Blink Rate 125
        Icon Spacing 125
        Sizing Grid 126
        Border Width 126
Network 126
Printers 126

Exercise 5.11

   Adding a Printer 127

International 138

Keyboard 145

Date/Time 145

Sound 146

386 Enhanced 146

Summary 148

CHAPTER 6: SETUP

What Is It? 149

Changing the Settings 150

Adding Programs 153

Problems with Setup 157

Summary 157

Keyboard Summary 158

CHAPTER 7: FILE MANAGER

What Is It? 159

Basic Actions 161

   To Switch to Another Drive: 161

   To Move or Resize the Directory Tree Window: 161

   To Page Through the Directory Listing: 161

   To Display Subdirectories Under a Directory: 163

   To Display the Contents of a Directory: 163

   To Close a Window: 164

   To Reduce a Window to an Icon: 164

   To Move Between Windows: 164

File Manager Menus 165

   File Menu 166

   Disk Menu 168

   Tree Menu 170

View Menu 171

Options Menu 173

Window Menu 174

Exercise 7.1
 Copying Files 174

Exercise 7.2
 Copying Files in One Window 177

Exercise 7.3
 Copying Files Using Search 179

Exercise 7.4
 Deleting Files 181

Exercise 7.5
 Renaming Files 183

Exercise 7.6
 Associating Files 184

Exercise 7.7
 File Attributes 185

Exercise 7.8
 Formatting Floppy Disks 187

Exercise 7.9
 Adding to the Program Manager 189

Exercise 7.10
 Pruning and Grafting 191

Exercise 7.11
 Closing File Manager 191

Summary 192

Keyboard Summary 192

CHAPTER 8: PRINT MANAGER

Behind the Scenes 195

Printing from DOS 196

Printing from Windows 197

Print Manager Menus 199
    Options Menu 199
    View Menu 201
Problems with Printing 202
Summary 203
Keyboard Summary 203

CHAPTER 9: ODDS AND ENDS

Clipboard 205
Exercise 9.1
  Grab an Image 207
Exercise 9.2
  Pasting to MS-DOS 209
Task List 211
DOS Window 214
Summary 215
Keyboard Summary 215

CHAPTER 10: PAINTBRUSH

What Is It? 217
Paintbrush Layout 218
Paintbrush Tools 220
Exercise 10.1
  Changing Colors 224
Exercise 10.2
  Draw a Line 225
Exercise 10.3
  Boxes and Circles 228
Paintbrush Menus 229
    File Menu 229
Exercise 10.4
  Changing Format 234

Edit Menu 234

View Menu 236

Text Menus 238

Pick Menu 240

Options Menu 241

Exercise 10.5

Pick a Piece 243

Exercise 10.6

Print a Picture 246

Summary 248

Keyboard Summary 248

CHAPTER 11: WRITE

What Is It? 251

Exercise 11.1

Setting the Format 252

Exercise 11.2

Ruler and Tabs 255

Exercise 11.3

Entering, Saving and Formatting Text 257

Cursor Keys 261

Highlighting Text 262

Changing Text 263

Exercise 11.4

Adding Graphics to Write 265

Exercise 11.5

Printing Your Document 265

Summary 267

Keyboard Summary 267

CHAPTER 12: ALL THE C'S

Calculator 271
Exercise 12.1
   Simple Sums 273
Calculator Summary 276
Calculator Keyboard Summary 276
Calendar 277
Calendar Menus 280
Exercise 12.2
   Pick a Date 282
Exercise 12.3
   Alarm Calls 285
Exercise 12.4
   Printing and Saving the Diary 288
Calendar Summary 290
Calendar Keyboard Summary 290
Cardfile..291
Cardfile Menus 293
Exercise 12.5
   Creating a Stack of Cards 297
Cardfile Summary 303
Cardfile Keyboard Summary 304
Clock 305

CHAPTER 13: GAMES PEOPLE PLAY

Reversi 307
Reversi Summary 311
Reversi Keyboard Summary 311
Solitaire 312
Playing the Game 314
Scoring 316
Let's Play 317

Solitaire Summary 321
Solitaire Keyboard Summary 322

CHAPTER 14: NOTEPAD

What Is It? 323
Exercise 14.1
  Using the Program 326
WIN.INI 330
Exercise 14.2
  Logging Your Files 338
Summary 338
Keyboard Summary 339

CHAPTER 15: MORE ACCESSORIES

PIF Editor 341
PIF Editor Summary 349
PIF Editor Keyboard Summary 349
Recorder 350
Macro Tips 352
Creating a Macro 353
Recorder Summary 354
Recorder Keyboard Summary 355
Terminal 355
Window Layout 356
Terminal Summary 359
Terminal Keyboard Summary 360

CHAPTER 16: PROBLEMS IN WINDOWS

What Problems? 361
Earlier Versions 361
MS-DOS Programs 362
Improving Performance 364

Extra RAM 364

Free Memory 364

Tidy Disk 364

Free Disk Capacity 365

Swap File 365

RAM Disks 365

APPENDIX

GLOSSARY

INDEX

Acknowledgements

Before going any further, I must take some time to thank those people who have supported, encouraged and otherwise assisted with the production of this book. No book is the work of any one person: many people make contributions, suggestions, and criticisms, and they should all be acknowledged. Therefore, I want to publicly thank them here.

Michael Cash, my editor, must be mentioned. He provided the initial impetus and encouragement that led to this book.

Brian Iddon, at Microsoft, provided the software and gave a number of valuable tips and suggestions.

Tim Kay at Arche Technologies arranged for me to borrow his 386SX machine.

Michelle Mathews, at Text 100 (Microsoft's PR company in the U.K.) supplied a vast amount of background information and was always very pleasant whenever I called.

Bryan Betts, at MicroScope magazine, made a number of suggestions. He also helped check things out on various machines.

Malcolm Brown, at Star Micronics, helped out with the printer problems. He and his team are to be thanked for solving most of them.

Michael Hearst

PREFACE

I can remember when the only way to get information into a computer was to feed it punch cards and tape. The very first computer I ever used was an ICL 1900 series; it had to be housed in a specially ventilated room, and I had to learn how to decipher the cards manually, because the card punch did not have a facility to print an English translation. Happily, those days are long gone. The computer I am using to write this book sits on one corner of my desk and has more computing power than that huge machine I first used. The way we enter information into the computer has also changed dramatically. With the advent of friendly machines and operating systems, using a computer has never been easier.

Be all that as it may, many people are still intimidated by a blank screen. A computer is simply a tool, like a hammer or a lawn mower: it allows you to do certain things better and more efficiently than you could without its help—try hammering nails with a brick or doing word processing with a typewriter and you'll see what I mean. Most people believe that computers are complex, frighteningly fast, superhuman and awkward to use, but these notions are only partially true. Yes, computers are complex, but the complexities are for the most part hidden from the user. Yes, they are fast, but speed is not everything. No, these machines are not superhuman: if anything, a computer is merely an idiot savant, processing electrical impulses at a rapid pace.

Unfortunately, it is true that computers are awkward to use. Turn on a computer that runs under MS-DOS (the acronym stands for Microsoft Disk Operating System, the most popular computer operating system in the world) and you'll see a thin flashing line called a system prompt. All the prompt does is echo what you type on the keyboard, just as a typewriter echoes what you type onto a sheet of paper. The computer assumes that whatever you have typed is a command; once you press the Enter or Return key the computer tries to carry out your instructions. It is only when it starts acting on that command that problems arise.

Microsoft has long recognized that many people are intimidated by the system prompt, and they have developed an alternative called Windows. In technical terms, Windows is a graphical user interface: in other words, it replaces the bare screen with pretty pictures. Instead of having to enter strings of commands from the keyboard, you use a mouse to point at an icon, click with the mouse to activate the icon, and then control the actions of the program using pull-down menus. Each program normally runs in its own separate window and you can switch from one to the other by simply clicking on it. At least that's the theory.

There have been three versions of Windows, each one tailored to the hardware available when it was introduced. The first version, released in 1983, ran on the original PC and its cousins, which used an 8088 or 8086 microchip. Windows 2.x came out in two versions in 1988; it was used mainly on the IBM PC-AT and other 80286-based machines. (Windows/386, intended specifically for 80386 machines, never really captured the imagination of PC users.) The latest version, Windows 3, is the best yet. It runs on any IBM-compatible PC, although it is most effective on 80386 machines. Quick and easy to use, simple and intuitive, Windows 3 is what Windows always should have been.

This book is about learning to use and master Windows 3. It is intended principally for those people who are new to Windows, new to computing, or both. The book will cover every aspect of the program and how it behaves on different machines; from the initial installation through using the programs that are part of the Windows package. I have deliberately written the book in a light, conversational style to avoid getting bogged down in technical terms. Each time a new term is mentioned it is defined and explained. All terms are also included in a Glossary at the back of the book. I hope you will enjoy reading it as much as I have enjoyed writing it.

Why This Book Is for You

This book is intended to be a hands-on tutorial guide to Windows 3. It will help you learn to use Windows and every one of the bundled programs that come with the main package. Throughout this book, I have included exercises that you can perform to help you get the most out of the software. In addition, each chapter ends with a complete reference guide to the program concerned.

During the course of writing this book, I installed and ran Windows on four separate machines to cover as many eventualities as possible. The machines used are listed below:

1. A Samsung 80286-based AT, running at 10 MHz and fitted with 1 MB of RAM. The machine has two 20 MB MFM hard disks and a single 5.25" 1.2 MB floppy drive.

2. An Arche 80386SX-based system running at 16 MHz and fitted with 8 MB of RAM. The machine has a single 1.2 GB SCSI hard disk and a single floppy drive. (The SCSI drive is phenomenally fast, with an access time that is less than half that of the other machines. Because Windows uses the hard disk extensively, this machine actually produces the best performance of all four machines.)

3. A Vtec Laser 80386-based machine running at 25 MHz and fitted with 2 MB of RAM. The machine has a single 70 MB RLL hard disk and two floppy drives—a 5.25" 1.2 MB drive and a 3.5" 1.44 MB drive.

4. An ALR 80486-based system running at 20 MHz with 4 MB of RAM and a 40 MB ERLL hard disk.

Introduction

Like it or not, MS-DOS is the most widely used operating system in the world. At last count, approximately 40 million computers worldwide used Microsoft's Disk Operating System. That's a phenomenal success story, considering that only ten years ago Microsoft was a tiny software company best known for its programming languages. But Bill Gates and his partner Paul Allen, co-founders of Microsoft, were in the right place at the right time.

In 1981, IBM decided to create a new breed of computers, ones that would sit on a desktop and so could be used by anybody. Because IBM wanted to build the new Personal Computer quickly, they decided to make it from readily available, off-the-shelf parts. IBM built its new machine, all right, but the Intel 8088 chip at its heart was so new that there was no operating system for the fledgling PC.

Gates and Allen had bought the rights to Seattle Computer Products' Q-DOS, an early operating system for the new Intel chips. Microsoft enhanced the product and sold IBM a license to use the operating system—and so the IBM PC was born. Since then Gates, who personally owns 45% of Microsoft, has become the youngest billionaire in the world, and Microsoft has gone from strength to strength. When the PC was launched, Microsoft employed less than 100 people at one site; today the company employs more than 4,000 people worldwide.

Despite its extraordinary success, MS-DOS has a big problem—it has earned a reputation as a very unfriendly piece of software. The operating system controls every aspect of the computer without you, the user, even noticing. And that's the problem. When you turn on the PC, it runs through its built-in tests, loads the operating system, runs your customizing files, CONFIG.SYS and AUTOEXEC.BAT, and then sits there... waiting.... All you can see is a little cursor flashing away rhythmically on an otherwise blank screen. Not the most inspiring introduction to the joys of computing.

In addition, the operating system has remained largely unchanged since its inception. Each new version of DOS has to be downwardly compatible—that is, it must be able to run any software that was written for a previous version—which places severe limitations on what MS-DOS can do. Since the original IBM PC there have been enormous advances in chip technology; the 80386 and 80486 are in widespread use, and the 80586 is due any day. But MS-DOS still has to operate as if the computer were an 8086. So what can be done? The answer is to work around the problem.

Realizing that many people are intimidated by the operating system's blinking prompt, Microsoft developed a graphical user interface (or GUI) called Windows. GUI is technospeak for a system that uses onscreen graphic images instead of a system prompt. The user (in the term GUI) refers to you, and the interface is the visual aspect of the program with which you interact.

A Brief History of Windows

Bill Gates has often said that he would like to see "a PC in every business and one in every home." Windows is one of the keys to making this dream come true. The system is designed to be easy and intuitive to use and to remove any latent fear that people might have with regard to computers.

Windows presents you with a series of pictorial icons, representing programs, files, disks and the like. You use a mouse and pull-down menus to select and run the software that you want to use. One major advantage of the system is that once you master Windows you essentially know how to use 80% of any software that has been designed to run under the environment. Because Windows provides a consistent interface for the software, there are only minor differences between Windows applications. This consistency is an enormous improvement over the confusing multitude of user interfaces common to MS-DOS programs.

Microsoft launched the first version of Windows in 1983. A number of leading hardware manufacturers decided to bundle the software with their machines; at the same time, various software companies saw Windows' potential and began developing applications for the new user interface. A new standard was born. Still, users complained that Windows was slow and there were few serious applications.

In early 1988, Microsoft introduced two new Windows versions almost simultaneously. Windows/286 offered a much-improved interface, with additional support for new printers, enhanced graphic resolutions and new machine configurations. However, because it had to be capable of running software from the original version, Windows/286 could not fully exploit the 286 chip's abilities. Windows/386 took advantage of the 386 chip's memory management capabilities to allow real multitasking, but it was still slow, difficult to set up and use, and hampered by a lack of application programs.

On May 22nd, 1990, Microsoft launched Windows 3 amid a fanfare of publicity. The launch was broadcast by satellite around the United States and is rumored to have cost over a million dollars. What makes this version worth the high-priced hype? Windows 3 is so far advanced from earlier versions that it might as well be an all-new product. Windows 3 provides full and total support for the 80386 microchip and its ability to control memory. On a 386-based system, providing you have sufficient memory, you can have full concurrency—that is, you can effectively run multiple programs simultaneously, as if each were running on a separate PC. Windows 3 is what Windows always should have been and further demonstrates Microsoft's commitment to end users.

What's the Point?

Windows 3 does much more than provide you, the end user, with a standardized interface. Beneath this colorful exterior, the heart of the system has been radically changed. For example, Windows 3 is downwardly compatible with previous versions of Windows only in a limited sense. True, the new program can run software from the earlier versions, but only in the underpowered real mode. Windows 3 is that rare thing in the computer industry—an upgrade that is so radically better than the original that it almost severs its connections with the earlier version.

Windows allows you to transfer images and text from one application to another with ease. Simply select the item you want in one application, copy it to the Clipboard, open the next application and paste the data into place. Because of the way in which Windows 3 works you can do this even from MS-DOS programs. Windows 3 allows you to open an MS-DOS window, letting Windows retreat into the background and operate the computer as if Windows weren't there.

Windows 3 provides three different modes of operation, depending on what type of hardware it's run on. Which mode you use can make a big difference in how Windows performs.

Real mode forces the PC, regardless of what chip it uses, to mimic the 8088/8086 chip that was the heart of the original IBM PC. This means that it can run standard MS-DOS software without any modifications. Any program running in real mode can access a maximum of 1 MB of RAM. If you are using an application that was developed for an earlier version of Windows, the only way you can use that program without encountering problems is to use this mode. You can force Windows 3 to start in real mode by entering WIN /R from the system prompt. On any machine that has less than 1 MB of RAM you can only run Windows 3 in real mode.

Standard mode is fully compatible with the 80286 chip's protected mode. In this mode Windows has access to extended memory and will allow you to switch between non-Windows programs—providing you have enough memory to do so. For example, one of the machines that this book is being written on is an 80386 with 2 MB of RAM. Because 256 KB is used for SMARTDRV.SYS and 768 KB is used for a RAM disk, there is insufficient memory to allow switching between MS-DOS programs from within Windows. I can switch from Windows to MS-DOS and back again, but I cannot have two or more MS-DOS programs open at the same time. If I try to do so the machine locks up tight and needs to be rebooted. To start Windows in standard mode, type WIN /s at the system prompt.

386 enhanced mode is brand new and a big part of what makes Windows 3 so special. Put simply, on an 80386, 80386SX or 80486 system, this mode allows Windows 3 to transform hard disk space into "virtual memory," thus allowing Windows to work with more memory than is actually present. In this mode Windows 3 can perform genuine multitasking of Windows applications and MS-DOS programs. Each program operates independently of the others and each is allocated its own 1 MB chunk of the available RAM. In essence, Windows can cause your computer to act as if it were really multiple PCs, with a number of programs all running simultaneously on the same machine.

Note, however, that if the machine possesses less than 4 MB of RAM then the multitasking will be severely limited or even nonexistent. The amount of RAM available will have a direct bearing on the number of programs that can be multitasked, as each one will require 1 MB for its own use. Thus, as a rule of thumb, if you have 4 MB you can have four programs running simultaneously, 8 MB gives you eight, and so on. (In fact you can do slightly better, but the principle remains the same.) Windows will start in 386 enhanced mode by default if your system hardware matches the specification required of it (see below). However, you can force the program to run in this mode on a machine with less than the optimum system resources, by entering WIN /3 at the system prompt. Under these circumstances, though, the program is likely to run appreciably slower than it would in standard mode on the same machine.

Each mode places a limit on the minimum hardware requirements as follows:

To run in real mode you can use any Intel-based computer, provided it has a minimum of 640 KB of RAM.

To run in standard mode you need an 80286 or better plus a minimum of 1 MB of RAM (640 KB of conventional memory and at least 256 KB of extended memory); the more memory you have, the better.

To run in 386 enhanced mode you must have an 80386, 80386SX or 80486 plus an absolute minimum of 2 MB of free RAM; again, more memory helps.

In addition, regardless of which mode you will be using, you must also have the following:

1. A hard disk with at least 5 MB, and preferably 10 MB, of free capacity.

2. At least one floppy drive.

3. A mouse. Using Windows without a mouse is like trying to dig without a

shovel—it's possible, but exhausting and unnecessarily difficult.

4. If you want to use the Terminal program (the telecommunications linker) you must also have a Hayes-compatible modem.

Notational Conventions

Throughout this book you will see references to certain keystrokes and actions that will produce specific effects. The following section details how these will appear.

Key Names and Labels

The names of the keys appear in bold type as they appear on the keyboard—e.g., **A, M, 1, 9, F3, F10**.

Key labels also appear in bold type, exactly as they appear on the keyboard—e.g., **Enter, Backspace, Del, Ins, Esc**, etc.

The cursor keys are referred to by their direction of operation—**Left, Right, Up** and **Down**—again in bold. On an Enhanced (101- or 102-key) keyboard, you may use either the dedicated cursor keys or those on the numeric keypad (that group of 17 keys to the extreme right of the main keyboard), providing you have **Num Lock** turned off.

Ctrl refers to the Control key. On the majority of keyboards this is placed at the bottom left-hand corner of the keyboard, on the same line that contains the spacebar. In some Windows menus you will see a caret (^) used to refer to the **Ctrl** key; thus, **^O** means to press **Ctrl-O**.

Key Combinations and Sequences

When it is necessary for you to press a number of keys together, they appear in the text joined by a hyphen—for example, **Alt-Space** means you press the **Alt** key and the **Spacebar** at the same time; **Ctrl-F4** means you press **Ctrl** and the function key **F4** at the same time.

If the keys are to be pressed sequentially, then they appear in bold but without a hyphen. Thus, **Alt-Space C** means you press **Alt** and the **Spacebar** together, release them, and then press **C**. **Ctrl Esc F4** means you press **Ctrl**, release it, press **Esc**, release it, and finally press **F4**.

Entering Commands

Throughout this book any text that you are expected to type verbatim appears in bold small caps—e.g., SETUP, WIN, or WIN SOL.

Any additional text or keystrokes that you have to supply as part of a command appear in the same format as the command but enclosed in square brackets. For example, **Alt-F S [filename]** means you press **Alt** and **F** together, press **S,** and then supply a name of your choice as the **[filename]**.

When you are required to press **Enter** at the end of a command you will normally be told to do so. However, when you see the phrase "Enter [text]," you should type the text string and then press **Enter**. For example, "enter WIN" means that at the system prompt you type WIN and then press **Enter** to activate Windows.

Keyboard Actions

Because this book contains hands-on exercises using both the keyboard and the mouse, I have included specific symbols for each one. Therefore, whenever you use the keyboard for an exercise, the symbol at left will appear.

Mouse Actions

When you use the mouse for an action, the symbol for the mouse will appear at the side of the text. Windows 3 has been purposely created to make using a mouse the main option; however, in many instances using the mouse and the keyboard together is faster and more precise. Thus you may find the words **Click-Alt F4** which means click the left-hand mouse button while pressing **Alt** at the same time, and then press **F4**.

Pointing means moving the pointer on the screen until it touches an object. Normally, the pointer appears as a white arrowhead that moves in the same direction you move the mouse. As the pointer moves across list items (filenames or choices on a pull-down menu, for example), these will normally turn inverse—that is, white letters on a black background.

Clicking simply means pressing one of the mouse buttons once. **Double clicking** means pressing one of the mouse buttons twice in rapid succession. Unless otherwise specified, the action always refers to the left-hand button. If you are left-handed you can swap the mouse buttons around (see Chapter 5 for details).

Dragging requires that you point to an object (an icon, a window or a filename, for example) and while still holding down the mouse button move the mouse so that the object moves with you.

Terminology

In this book, certain words and phrases have specific meanings or embody important assumptions. The following section details what these are.

Application programs are, generally, those programs that have been specially written to take advantage of the way in which Windows 3 operates, especially in its use of memory and disk storage. A number of application programs are included with the Windows package. Other application programs include Microsoft Word for Windows, Aldus PageMaker, Microsoft Excel and Amí Professional.

Boot means to supply the machine with power so that it operates. **Reboot** means to restart the PC, either by pressing **Ctrl-Alt-Del** or turning the computer off and then on again. (Make sure you allow the disk to stop spinning before you restore the power if you do the latter.)

Copy means to duplicate something—a file or an icon, for example. The duplicate will be identical to the original. You should note that the normal MS-DOS rules about duplicate filenames and directory names apply under Windows—that is, you cannot have two files or subdirectories of the same name in the same directory.

A **group** is a collection of files that have been gathered together as a single entity. In Windows 3 all groups share a number of characteristics as well as the menus that appear on the group window.

Hard disk means drive C:, the disk that you would normally boot from. To use Windows, you absolutely must have a hard disk. And that hard disk must have between 5 MB and 10 MB of spare capacity—you'll need nearly 4 MB just to install Windows!

Icons are simply pictorial representations of things. Thus the MS-DOS icon is shown as a monitor with DOS written on it, Paintbrush appears as a colorful palette, Clock appears as a clock face, and so on. Windows 3 allows you to change the icons that many programs use.

A **Menu** is a list of commands, options or items. Normally hidden away so that it cannot be seen, it will appear when you click on the menu name or when you press **Alt** and the underlined key letter of the menu.

Modes are the three different ways in which you can operate Windows 3. The most important factor influencing which mode you use is the type of processor chip used in your PC. On any machine that uses an 8086 chip, Windows can run only in **real mode**. On an 80286-based machine the program will normally run in **standard mode**—provided there is sufficient memory available. On machines built around the 80386SX, 80386 or 80486, Windows 3 can operate in **386 enhanced mode**, but to do so effectively you must have at least 4 MB of RAM.

Move means just what it says. Under Windows 3 you can pick up a file, directory, icon or group in one location and move it to another one in a single action. This has the same effect as copying an item and then deleting it from the source location.

MS-DOS means MS-DOS or PC-DOS version 3.2 or later. Whenever possible, Windows has been tested with MS-DOS versions 3.1, 3.2, 3.3 and 4.01.

MS-DOS programs are those programs that are intended to be run from the DOS system prompt and which have not been designed to run under any version of Windows.

Selecting means marking one or more items (such as those in a list of files) ready to be acted upon. Only after the items have been selected do you initiate an action.

Windows means Windows 3, and refers to the program as a whole. When the uncapitalized word **window** appears, it refers to a window in which a program is running.

CHAPTER 1

Installing Windows 3

Open the Box

Inside the Windows 3 box you will find an envelope containing a packet of disks and the license agreement, a manual, a runtime version of Asymetrix Toolbook, and half a dozen pieces of paper. Normally you probably wouldn't bother with the pieces of paper, but in this case I suggest you read them.

One sheet contains an impressive list of hardware that has been tested for compatibility with Windows 3. Some of the names on the list are prefixed by an asterisk, which means that the machines concerned need to be dealt with in a specific way during installation.

Another sheet offers a list of companies that have begun production of, or have already released, Windows 3-compatible versions of their software. At the latest count well over 500 companies were preparing Windows 3-based software, and the number is growing daily—proof positive that Windows 3 is the most significant software development of the decade.

The most important piece of paper in the package is probably the registration card. Even if you have never registered a program in your life, you should register your copy of Windows 3. Why? Registering software allows the manufacturer to gauge the public acceptance of the program and to build a picture of where the program is being used and by whom. From the user's point of view, returning the registration card brings a range of privileges to make life easier. Registered users get advance notice of new products, preferential prices on upgrades and better technical support, among other benefits.

When you open the envelope you will find either five 1.2 MB 5.25" floppies or seven 720 KB 3.5" ones. The 360 KB 5.25" disks have to be specially ordered, which implies that Microsoft intends that the program be used only on machines with high-density drives—that is, systems at least as powerful as the PC-AT.

Before You Begin

You will need about 20 to 30 minutes to install Windows 3 completely, depending on how many printers you include. You cannot interrupt the installation once it has begun. You cannot go partway through the routine, stop and use your PC for something else, and then continue where you left off. Either you're installing the software or you're not!

If you are updating from a previous version of Windows, I suggest you rename the directory that contains the old files. If you don't have a utility that will allow this, you can create a new directory by entering MD C:\WIN-OLD at the system prompt. Assuming that the Windows version you're updating from is in a directory named WINDOWS, you can copy all the files to the directory you just created by entering COPY C:\WINDOWS*.* C:\WIN-OLD. Once the files have been copied enter DEL \WINDOWS to delete the files from the original directory. Answer **Y** when prompted and all the files will be erased. Finally, enter RD WINDOWS to remove the old directory. (If you have subdirectories under your WINDOWS directory, you'll need to repeat this process for each of them before DOS will let you remove the directory.)

To install Windows 3 you'll need at least 5 MB (that's 5,242,880 bytes) of free space on your hard disk. You can install it in less space than that, but in the end it's not worth it. To find out how much free disk space you have available, enter DIR or CHKDSK at the system prompt.

A Word of Warning

There is a well-documented incompatibility between Windows 3 and certain PCs equipped with specific types of hard disks. On these systems, using the Windows 3 disk-caching program, SMARTDRV.SYS, can cause damage to the hard disk's File Allocation Table, resulting in irretrievable data loss. This damage can be substantial and far-reaching. The problem has been found to occur on hard disks which have been partitioned using Ontrack Computer Systems' Disk Manager program and the device driver DMDRV.BIN. Apparently, the problem can also occur on other hard disks that have more than the 1024 cylinders DOS can deal with.

At this time there is no easy answer available. If you have a nonstandard hard disk, or one that has been partitioned using Disk Manager, your best course of action is to avoid the problem by not installing SMARTDRV.SYS. Microsoft has promised to release an updated version of SMARTDRV.SYS to all registered users—which is a good reason for filling in and returning the registration card.

On the plus side, some MS-DOS programs seem to work much faster when used from the Windows environment. In particular, those that are heavily keyboard dependent, like word processors, seem to run about 50% faster. Why? I'm not sure. Windows offers better control over the keyboard than MS-DOS itself; perhaps the fact that you can vary the keyboard speed results in better performance.

Before you install Windows, make a checklist of the hardware that is included in your system. It's particularly important that you know what type of display adapter (VGA or EGA, for example) and monitor you are using and what kind of memory you have. The Windows Setup program will check your hardware and take its best guess, but you'll need to confirm that it has guessed correctly.

Running Setup

Assuming all's in order, take the Windows 3 disk labeled Disk 1 and place it into the corresponding drive (usually drive A:). Log onto the drive by entering **A:**, and then enter **SETUP** to begin the installation routine.

After a short time you will be presented with a message bidding you welcome to Setup. From here you can press **F1** for on-line help. Pressing **F3** will terminate the installation, both at this screen and at any time further on into the installation. To begin the installation, just press **Enter**.

You will be asked to specify a drive and directory where you want Windows 3 installed. By default this is always **C:\WINDOWS**—hence the reason for renaming any directory containing an older version of Windows. If you want to designate another drive, use the cursor keys to move back to the drive letter, delete it, and then type the new drive designator. If you want to use a different directory, erase the default and type your preference. When you are satisfied with the choice, press **Enter** again.

The next part of the program is quite perceptive. It will check all your system resources, from the monitor type to the keyboard configuration, and present you with a list of what it finds. If you are installing the program on a computer configured to the American standard, the list will almost certainly be correct.

```
Windows Setup

    Setup has determined that your system includes the following hardware
    and software components. If your computer or network appears on the
    Hardware Compatibility List with an asterisk, press F1 for Help.

        Computer:          MS-DOS or PC-DOS System
        Display:           EGA
        Mouse:             No mouse or other pointing device
        Keyboard:          Enhanced 101 or 102 key US and Non US keyboards
        Keyboard Layout:   US
        Language:          English (American)
        Network:           Network not installed

        No Changes:        The above list matches my computer.

    If all the items in the list are correct, press ENTER to indicate
    "No Changes." If you want to change any item in the list, press the
    UP or DOWN ARROW key to move the highlight to the item you want to
    change. Then press ENTER to see alternatives for that item.


  ENTER=Continue  F1=Help  F3=Exit
```

Windows Setup System Identification

If your computer is configured for another country's standard, the list may well be wrong in minor details. I've never seen the keyboard layout selected for anything except a U.S. keyboard. For PC users in the U.K. (like me), that choice won't work properly. On a U.K. keyboard, for example, **Shift-3** produces a Sterling Pound sign (£), whereas in the U.S. it normally produces a crosshatch (#).

To change this setting, or any of the others, move the highlighter bar up using the cursor keys until it overlays the area you want to change. Once there, press **Enter** to pop up a menu of possible configurations. Select the one you want, again using the cursor keys, then press **Enter** again. You will be returned to the Setup screen with your choice now set as the new default. Once you're satisfied with the list of parameters, press **Enter** to begin the actual installation.

The program creates the necessary directories on your hard disk and begins copying the files. After a while it will ask you to remove Disk 1 and replace it with Disk 2. Do so and press **Enter** to continue the process.

Suddenly the screen vanishes and you find yourself in a true GUI window. You

18

are not yet truly into Windows 3; this step of the installation is a sort of proto-Windows. At this point you cannot use the program to do anything other than continue the installation. A word of warning: don't try to activate any memory-resident program you may have loaded, or you may cause the machine to hang up completely.

The screen contains three pre-checked options:

Set up Printers
Set up Applications Already on Hard Disk
Read On-line Documents

You can deselect any option by clicking on it. However, as this is the first time you are installing Windows, I suggest that you accept all three options by just pressing **Enter**.

The installation continues with more files being copied. After a while you will be asked to remove Disk 2 and replace it with Disk 3. Do so and press **Enter** again or click on the button that says **OK** to continue the installation. Setup continues to prompt you for new disks and copy files until all the necessary ones, plus those device drivers you selected (whether you knew it or not) on the previous screen, have been installed.

In the next stage, Windows Setup needs to change your CONFIG.SYS and AUTOEXEC.BAT files. You can allow the program to do this for you (the fastest option), or you can review the changes before they are made (a better option, because you can see what is going on). If you'd like, you can choose to make the changes later by having Setup write the recommended files to the disk for you.

Click on the second option using the mouse. Or, if you prefer to use the keyboard, press **Down**, and then press **Enter**. You will see two windows, one above the other, the top one containing your current AUTOEXEC.BAT and the bottom one containing the suggested changes. The usual change at this point is to ensure that the WINDOWS directory is in your PATH statement. If you don't have a PATH statement, the program will create one for you. Press **Enter** to accept the changes and your original AUTOEXEC.BAT will be renamed to AUTOEXEC.OLD while the new file will be written to your disk as AUTOEXEC.BAT.

Allocating Memory

Next come the changes to CONFIG.SYS. Windows 3 is a memory-hungry little beast that needs enormous amounts of RAM to operate correctly; therefore, it will hog as much of the available memory as possible. Exactly what changes it will suggest depend on the type of machine you are using.

On the Samsung, for example, I had a RAM disk of 320 KB set up. Windows reduced it to 128 KB in size and took the remaining 192 KB of RAM for itself. There was no room for SMARTDRV.SYS, so the program didn't bother with it. It did replace the HIMEM.SYS device driver—the version supplied with Windows 3 differs from that supplied with previous versions. You can use old versions of Windows with the new HIMEM.SYS but not vice versa. One annoying note: Setup copied the HIMEM.SYS file into the root directory of the hard disk and amended the CONFIG.SYS file accordingly with the line **DEVICE=C:\HIMEM.SYS**. I like to keep the root directory as clean as possible, but Setup has no provision for placing the device driver anywhere else. The result is that I had to move it myself later and manually edit CONFIG.SYS to accommodate the change. The funny thing is, Setup stores SMARTDRV.SYS in the WINDOWS directory, so why can't it do the same thing with HIMEM.SYS?

The Arche 80386SX had more than enough memory available for SMARTDRV.SYS to be fully installed—after all, 8 MB should be enough for just about anything. The machine originally had all of its extended memory configured as a RAM disk. The original CONFIG.SYS looked like this:

```
FILES=30
BUFFERS=30
COUNTRY=044,,C:\DOS\COUNTRY.SYS
INSTALL C:\DOS\SHARE.EXE
DEVICE=C:\WINDOWS\RAMDRIVE.SYS 7168 /E
```

The Windows Setup program added two lines, the first installing HIMEM.SYS and the second installing SMARTDRV.SYS with a normal cache size of 2048 bytes and a minimum cache of 1024 bytes. In other words, it took 2 MB of RAM and this speeded up Windows enormously. While the Arche machine is only a 16 MHz 80386SX, it has the greatest system resources of all the machines used for this book.

This is the only one of the four machines that will allow Windows to run in 386 enhanced mode by default—but for all, that the program still runs slower on this machine than it does on the Laser 80386.

The Laser 386 has 2 MB of RAM, of which 64 KB is used as a system cache. The remaining 1344 KB was originally set up as a RAM disk. During the Windows 3 Setup, the program installed SMARTDRV.SYS using 256 KB of the RAM and then reduced the size of the RAM disk to 256 KB—ignoring the remaining 832 KB of extended memory.

As an experiment, I reinstated the RAM disk with all 1088 KB—the Windows allocation of 256 plus the unused bit. When I rebooted, however, Windows wouldn't run in any mode, because there wasn't enough memory for it! Gradually, through trial and error, I found that using a RAM disk of 768 KB allowed sufficient memory for everything. But why didn't the Windows setup allow this much? I don't know and haven't been able to find out.

The CONFIG.SYS on the Laser 386 now looks like this:

```
FILES=30
BUFFERS=10
COUNTRY=044,,C:\DOS\COUNTRY.SYS
INSTALL C:\DOS\SHARE.EXE
DEVICE=C:\DOS\HIMEM.SYS
DEVICE=C:\WINDOWS\SMARTDRV.SYS 256 256
DEVICE=C:\WINDOWS\RAMDRIVE.SYS 768 /E
```

The Files command, which specifies how many different files can be open at any one time, must be set to a minimum of eight for running MS-DOS. Because I use WordStar, which is heavily file dependent, and PageMaker, which is even more so, I have had to increase the number of files to 30. Each one above the minimum eight uses an additional 48 bytes of RAM. Therefore the 30 files use up 1056 bytes or just over 1 KB.

Each buffer takes up 528 bytes; in this configuration, therefore, the 10 of them use 5280 bytes, or just over 5 KB. Normally, on an 80386 machine with a 70 MB hard disk, you would set the number of buffers to at least 20 and preferably 30. But because SMARTDRV.SYS takes over some of the activities of the BUFFERS command, you can safely reduce the number to 10. Don't make it less than this or you will run into problems.

On the ALR machine, which had 4 MB of extended memory, I had a lot of problems getting the machine to recognize that it had this much RAM in the first place. Eventually, after much messing about and numerous phone calls to ALR, I managed to convince the system to recognize the extra RAM. Only then was I able to install Windows. As with the Arche machine, SMARTDRV.SYS took 2 MB for itself and left 2 MB for a RAM disk. The strangest thing of all was that this 486 machine was actually slower at running Windows than either of the 386 machines.

Some Conclusions about Memory

Having played about with various memory configurations, RAM allocations, and what have you, I found that Windows would run in standard mode by default on both the Laser and the ALR machines, but each could be forced to run in 386 enhanced mode if I entered WIN /3 at the system prompt. In this mode the Laser ran Windows faster than the ALR machine, even though the latter uses a superior chip.

On the Samsung AT, Windows ran in real mode only; it was impossible to get it to run in any other mode. Using Windows 3 on this 80286, with its very limited resources, was a disaster. It worked, but only barely, and the program was dreadfully slow, cumbersome, unwieldy and uncooperative. That's not to say that the Samsung 80286 is an inferior machine—but Windows needs much more in terms of resources to run properly.

On the Arche 80386SX-based machine, Windows ran in 386 enhanced mode by default, because there is so much RAM available. Still, the program actually ran noticeably more slowly in this mode than it did in standard mode on either the 80386SX or the 80386. It appears that Windows always runs slower in 386 enhanced mode, regardless of the system resources available and the type of chip being used.

Installing a Printer

At the next stage of the installation, Setup allows you to install a printer. To be more precise, it installs one or more printer drivers—you'll have to configure each printer separately. From this point on, it looks as though you are already in Windows, but you are still not there. The screen display shows a large box, covering almost half of the screen area, with a highlighter bar covering the first name in the list of printers. Using the cursor keys, move this highlighter to the name of the printer you want to install. If your printer isn't listed, you will have to choose an emulation. For example, most laser printers can emulate a Hewlett-Packard LaserJet Series II. My StarScript printer (actually a Star Laser 8II with added PostScript emulation) is not on the list, but because it emulates an Apple LaserWriter I can install it as that.

If you've been using a previous version of Windows, don't assume that your printer emulation will remain the same—Microsoft has completely rewritten the printer drivers for Windows 3. Under Windows/286, my StarScript used to run perfectly well as an Apple LaserWriter NTX. So when I first installed Windows 3, I used that emulation for the printer. The result? The printer began throwing out error messages as if there were no tomorrow. In the end, by trial and error, I found that it had to be installed as a plain Apple LaserWriter. Oddly enough, that emulation didn't work correctly running from Windows/286!

Select the name of the printer driver you want to install and then press **Enter**. You may have to swap disks as part of the printer installation. If you want to install additional printers you can do so in exactly the same way. When you're finished, click on the button marked **OK**. (If you're using the keyboard, press **Tab** until the **OK** key is highlighted and then press **Enter**.)

Setting Up Existing Applications

The next stage of Setup looks on your hard disk for existing programs—Windows applications and MS-DOS programs alike—and configures them to run within the Windows environment. This part of the program is much faster and more accurate than you could possibly be if you were to install applications one by one. You have three options: All Drives; Path Only (that is, only those directories listed in your system's PATH statement); or specific drives.

Which option you select depends on how you have set up your hard disk. After you make your choice and click on OK, Setup searches for programs in the specified area. As it searches, you'll see a display telling you, in percentage terms, how much of your disk the program has searched. The Setup program is almost certain to find any Windows applications you have installed on your system. It will also look for MS-DOS programs about which it has information; many, but not all, major non-Windows applications are on this list. Once the search is finished the screen changes to display a list of the applications that have been found.

You now select which of these will be set up for use in Windows. Chances are the program will have found many more applications than you will want to include. You can select the specific ones you want to set up by clicking on each program's name in the list box—as you make your selections, each name will be highlighted in inverse video. When you have finished, click on **Add->**. The names of the programs you selected will move from the left-hand window to the right-hand window. (If you make a mistake, just reverse the process: Select the names in the right-hand window and click on the **<-Remove** button.)

Because the Setup program can only search for programs it knows about, you will find that many of your current programs are not included. It is also possible that some programs you didn't know existed will be displayed. If you want to include all your programs and run them from within Windows, you will have to install them separately. (We'll cover this topic later.)

Once you press **Enter**, or click on **OK**, Setup creates an icon for each application and organizes the icons into program groups; for each MS-DOS program, it creates a PIF file. (PIF stands for Program Information File, a special file that Windows needs in order to run most MS-DOS programs properly. See Chapter 15 for more details.) A program group is, basically, a collection of programs that share certain attributes. The process is automatic and uninterruptible. You can change the groups later, but for now just let Setup get on with it.

Once the groups have been created, Setup activates the Windows Notepad and begins to display the .TXT files that have been installed. These "read me" files contain a wealth of information that is not included in the manual. You can read them now or leave them until later. After you have finished reading a file, press **Alt-Spacebar C** or **Alt-F4** to close the Notepad.

You now get a message telling you that Windows 3 has been installed, and you are provided with three options:

Reboot will restart your machine (just as if you had pressed **Ctrl-Alt-Del**) and activate the changes that have been made within your CONFIG.SYS and AUTOEXEC.BAT files. This is the preferred option.

Restart Windows will end the Setup program and activate Windows immediately. You may find, however, that Windows does not work correctly. In some cases it may not work at all—especially if Setup has changed the memory allocations. This is the least preferred option.

Return to MS-DOS takes you out of the Setup program and drops you back to the system prompt. When I first installed Windows 3 I chose this option, because I used The Norton Utilities' Format Recover program to save crucial information about the files on my disk. I also used Norton's Speed Disk program to compress the files on the disk in preparation for the next step in the Windows installation process. (As you'll see, once you start Windows you need to add a huge file to your disk, and it's best to compress the disk first.)

Select whichever option you wish by clicking on it. Windows is now installed and ready for use—but you will probably have to fiddle around with things first to get optimum performance.

Summary

There is a known incompatibility between SMARTDRV.SYS and certain types of hard disks, including those partitioned with Disk Manager.

Fill in and return the registration card. It is more than worth your while.

If you are replacing an old version of Windows, rename the old directory before installing Windows 3. (You may have to physically move the old files to accomplish this step.) Don't delete the old version until you're certain that Windows 3 and all your old applications run smoothly on your system.

Before you install Windows, make a note of what hardware you are using. In particular, be sure you know what type of monitor you are using and what kind of memory you have installed, as these components can have a marked effect on Windows.

Install your printer as part of Setup. It's quicker and easier to do it here at this point rather than later. However, if your printer is not on the list of supported models, you will need to choose another printer that emulates the one you have.

Existing Windows applications may not run properly in Windows 3 if you use anything other than real mode. Make sure you get updated versions of old Windows software if you want to use Windows 3 to its full advantage.

After you have installed Windows, reboot your system to activate any changes the Setup program has made. You may wish to return to the MS-DOS system prompt and compress the files on your hard disk before you reboot.

CHAPTER 2

Inside Windows

One of the most appealing aspects of Windows is its consistent set of commands. Someone once dubbed Windows a WIMP interface—a humorous acronym for "windows, icons, mice and pull-down menus." There's nothing wimpy about Windows, but those four elements are indeed at the heart of the program.

Because every Windows application has a similar look and feel, when you've learned how to use one program, you know how to get started in any program. Before going any further, let's take a close look at the features and elements you're likely to see in every Windows application.

What's a Window?

Windows applications, as the name implies, run in windows—rectangular areas of the screen that can be opened, closed, moved and resized as you wish. You can have multiple windows open and visible onscreen; in 386 enhanced mode, you can even run MS-DOS applications within windows.

There are two main types of windows. Although they share certain similarities, there are slight differences in the way you work with them.

Application windows are those in which programs run. This type of window always has a menu bar, and it can be shrunk to an icon that sits on the main Windows background.

Document windows are used within applications. In a Windows word processing program, for example, you might be able to edit two or more documents at a time, each in its own window. This type of window has no menu bar; you execute commands using the application's menus. Some document windows can be shrunk to an icon, but the icon remains within the application window.

Every window consists of a number of subsidiary elements, most of which you can control to some extent. Although there are exceptions, most windows contain the following common elements.

The entire window is surrounded by a **border**. By default, an active window's border is gray, while the border of an inactive window is white. You can resize most windows by clicking on this border and then dragging it. If you click on a corner, you can drag the two sides of the window that are associated with that corner. For example, clicking on the bottom left corner allows you to resize the base and the left side of the window at the same time.

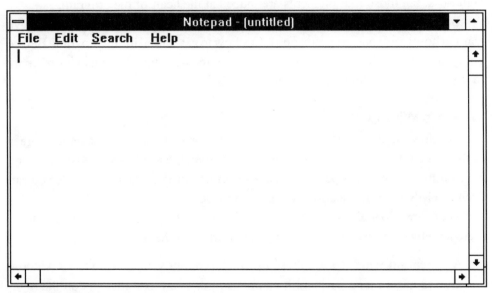

Typical Application Window

Inside the border, at the top left-hand corner of the main window, is a small box containing a horizontal line. Click on this box to drop down the **Control menu**, which allows you to control the major aspects of the window. Every window— application windows, document windows, and dialog boxes—will normally have its own Control menu. An application window typically contains the following commands:

Restore is used to expand an icon to a window, or to shrink a full-size application to a window, in its former size and position.

Move allows you to move the window using the keyboard.

Size allows you to change the size and shape of the window using the keyboard.

Minimize is used to reduce a window to an icon.

Maximize enlarges a window or an icon so that it fills the entire screen.

Close can be used to close a window and shut down the program running within it. If you execute this choice from the Program Manager, you will quit Windows itself.

Switch To... calls up the Task List, which allows you to move directly to another program.

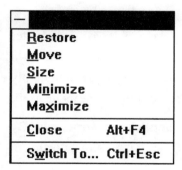

Control Menu

The Control menu for a document window may contain the **Next** command, which allows you to move between document windows.

Running along the top of the window is the **title bar**. The window title may be the name of the program that is running within the window, the name of a document, or the name of a group of icons. By default, the title bar for an active window is a hazy cyan color. You can move an open window, as long as it is not maximized, by dragging the title bar. Move the mouse pointer to the bar, click and hold the mouse button, and then move the mouse. The open window will follow your movements. Depending on the speed of the computer and the monitor, you may notice a slight delay as the screen is refreshed, especially if you move the mouse rapidly.

At the top right-hand corner of the window, to the right of the title bar, are two boxes. The first contains an arrow that points downward; it is called the **Minimize** button. Clicking here will reduce the window to an icon at the bottom of the screen. Next to it is an arrow that points upward; this is known as the **Maximize** button. Clicking here will enlarge the window so that it fills the entire screen. When an application is running in this mode, the Maximize button is replaced by the **Restore** button, which contains a two-headed arrow. Clicking on this button will return the window to the size and position it occupied before it was enlarged.

Immediately below the title bar is the **menu bar**. The choices available differ from application to application. Clicking on any of these choices will pull down a menu from which you then select commands. If you open a menu inadvertently you can close it again by clicking anywhere on the screen outside the menu itself.

Within the border, and below the menu bar, is the **application workspace**. By default, this appears as a very pale yellow. It is within this area that document windows operate for specific applications.

Somewhere on the screen you will see a white arrow. This is the **mouse pointer**; you use it to manipulate the menus, icons and windows themselves. Any movement you make with the mouse will be reflected by the pointer—move the mouse left and the pointer moves to the left side of the screen. The pointer moves only when you move the mouse. When the mouse pointer is within a document window where you can edit text or graphics, it may change to a thin line called a **selection cursor**.

Scroll bars are horizontal or vertical regions that appear at the side or bottom of an active window when there is more material than can be shown. Each scroll bar contains a square marker and terminates in a pair of arrows that point in opposite directions; you click on these arrows to move through the display and view the missing material. You can use scroll bars to page through list boxes and text as follows:

a. Clicking on the arrowheads scrolls the display (usually one line at a time) in the direction of the arrowhead you click on.

b. Clicking on the scroll bar itself will page through the list or text a screenful at a time. The direction in which the window scrolls depends on whether you click above or below the marker.

c. You can drag the marker button along the scroll bar. As you do so, the material in the window moves with you. This facility is extremely useful for very quick searches through a list box.

d. In some (but not all) list boxes, you can click on any name in the list and then type the initial letter of the entry you're looking for. The highlight will immediately jump to the first entry in the list that begins with that letter.

Dialog Boxes

A **dialog box** is a special sort of window that lets you exchange information with an application. Typically, it contains a list of options, as many as a dozen or so, from which you make selections. You can point directly to different areas of a dialog box with the mouse, or you can use the **Tab** key to move from one area to another. If an option includes an underlined letter, you can select that option by pressing **Alt** and the letter simultaneously.

Windows gives you different ways to use a dialog box, depending on the type of information you are expected to supply.

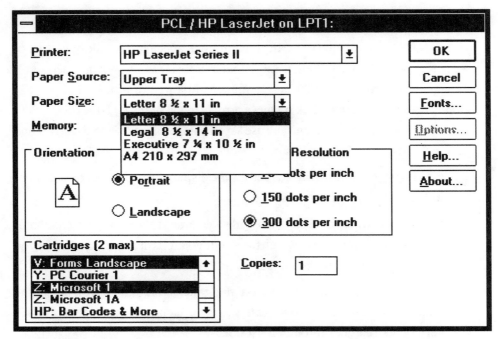

Typical Dialog Box

Command buttons carry out commands or run programs. Many dialog boxes include command buttons labeled **OK** and **Cancel**. To accept the choices you've made in the dialog box, click on **OK**. To close the dialog box without taking any action, click on **Cancel**. Using the keyboard, you can choose a command button by pressing the **Tab** key until the button is highlighted, and then pressing **Enter**. An ellipsis (**...**) means pressing the command button will reveal another dialog box. A pair of right brackets (**>>**) means that pushing the button will expand the dialog box.

Text boxes let you type information directly into the dialog box. Windows may suggest a default entry for you.

Check boxes let you decide whether an option should be turned on or off. When the option is turned on, the box contains an X. To change the setting for a check box, click on it with the mouse, or highlight the option and press **Spacebar**.

Option buttons (sometimes called **radio buttons**) let you select a single option from a group of available choices. The different alternatives are depicted by small circles; when you select one, a black dot appears within the circle.

List boxes let you choose one or more entries from a list. Whenever you open a file, for example, you will typically choose the filename from a list box. You can click on your choice with the mouse, or scroll through the list with the cursor keys and highlight your choice using the **Spacebar**.

Drop-down list boxes are a special form of list. When one first appears, you will see only a single line. You can scroll through the entires in the list using the cursor keys. Clicking on the arrow at the right of the box or pressing **Alt-Down** causes the list to expand.

System Messages

Windows issues a **system message** when something goes wrong, or is about to go wrong—for example, when the printer runs out of paper. Windows displays the message to tell you what has happened, and it may suggest possible methods of fixing the problem. A system message will pop up over any active application.

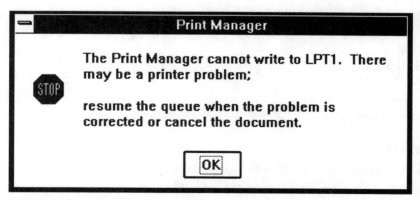

System Message

The Icons Have It

Windows uses icons—pictorial representations of programs and windows—to eliminate the need to type command strings. You can't change the size of an icon, but you can move them around the screen. There are three types of icons.

You can shrink any active program to an **application icon** that sits on the Windows desktop. A single click on the icon brings up the program's Control menu; a double click restores the application.

Some programs allow you to shrink an open file to a **document icon**. You can move and rearrange these icons only within the application window of the program that created them. Mouse clicks work the same here as they do with application icons.

Within the Program Manager only (see Chapter 5), you can create a special type of document icon called a **program item icon**. This type of icon contains all the information needed to start a program by double clicking or pressing **Enter**.

```
┌─────────────────────┐
│ File                │
├─────────────────────┤
│ New                 │
│ Open...             │
│ Save                │
│ Save As...          │
│ Print               │
│ Page Setup...       │
│ Printer Setup...    │
├─────────────────────┤
│ Exit                │
└─────────────────────┘
```

Typical Pull-down Menu

Of Mice and Menus

To carry out commands within Windows applications, you make selections from pull-down menus. The options you see on the menu bar will vary between applications, but almost all programs have a **File** menu, which lets you open, close and save files, as well as a **Help** menu.

The choices available from a pull-down menu are shown by bold-faced words. Additional information about menu choices is shown by the following distinctive typographic treatments.

- When a menu option is currently unavailable, it is shown in light gray letters.

- An ellipsis (...) to the right of the selection means that the choice pulls up a dialog box.

- A checkmark means that the selection is a toggle that is currently turned on.

- If there is an optional keyboard shortcut, the key combination is shown to the right of the menu option.

- A solid triangle at the right of a selection means that choosing it will cause a second, cascading menu to appear.

To select a menu option using the mouse, simply click on the name in the menu bar, and then click on the menu item.

You can use the keyboard to make menu selections as well. If the menu name has an underlined letter, press **Alt** and the letter to pull down the menu. You can also press **Alt** or **F10** to move the highlighter to the menu bar and then use the **Left** and **Right** keys to step from one menu item to the next. Once the menu is revealed, use the **Up** and **Down** arrows to move among the items, pressing **Enter** when your choice is highlighted. If the menu item has an underlined letter, you can press the letter to select the item immediately.

Moving and Editing

To move between windows using the mouse, simply click anywhere within the window you wish to activate. You can also double click on the background or select **Switch To...** from the Control menu to display the Task List, a pop-up dialog box that lets you move quickly between open application windows.

A collection of keyboard shortcuts let you switch windows easily without the mouse. **Alt-Esc** and **Alt-Tab** cycle between open application windows. **Ctrl-Tab** (or **Ctrl-F6**) does the same for document windows. To select the Control menu for an application window, press **Alt-Spacebar**; for a document window, the keyboard shortcut is **Alt-Hyphen**. From anywhere in Windows, you can press **Ctrl-Esc** to pop up the Task List.

Positioning the editing cursor with the mouse is easy—just point and click. When it comes to moving through text, certain keyboard shortcuts are useful throughout the Windows environment. The **Up** and **Down** keys move one line at a time, while the **Left** and **Right** keys move one character at a time. **Home** and **End** move the insertion point to the beginning and end of the current line, respectively. **Page Up** and **Page Down** move the cursor up and down by a screenful; **Ctrl-Left** and **Ctrl-Right** move a word at a time; and **Ctrl-End** and **Ctrl-Home** jump to the beginning or end of a document. **Delete** erases the character to the right of the cursor, while **Backspace** erases the character to the left of the cursor.

In most Windows applications, you select a block of text and then act on it. To highlight text using the mouse, point to the beginning of the block, then click and drag the mouse to the end of the block. You can also highlight a text block by clicking on the beginning point and then holding down the **Shift** key and clicking on the end point. A double click highlights the current word.

Using the keyboard, you can extend a selection by pressing the **Shift** key and moving the cursor—for example, **Shift-Home** selects from the current insertion point to the beginning of the line, while **Shift-Ctrl-Right** extends the selection one word to the right.

When a block of text is highlighted, pressing **Delete** or **Backspace** will erase the selection, as will typing any character. **Shift-Delete** cuts the selection and places it on the Clipboard, while **Ctrl-Ins** leaves the selected text in place and copies it to the Clipboard. **Shift-Ins** inserts the contents of the Clipboard at the insertion cursor. (See Chapter 9 for more details about this aspect of Windows.) One of Windows' friendliest functions is **Undo**—pressing **Alt-Backspace** will restore an inadvertent deletion or remove the most recently typed text.

Summary

- Windows' consistent user interface means that keystrokes and commands work the same in all applications.

- There are two classes of windows: application windows and document windows.

- Most windows have certain common features, including borders, a title bar, a Control menu, and Minimize and Maximize buttons.

- Dialog boxes allow you to exchange information with Windows in consistent ways.

- System messages provide notice of a fault and may suggest possible causes and cures.

- Icons are pictorial representations of windows programs and documents. They can be moved, but not resized.

- Most Windows commands can be executed by using pull-down menus. You can navigate through these menus using a mouse or the keyboard.

Keyboard Summary

Alt	Move highlighter to menu bar.
Alt-Backspace	Undo previous edit.
Alt-Esc	Switch to next application window.
Alt-F4	Terminate the current program or dialog box.
Alt-Hyphen	Open document window Control menu.
Alt-letter	Choose menu, dialog box option, or menu item identified by underlined letter.
Alt-Spacebar	Open application window Control menu.
Alt-Tab	Switch to next application window.
Backspace	Delete character to left.
Ctrl-End	Move to end of document.

Ctrl-Esc	Activate Task List.
Ctrl-F4	Close document window.
Ctrl-F6	Move between document windows.
Ctrl-Home	Move to beginning of document.
Ctrl-Ins	Copy selected text to Clipboard.
Ctrl-Left	Move one word to left.
Ctrl-Right	Move one word to right.
Ctrl-Tab	Move between windows and icons.
Delete	Delete character to right.
Enter	Execute highlighted command or program.
Esc	Cancel current operation.
F1	Activate Help program.
F10	Move highlighter to menu bar.
Shift-	With direction key, extend text selection.
Shift-Del	Cut text to Clipboard.
Shift-Ins	Paste text from Clipboard.
Shift-Tab	Move between dialog box options in reverse order.
Spacebar	Selects or clears the highlighted option in a check box or list box.
Tab	Move between dialog box options.

CHAPTER 3

Starting Windows

Select a Mode

Now that you've installed Windows and have experimented with different ways of allocating system resources, you are finally ready to run Windows itself. Windows can be run in any of three different modes; which mode you choose depends to a great extent on what kind of PC you're using.

Real mode is the most basic choice. This is the only method of operation available on an 8086- or 8088-based machine, or any PC with less than 1 MB of free memory. When Windows is running in real mode, your computer—regardless of which processor it contains—is essentially operating as if it were an 8086 machine. In real mode, any application is allowed to use only those system resources that would be available under MS-DOS itself. In other words, each application is limited to 640 KB of conventional memory, and any extended memory is best used as a RAM disk. If you have expanded memory available, however, Windows will make effective use of it in real mode.

Standard mode is the normal operating condition on any machine that uses an 80286 or better chip and has at least 1 MB of memory available. In this mode Windows has full access to all extended memory in your PC, allowing you to run more Windows applications. Certain memory-hungry applications written especially for Windows 3 will only run in standard or 386 enhanced mode.

386 enhanced mode is a real RAM hog, but the benefits are well worth it. As in standard mode, Windows has full access to any extended memory in the system; it can also use the 386 chip's advanced capabilities to turn disk space into "virtual memory." Windows operates in this mode by default only if you have at least 2 MB of free RAM on an 80386SX or better, although 4 MB is a more realistic estimate of what this mode really requires. In 386 enhanced mode, Windows can multitask applications and run MS-DOS applications in a window. If you have less than 3 MB available, this mode is much slower than standard mode.

At startup, Windows will accept command line switches and instructions to run specific programs; in other words, you can force Windows to start in a given mode and automatically run a Windows program as part of the same command line. There are three command line switches available:

WIN /R starts in real mode.

WIN /2 or WIN /s launches Windows in standard mode.

WIN /3 runs in 386 enhanced mode.

You can follow the command line switch with the name of a Windows program; for example, entering WIN SOL will load Windows and immediately run the Solitaire program. If you enter just WIN, then Windows will run in its default mode as defined by the available system resources.

From within Windows, you can check which mode you are in by clicking on **Help** on the Program Manager menu bar and then clicking on **About**. (Using the keyboard, you can press **Alt-H A**.) The message box that pops up includes details about the current mode and gives you a summary of available resources.

Swap Files

As we have seen, Windows 3 can use space on your hard disk to simulate memory. To accomplish this trick, Windows uses a special file called a *swap file*. It is important to understand that this type of swap file is only used if you are running in 386 enhanced mode. By giving Windows the ability to swap information from memory to the disk, a swap file lets you do more with Windows. When you start Windows in real or standard mode, on the other hand, Windows uses temporary application swap files for any non-Windows program you run.

A swap file can be either temporary or permanent. In either case, it consists of hidden, system files that can't normally be seen using the **DIR** command. When you start Windows in 386 enhanced mode the program searches your hard disk for a permanent file; if it cannot find one then it automatically creates a temporary swap file. When you close Windows this temporary file is erased.

If your system uses an 80386SX, 80386, or 80486 processor and you want to use a permanent swap file, you'll have to create it via the Windows environment. There are several advantages to using a permanent swap file: Windows loads faster, because the program doesn't need to create the temporary file as part of the startup process. Because the file is contiguous—that is, it occupies sequential sectors—reading from and writing to the file can be faster. And it ensures that Windows always has a predictable amount of disk space. Of course, if you need the disk space back you can easily modify the file size or remove it altogether.

The only real disadvantage to using a permanent swap file is that it reduces the amount of free space on your hard disk, but the advantages far outweigh this drawback. Note that you cannot create a permanent swap file on a network, because more than one person is likely to access it at the same time, nor can you use a RAM disk for a permanent swap file.

Creating a Swap File

Before you create a permanent swap file you must compress your hard disk—the size of the swap file to be created is limited by the amount of contiguous disk space. To compact the disk, you will need a utility like The Norton Utilities' Speed Disk or PC Tools' Compress. Once the disk has been compacted you can create the swap file using the following steps.

First, verify that your system runs in 386 enhanced mode. From the system prompt, enter WIN without any command-line parameters, because you want the program to run in its default mode.

Once Windows has loaded, press **Alt-H A** to see what mode Windows operates in by default.

Click on **Help** and then on **About Program Manager...** to pop up a message box with Windows mode information.

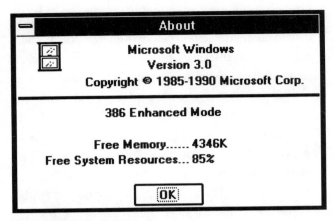

Windows Mode Information

If the message box tells you you're running in real or standard mode, don't bother creating the swap file. If Windows is operating in 386 enhanced mode, you'll need to exit and restart in real mode to carry out the next step in creating a permanent swap file.

Press **Enter** to close the message window.

Press **Alt-Space C** or **Alt-F4** to close Windows.

Click on **OK** to close the message box; then double click on the small box in the top left-hand corner of the Program Manager window to close Windows.

Once you are back at the system prompt, enter WIN /R to start Windows in real mode. You can only create or modify a swap file when running in this mode! If you try to activate the Swapfile program in any other mode you'll get an error message.

Press **Alt-F R** to open the File menu and select Run; a dialog box will appear.

Click on **File** in the menu bar and then click on **Run** to open the dialog box.

Now type SWAPFILE and press **Enter**. You will see a dialog box that looks like this:

```
┌─────────────────────────────────────────────────────────────┐
│                          Swapfile                            │
├─────────────────────────────────────────────────────────────┤
│ Swapfile has found a suitable location for a swap file        ┌──────────┐
│ on drive C:                                                  │  Create  │
│                                                              └──────────┘
│ Largest possible swap file size:    12442K bytes             ┌──────────┐
│ Total free disk space:              17418K bytes             │ Next Drive│
│                                                              └──────────┘
│ Recommended swap file size:     8192  ▲▼ K bytes             ┌──────────┐
│                                                              │  Cancel  │
│                                                              └──────────┘
│                                                              ┌──────────┐
│                                                              │  Help... │
│                                                              └──────────┘
└─────────────────────────────────────────────────────────────┘
```

Swapfile Dialog Box

The Swapfile dialog box tells you three things: how much space is free on your disk; the largest swap file you can possibly create, as determined by the amount of contiguous space on the disk; and the recommended size for the swap file. The recommended size will never be more than 50% of the total available space, and it may be less—again depending on the amount of contiguous space available. Most people are best off accepting this suggested size; however, you are free to adjust the swap file size depending on your needs.

Click on the arrows at the side of the proposed size to increase or decrease the swap file size, or type in a number that is less than that shown next to **Largest possible swap file size**. Click on **OK** or press **Enter** to create the swap file. A message box confirms the size and location of the swap file.

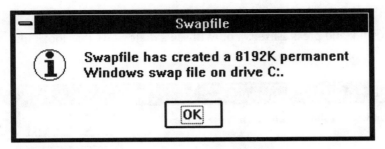

Swap File Created

Click on **OK** or press **Enter** to remove the box from the screen.

Close Windows by pressing **Alt-F4** or by clicking on **File** and again on **Exit**.

When the **Exit Windows** dialog box appears, press **Enter** or click on **OK** and you will return to the system prompt. Now, whenever you run Windows in 386 enhanced mode, you will be able to use this swap file to make Windows run faster.

Windows Layout

Decide which mode you want Windows to run in and, from the system prompt, enter the necessary command. Throughout the remainder of this book it is assumed that you will start Windows by simply entering WIN. However, if you wish to use a specific mode then you may need to add the parameter for that mode.

Once the command has been issued, Windows checks through your system resources before actually running the program. It does this for two reasons:

1. To make sure that the settings you established when you installed the program still exist—that you haven't changed the directory name without modifying the PATH statement, for example.

2. To ensure that there is sufficient memory for the program to run. Even having a small memory-resident program loaded can reduce the amount of available memory to a level where Windows simply will not run.

Assuming the necessary resources are available, you can expect to wait for a few moments as the program and its associated files load. After this brief delay, the Windows 3 logo appears, followed by the Windows program. The first time you run Windows, you should see the Program Manager window, as shown below.

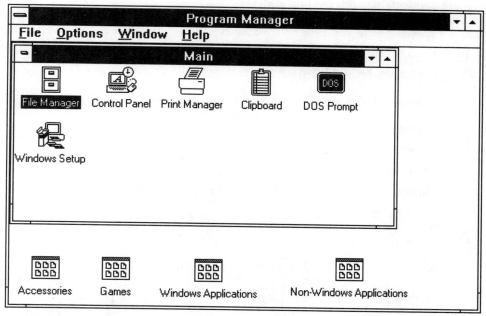

Windows First Time

On the screen is an open window containing a subsidiary window plus four icons. (Your screen layout may differ slightly, depending on how you originally installed applications.) Behind the main window is the background, which by default is a dull gray on all monitors. You can change the background to any one of a vast range of colors, or even incorporate a graphics file as the background if you wish. (We'll cover how to do this in Chapter 5.)

Exercise 3.1
The Window Dance

Moving windows is something that you will almost certainly want to do from time to time. You can use the keyboard or the mouse to do so. Try each method until you are comfortable with the process.

1. Make sure the Program Manager is running in a window and is not maximized. If you see a two-headed arrow in the upper right-hand corner of the screen, press **Alt-Space R** to restore the Program Manager to a window.

2. Press **Alt-Space M**. The pointer becomes a four-headed cross.

3. Press the **Right** key once. The window remains where it is but a frame that corresponds in size to the window borders appears and shifts slightly to the right. As soon as you press **Enter**, the frame disappears and the window shifts to this new position. Pressing **Esc** cancels the operation and leaves the window in its original position.

4. Press the **Up** key twice and the frame moves toward the top of the screen.

5. Press **Down** twice and the frame moves back down.

6. Press **Left** once and the frame returns to its original position.

Notice that each time you press a cursor key the window frame moves by the same increment. If you want to make a finer adjustment in the window position, hold down **Ctrl** as you press any cursor key and the window frame will move very slightly in that direction.

7. Press and hold **Up**. The window frame will move up until it reaches the top of the screen and then keep right on going. It may even vanish from the screen completely. Eventually it can go no further, at which point the computer may sound a warning beep.

8. Press and hold **Left**. The frame moves as far to the left as it can go; again, it may disappear from view.

9. Move the frame to the bottom right side of the screen. Note that you can only move the window frame using the **Left**, **Right**, **Up** and **Down** keys.

10. When you are satisfied with the window's new position, press **Enter.** To cancel the Move operation and leave the window in its original position, press **Esc.**

1. Make sure the Program Manager is running in a window and is not maximized. If you see a two-headed arrow at the upper right-hand corner of the screen, double click on it to restore the application to a window.

2. Move the mouse pointer to the title bar.

3. Click and hold the mouse button. As you do so, a frame that corresponds in size to the window borders will appear, although it may be difficult to distinguish at this point.

4. Move the mouse in any direction and the window frame will follow your movements. Using the mouse it is impossible to make the entire frame leave the screen.

5. When you have the frame where you want it, release the button and the window will move to that position.

Exercise 3.2
Imagine That

One of Windows' biggest attractions is its ability to run multiple applications simultaneously. When you have more than one window open at a time, you can reduce the onscreen clutter by shrinking any window to an icon. Again, you can do this using the keyboard or the mouse.

1. Press **Alt-Space N** and the window instantly shrinks to an icon at the bottom left-hand corner of the screen. Immediately below the icon you'll see the window title—in this case, Program Manager. (A bit unnecessary here, perhaps, but when you have a number of icons onscreen it is useful to know which is which.)

2. Press **Alt-Space R** or **Alt-Space Enter** to restore the icon to a window. (You can use the latter option because Restore is the highlighted option on the Control menu.) The window will be the same size and occupy the same position it did before you reduced it to an icon.

1. Click on the **Minimize** box—the one containing an arrow pointing downward—to the right of the title bar. The window instantly shrinks to an icon at the bottom of the screen.

2. Double click on the icon and the window is restored to its former position and size.

3. Click on the box at the left of the title bar to reveal the **Control menu**. Click on **Minimize**.

4. Double click on the icon again to restore the window.

By the way, you can move the icons themselves by simply dragging them. You can position icons anywhere on the screen, although they will be hidden by an active window. A command on the Task Manager menu (to be covered in Chapter 4) lets Windows arrange icons in a neat row along the bottom of the screen.

Exercise 3.3
A Whole Lot of Window

When you're working with a single application, there will be times when you'll want a window to be as large as possible. Here, too, you can use either the keyboard or the mouse to expand the active window.

1. Make sure the Program Manager is running in a window. If you see a two-headed arrow in the upper right-hand corner of the screen, press **Alt-Space R** to restore the Program Manager to a window.

2. Press **Alt-Space X** and the window will enlarge to cover the entire background area. Any icons or other windows will be covered up in the process.

3. Restore the window to its former size and position by pressing **Alt-Space R** or **Alt-Space Enter**.

1. Make sure the Program Manager is running in a window. If you see a two-headed arrow at the top right corner of the screen, double click on it to restore the application to a window.

2. Click on the **Maximize** button—the box containing an upward-pointing arrow—at the extreme right-hand edge of the title bar, and the window expands to fill the screen. (Double clicking on the title bar has the same effect.) The Maximize button is replaced by the Restore button, with its double-headed arrow.

3. Click on the **Restore** button and the application window reappears in its former size and position.

4. Click on the **Control-menu box** and then on **Maximize**. The window expands.

5. Click on the **Control-menu box** again and then click on **Restore** to return to the familiar window.

Exercise 3.4
All Sizes and Shapes

In addition to minimizing and maximizing them, you can also change the size and shape of most windows. (Some windows, like the Control Panel, cannot be resized.) It's much easier to do this with the mouse, but it can be done using the keyboard, too. The process is similar to that involved in moving a window.

1. Make sure the Program Manager is running in a window. If the application is maximized, press **Alt-Space R** to restore it to a window.

2. Press **Alt-Space S.** The mouse pointer becomes a four-headed arrow and the window frame appears over the borders.

3. To begin resizing the window, press the cursor key that points to the side you want to act on. For example, pressing **Right** allows you to move the right side of the window, while **Down** lets you move the base of the window. For this exercise, press **Right**. The four-headed arrow turns to a smaller, two-headed arrow atop the window's right border.

4. Press **Left** and the right side of the window frame begins to move toward the center of the window. If you hold down the **Left** key you will find that there is a minimum width of just over an inch, at which point the window frame will stop shrinking. Position the frame so that it lies about halfway across the open window.

5. Now press **Up**; the pointer moves to the top right-hand corner of the framework.

6. You can now adjust the window size using all four cursor keys—the **Left** and **Right** keys change the width, while the **Up** and **Down** keys let you vary the height. You will find that there is a minimum height for the window as well. To make fine adjustments in size, hold down the **Ctrl** key while pressing one of the cursor keys.

7. Press **Enter** to accept the new window size, or press **Esc** to cancel the Size operation and leave the window in its current size and position.

Note that when you use the Size command you establish a new default size for that window. The Restore command will switch an application from its maximized or iconized state to this window size, but there is no way to return the window to its former size other than by going through this whole process once more.

1. Make sure the Program Manager is running in a window. If the application is maximized, double click on the **Restore** button to run it in a window.

2. Move the mouse pointer to the left border. As the pointer crosses the border, it will turn to a two-headed arrow. Click on the border and hold down

the mouse button; the window frame will appear.

3. Move the mouse to the right (keeping the left button held down) and watch the left side of the frame move toward the center of the window. Once you release the mouse button, the window assumes the new size set by the frame. To keep the window from being resized, press **Esc** before releasing the mouse button. To make fine adjustments in the window size, hold down the **Ctrl** key as you drag the borders.

4. Click and hold on the top left-hand corner of the border. The pointer becomes a diagonal two-headed arrow.

5. Move the mouse in any direction and both the top and the left side of the window frame will be dragged along with it. Again, unless you press **Esc** first, as soon as you release the button the window assumes the size and shape of the frame.

Exercise 3.5
Ending It All

You should always quit Windows before you turn off your computer. Exiting properly lets Windows close any files you might have been working with and clean up any temporary files it might have created. It also lets you park the heads of your hard disk, if necessary.

1. Press **Alt-Space C**, **Alt-F4**, or **Alt-F X**—all three commands have the same effect.

2. A dialog box appears asking if you want to end your Windows session. It also contains a check box next to the words **Save Changes**. If you select this option, the program will remember the size and position of each of your Program Manager group windows so that they appear the same way the next time you start Windows.

3. Press **Tab** until the **Save Changes** command is outlined. Now press the

Spacebar to toggle the selection on or off. (I suggest that at this point you turn it off.)

4. Press **Enter** to exit Windows and return to the system prompt.

1. Double click on the **Control-menu box**; or click on the **Control-menu box** and then on **Close**; or click on **File** and then on **Exit**. All of these actions have the same effect.

2. Toggle the **Save Changes** option on or off by clicking on it.

3. Click on **OK** to exit Windows.

If you selected **Save Changes**, you'll notice your hard disk working away for at least a few seconds as Windows saves the environment information. Otherwise, Windows shuts down almost immediately.

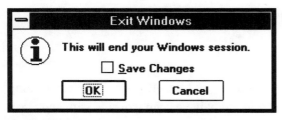

Close Windows

Summary

In real mode, Windows treats your computer as if it were an 8086-based machine, regardless of its actual processor. To force Windows to run in real mode, enter WIN /R from the system prompt.

Standard mode allows Windows to take advantage of all the extended memory in your system, but it needs an 80286 or better and at least 1 MB of memory to do so. To launch Windows in standard mode from the system prompt enter WIN /2 or WIN /s.

On a PC with an 80386SX or better and at least 2 MB of memory, Windows' 386 enhanced mode uses all of your system's extended memory and creates "virtual memory" out of space on the hard disk. You can multitask applications, with each behaving as if it were running on its own PC. To force Windows to start in 386 enhanced mode, enter WIN /3 from the system prompt.

A permanent swap file allows Windows to operate faster and more dynamically, but only in 386 enhanced mode. Paradoxically, before you can create a swap file you have to start Windows in real mode.

A window can be resized by clicking and dragging on its borders. It can be moved by dragging the title bar.

Keyboard Summary

Alt-F4	Terminate Windows and return to system prompt.
Alt-H A	Display copyright notice and check mode information.
Alt-Space	Open Control menu.
Alt-Space M	Move current window.
Alt-Space N	Shrink application to an icon.
Alt-Space R	Restore icon or maximized application to window.
Alt-Space S	Change size of current window.
Alt-Space W	Activate Task List.
Alt-Space X	Enlarge icon or window to cover entire screen.
Ctrl-Esc	Activate Task List.

CHAPTER 4

Program Manager

Windows in Use

The Program Manager is the heart of the Windows 3 environment. It replaces the MS-DOS Executive found in previous versions of Windows and is much easier to use. By default, the Program Manager will be run whenever you start Windows, although you can change things so that the File Manager will run by default instead (see Chapter 7 for details). Microsoft designed Program Manager to be used as the front end of the Windows environment, and their programmers have put a lot of thought and work into getting it right.

Program Manager is a social tool (using the word *social* in its broadest sense) that controls how Windows handles programs and files. It is not a disk manager or utility; rather, it is a way of classifying and carrying out requests from the user. Program Manager allows you to create groups of programs and items according to your own preference, then lets you display the groups in windows, as icons or as a combination of the two.

Like all Windows applications, Program Manager runs in an application window. Within this main window are a number of subwindows, each of which contains a group of program items. You can reduce any group window to an icon, which allows you to keep only specifically required windows open. When you install Windows 3 it will create a number of groups automatically; if you prefer, you can change or even delete these groups and add your own. There are no hard and fast rules about what belongs in which group, or even about the number of groups you can create. How you organize the groups and arrange the items within them is purely a matter of your own taste.

There is no apparent limit on the number of groups you can create in Program Manager. As a test, I have created (and subsequently deleted) 60 groups, in addition to the ones automatically created by Setup, without experiencing any problems. Of course, it is really in your best interest to keep the number of groups to a minimum. The more groups you create, the more cluttered your screen will be. With many groups shrunk to icons or displayed in small windows, you will not be able to see what they contain.

Microsoft recommends that you not have more than 40 files in any one group. That's good advice purely from an aesthetic viewpoint—having that many icons in one window means you wouldn't be able to see them all, even with the window maximized. Personally, I prefer to limit the number of files in each group to an essential few and to have all the group windows visible at the same time without any of them being an icon.

When Program Manager is on the screen you can quickly and easily run any program. Just double click on the program icon (or select an icon and press **Enter**). As the selected program is being run, Program Manager slips into the background.

Because Program Manager is the Windows front end, you must return there to exit Windows. You cannot quit from anywhere else.

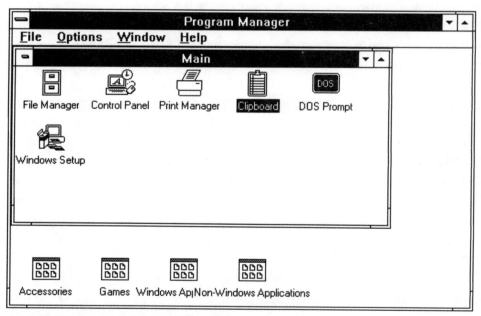

Program Manager Created by Setup

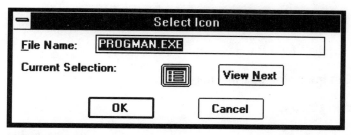

Select an Icon

12. Back at the Properties dialog box, press **Tab** until **OK** is highlighted and then press **Enter**. The program you have chosen, represented by the icon you selected, will now appear in the group window that was active when you started the selection process.

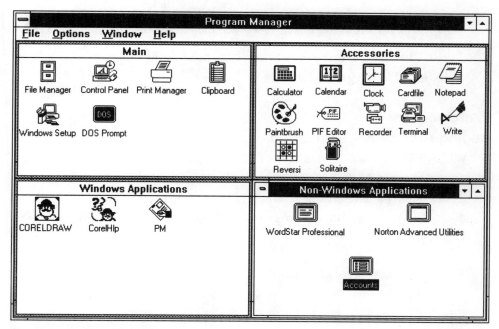

New Program Item Added

1. Click on the window to which you want to add the program.

2. Click on **File** in the Menu Bar and then on **New**.

3. Click on **OK** in the dialog box that appears.

4. Double click on **Browse**.

5. The directory listing defaults to the main Windows directory. Use the list box to log onto the directory containing the program you want to add. To go up a directory level, double click on **[..]**.

6. Double click on the directory that contains the file you want to add.

7. Double click on the file name of the program you want to add.

8. Type the description and then click on **Change Icon**.

9. Click on **View Next** until you reach the icon you want. Click on **OK**.

10. Click on **OK** in the Properties dialog box and the program, with its icon, is added to the group window.

Exercise 4.7
Adding Programs Using Setup

When Windows was installed, the Setup program copied part of itself into the Windows directory. At the end of the installation this file was updated to include the details of system parameters under which Windows runs. You can use the resulting Windows Setup program to add programs to the groups within Program Manager.

1. Activate the Main Group window.

2. Using the cursor keys, highlight Windows Setup and press **Enter** to bring up the Windows Setup dialog box.

```
┌─────────────────────────────────────────────────────┐
│ ▬                    Windows Setup              ▼     │
│ Options    Help                                       │
├─────────────────────────────────────────────────────┤
│   Display:        VGA                                 │
│   Keyboard:       Enhanced 101 or 102 key US and Non US │
│   Mouse:          Microsoft, or IBM PS/2              │
│   Network:        Network not installed               │
│   ─────────────────────────────────────────────────  │
│   Swap file:      Permanent (7506 K bytes on Drive C:) │
└─────────────────────────────────────────────────────┘
```

Windows Setup Details

3. Press **Alt-O** to activate the Options menu, followed by **S** to choose **Set Up Applications**. This brings up a new dialog box.

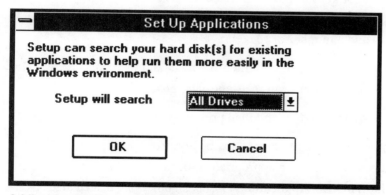

Adding Applications with Windows Setup

4. You can use the cursor keys to select which drives you will search to find programs. You can choose all drives, designate specific disks or search the PATH only. After you have made your selection, press **Enter** to begin the search.

5. The program searches the designated area and then produces a dialog box containing a list of the programs it has found.

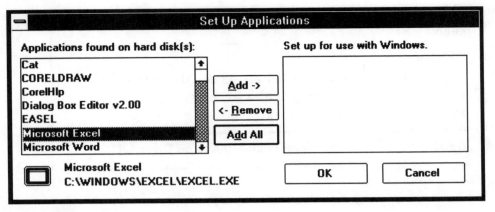

Programs Found

6. Use the cursor keys to move the selection box to the program you want to add. Press **Space** to select it. Repeat this process as often as necessary if you want to add a number of files.

7. Press **Tab** to move the highlighter to **Add->** and then press **Enter**. The selected program(s) appear in the right-hand box.

8. Use **Tab** to move to **OK** and then press **Enter**.

9. The Program Manager comes to the forefront as the programs you selected are added to their appropriate groups—Windows programs are added to the Windows Applications Group; all others are placed in the Non-Windows Applications Group. As the Setup program finishes with each group it shrinks the group to an icon.

10. Once all the programs have been added, the Windows Setup dialog box reappears. To remove it press **Alt-F4**.

11. Use **Ctrl-Tab Enter** to reinstate any window that has been shrunk to an icon. The icons will reappear as group windows in their former positions.

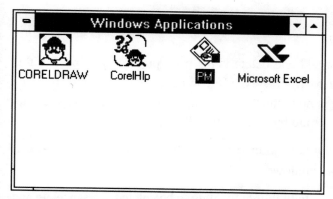

Program Added to Windows Group

1. Double click on **Windows Setup** in the Main Group window.

2. Click on **Options** and again on **Set Up Applications**.

3. If necessary, click on the drop-down list box to change the selection of drives to be searched, and then click on **OK**.

4. Click on the programs you want to add, using the scroll bars if necessary to move through the list. Click on **Add->**.

5. Click on **OK** and the programs are added to the groups.

6. Double click on the Control menu box at the top left-hand corner of the dialog box to terminate the Setup program.

7. Double click on any icons to restore them to windows.

Deleting Items from Groups

To delete an item from a group, all you have to do is select the item and then press **Delete**. You will be asked to confirm your decision to delete the item before it is actually removed.

Exercise 4.8
Deleting Items

It's a simple process to add and delete items from program groups. For this exercise, let's delete the icon for Microsoft Excel. Items can only be deleted from the groups one at a time; there is no method of deleting multiple items from a group, unless you delete the entire group by erasing the .GRP file.

 1. Select the appropriate group window, using **Ctrl-Tab** or **Ctrl-F6** if necessary to change windows.

2. Use the cursor keys to highlight the item to be deleted. Press **Delete** and a dialog box appears, asking you to confirm your decision.

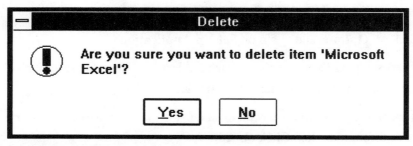

Delete Item Dialog box

3. Press **Enter** and the item is removed from the group. (Note that the program itself is not deleted from the disk—it is simply no longer part of the group and thus cannot be started from the Program Manager.)

 1. Click on the file to be deleted. Press **Delete**. Click on **OK**.

Creating a New Group

As part of the installation routine, Setup created five groups that should include most of the Windows and non-Windows programs you normally use. These five groups will be sufficient for most people, but depending on your needs you may wish to create additional groups.

The items within a group do not have to be limited to just programs; you can also create items based on files that are associated with a program. For example, suppose you are working on a project about global warming. You use Write to produce documents, Paintbrush to create graphics, Cardfile to collect basic data and Aldus PageMaker to produce the finished report. All these programs and their related files can be put into a single group.

The secret is to create items that load a specific file along with its associated program every time you select the icon. You do this by linking the file directly to the program using the Properties command. Here's how to do it.

Exercise 4.9
A New Group

1. Press **Alt-F N** to bring up the New Program Item dialog box. Press **Alt-G** to select **New Program Group** and then press **Enter**.

2. In the Program Group Properties dialog box enter the name of the new group. (For this exercise, let's call it *Project*.) There's no need to fill in a filename in the Group File text box; Windows will give the newly created group file a unique name.

3. Regardless of how the existing groups are arranged, the new group window will appear in the position it would occupy if all the windows were cascaded. Press **Shift-F4** to tile it into the other windows.

4. Use **Ctrl-Tab** or **Ctrl-F6** to move into the Accessories group. Then use the cursor keys to select the Cardfile.

5. Press **Alt-F C** to begin the process of copying the Cardfile to the new group. This command brings up a dialog box that looks very much like the one used to move items.

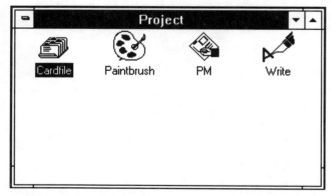

Copy Program Dialog Box

6. Use the cursor keys to change the target group name. By default, the destination is the currently active group—in this case, Accessories. You'll need to change the destination to the Project group or the program will simply make another copy of Cardfile in the Accessories window.

7. Select each of the other programs to be included in this group—Write, PageMaker and Paintbrush—and copy them into the Project group.

Project Group Created

8. Now for the fun part. Let's suppose you have three data files, each created by Cardfile. Make two extra copies of the Cardfile icon within the Project group. (Remember, any program can appear in a group as many times as you like.)

9. With one of the Cardfile icons selected, press **Alt-F P** to bring up the Program Item Properties box. Change the description on the first line to read *Data 1*.

10. In the second line, add the name and extension of the data file after the program name. (Be sure to leave a space between the two!) If the data file and CARDFILE.EXE are located in different directories, you must include the full path for the data file.

11. Once the name of the data file has been added, press **Enter** and the icon within the Project group will be renamed.

12. Rename the other Cardfile icons in the same way. Make as many copies of the other programs as you need so that each loads a file automatically. When you're finished, the Project group should look something like this:

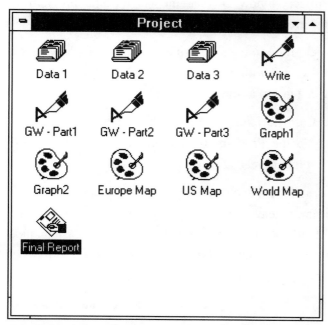

Project Group Completed

1. Click on **File** in the menu bar, then click on **New** to bring up the New Program Item dialog box. Select the **New Program Group** option and click on **OK**.

2. In the Program Group Properties dialog box enter the name of the new group. (For this exercise, let's call it *Project*.) There's no need to fill in a filename in the **Group File** text box; Windows will give the newly created group file a unique name.

3. The new group window appears in the position it would occupy if all the windows were cascaded. Click on **Window** and then on **Tile** to arrange the windows neatly onscreen.

4. Click on the Accessories group to make it the active window. Point to the Cardfile icon and hold down the **Ctrl** key. Now you can click and drag a copy of the icon into the Project window. Do the same with the other programs to be added into the new group—Write, PageMaker and Paintbrush.

5. Click on the Project group to make its window active. Make two extra copies of the Cardfile icon within the Project group. (Remember, any program can appear in a group as many times as you like.)

6. With one of the Cardfile icons selected, click on **File** and then on **Properties** to bring up the Program Item Properties box. Change the description on the first line to read *Data 1*.

7. In the second line, add the name and extension of the data file after the program name. (Be sure to leave a space between the two!) If the data file and CARDFILE.EXE are located in different directories, you must include the full path for the data file. Click on **OK** to rename the icon.

8. Rename the other Cardfile icons in the same way. Make as many copies of the other programs as you need so that each loads a file automatically.

Now, whenever you activate one of the programs within the Project group, the associated data file will be loaded automatically. Using this approach can be a tremendous time saver, but there are two potential problems with it: First, every time you click on one of these icons it loads another copy of the application, which may cause memory problems; second, some applications won't allow you to load a second copy, which means you'll sometimes see an error message.

Exercise 4.10
Deleting Groups

There is an easy way to delete a number of items at once without having to select them all individually. This method makes use of the fact that you can delete an entire group. Remember that the program files are not deleted from your hard disk—only the group is removed from Program Manager.

1. Create a new group just as you did in Exercise 4.9. Call this group *Junk*.

2. Use the steps outlined in Exercise 4.5 to move the items you want to delete into this group.

3. Press **Ctrl-F4** to reduce the Junk group to an icon.

4. With the icon highlighted, press **Delete Enter** and the group with its entire contents will be deleted.

1. Create a new group just as you did in Exercise 4.9. Call this group *Junk*.

2. Cascade the windows and then move the items to be erased into the new group.

3. Click on the **Minimize** button to reduce the group window to an icon.

4. Press **Delete** and click on **OK** to delete the group and the files it contains.

Menus

Program Manager is the main program that will be loaded whenever you activate Windows. Each group window contains its own Control menu, title bar, and Minimize and Maximize buttons, but no group window contains a menu. Instead, each group shares the Program Manager menu.

The menus in general allow you to use either the keyboard or the mouse, although for some actions you must use the mouse and keyboard in combination. The menus and their contents are as follows.

```
 New...
 Open            Enter
 Move...
 Copy...
 Delete          Del
 Properties...
 Run...
 Exit Windows...
```

Program Manager File Menu

The **File** menu lets you add, edit and delete program items and groups. The commands it contains, and their actions, are:

New allows you to create a new group or add a new program item to an existing group. It brings up a dialog box that allows you to name the new item or group.

Open applies specifically to program items; it simply means start the program. It's usually much simpler to use the cursor keys to select the program you want to run and then just press **Enter.**

Move lets you move a program from one group to another.

Copy allows you to duplicate a program item in another group, or even copy it into the same group as many times as you wish.

Delete is used to remove an item from a group. You can also use this command to delete a group in its entirety, but how you do so depends on whether or not the group contains any items. If the group window is open, you must remove all the items within it, one by one, before you can delete the group. If the group is reduced to an icon, however, you can delete it—items and all—in a single action.

Properties calls up a dialog box that lets you change the description, program details and icon of any program item. It also allows you to change the description of a group. You can include the name of a file to be loaded along with the program whenever you choose that program item.

Run lets you run programs that are not associated with icons. To use this command, type the name of the program—and, if necessary, the associated data file—just as you would enter it at the system prompt. If the program directory is not available in the PATH, you'll need to type the full pathname of the program file.

Exit Windows lets you end your Windows session. When you choose this command you will be asked to confirm that you really intend to quit Windows. You will also be provided with the option of saving the changes you have made in the arrangement of Program Manager group windows.

The **Options** menu allows you to automatically arrange the items in a group window, and to control how Program Manager behaves when you run an application. It contains only two commands:

Auto Arrange, as the name implies, automatically repositions the icons in a group window whenever you resize the window (a check mark tells you whether the option is toggled on or off). The new positions of the icons are subject only to the setting in the Control Panel that determines the spacing between icons. Whether this will affect your system setup depends on how many icons you have in a group. In a window with 10 or 12 items, for example, it is possible to arrange all the icons so that they fit snugly within a window of a certain size. If the group is reduced to an icon and then restored to a window with the **Auto Arrange** option selected, the icons may shift around and the scroll bars may appear, thus undoing all the arranging you have done.

Minimize on Use is another toggle that instructs Windows to shrink the Program Manager to an icon whenever you launch a program. When you have finished with the program you restore the Program Manager icon. This option keeps your screen uncluttered; however, you still have access to the Program Manager, using **Ctrl-Tab**, and it can be restored to a window at any time.

<u>C</u>ascade	Shift+F5
<u>T</u>ile	Shift+F4
<u>A</u>rrange Icons	
<u>1</u> Accessories	
√ <u>2</u> Windows Applications	
<u>3</u> Main	
<u>4</u> Non-Windows Applications	

Program Manager Window Menu

The **Windows** menu, not surprisingly, controls the windows and how they appear. It contains the following commands:

Cascade displays open Program Manager windows so that they stack neatly, with the title bars visible and the active window at the front of the stack. To select another window you simply click on it and it becomes active. However, it does not change its position within the stack unless you issue the command to cascade the windows again. The command has no effect on any group that is being displayed as an icon.

Tile arranges the windows side by side, with the active window at the top left corner. When the display is tiled, Windows tries to fit the open windows into the main Program Manager window so that they occupy an equal amount of space. Here, too, the command has no effect on any group that is being displayed as an icon.

Arrange Icons does exactly what it says: this command organizes the icons in the active window into neat lines and columns. The order in which the icons are arranged is based on where they lay when you issued the command. The icon that is nearest the top left-hand corner of the window is moved into that position, the icon nearest to that is then moved next to it, and so on. This command does not ordinarily rearrange groups that are displayed as icons; however, if all the groups are displayed as icons, without any windows active, then the command will cause all the icons to be arranged in a line along the bottom of the Program Manager window.

The remainder of the Windows menu contains a numbered list of the groups that are contained with the Program Manager (a check mark appears beside the group window that is currently active). You can activate any group window by pressing **Alt-W** and then the number corresponding to that group.

Restore	
Move	
Size	
Minimize	
Maximize	
Close	**Ctrl+F4**
Next	**Ctrl+F6**

Group Control Menu

Each group window also contains its own Control menu, which includes a list of commands similar to those in the Program Manager Control menu. You activate a group window's Control menu by pressing **Alt-Hyphen**. It contains the following commands:

Restore returns a group icon to its former position and size within the Program Manager application window.

Move lets you reposition the group window or icon within Program Manager.

Size allows you to change the size of the group window using the cursor keys.

Minimize reduces the group window to an icon.

Maximize expands the group window so that it fills all the available space within the Program Manager application window.

Close reduces the group window to an icon.

Next switches to the next group window. (The sequence of windows is shown in the Windows menu.)

Exercise 4.11
Tidy Icons

This exercise will show you the effect of rearranging icons.

1. Reduce all but the Accessories window to icons. Use **Ctrl-Tab** or **Ctrl-F6** to move between windows and press **Ctrl-F4** to minimize each window.

2. Enlarge the Accessories window to the maximum size by pressing **Alt-Hyphen X**.

3. Invoke the Arrange Icons command by pressing **Alt-W A**. The icons within the window will rearrange into neat lines.

4. Toggle the Auto Arrange option by pressing **Alt-O A**.

5. Return the Accessories window to its original size by pressing **Alt-Hyphen R**. The window is restored and the icons automatically reposition themselves.

6. Restore the other group icons. Use **Ctrl-Tab** or **Ctrl-F6** to select each in turn and then press **Alt-Hyphen R** for each one. As each window returns to its former position the icons within it will be reorganized.

7. To turn the Auto Arrange facility off, press **Alt-O A** again.

1. Reduce all group windows, except Accessories, to icons by clicking on each window's **Minimize** button.

2. Click on the **Maximize** button of the Accessories window.

3. Click on **Window** in the Menu Bar and then again on **Arrange Icons**.

4. Click on **Options** and then on **Auto Arrange** to toggle this option on. (A small check mark will appear next to the menu choice.)

5. Click on the **Restore** button in the Accessories window to restore it to its former position and size. The icons within the window will be rearranged as the window changes size.

6. Restore the other group windows by double clicking on the group icons. Again, the program icons will be rearranged.

Help

Windows 3 provides a continuous, context-sensitive on-line help facility for just about every area of the program. The help facility can be activated at any time by pressing **F1** or by clicking on **Help**. Once you have activated help you use the pointer, which changes into a pointing finger, to select the topic you want help with. Along the top of the screen is a set of buttons that allow you to navigate your way around the help system.

The help facility is superb, far superior to what was available in Windows/286, but it does take some getting used to. Because the help system now covers every aspect of the program, you can very easily get lost as you move through the various screens.

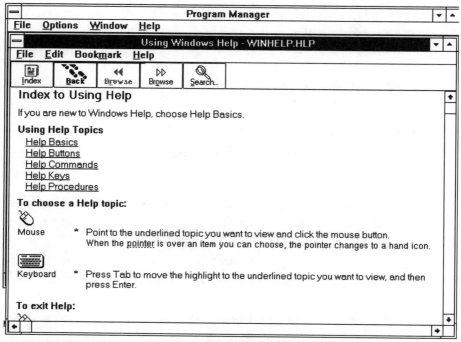

Program Manager Help

When you choose Help from the Program Manager menu bar, a pull-down menu appears containing the following commands :

Index takes you directly to the main Help index for the Program Manager. From here you can access any part of the Help system.

Keyboard provides help with those commands and actions that can be accessed from the keyboard.

Basic Skills helps beginning users get up to speed quickly.

Commands provides a full list of the commands available under Windows, broken down into convenient subsections.

Procedures helps explain the philosophy and techniques used in the application. Here, too, you can select specific areas to look at.

Glossary defines essential Windows terms.

Using Help may come in handy if you get lost!

About Program Manager... provides copyright details and other important information about the program you are running. Within Program Manager this menu choice tells you which mode Windows is running in and how much memory is available.

Within the Program Manager help system, as is true with the help facilities throughout Windows, you can add comments to a file by clicking on **Edit** and then on **Annotate**, or by pressing **Alt-E A**. You can type your comments into the Help Annotation dialog box and then add the comments to the help screen by pressing **Enter** or clicking on **OK**. The presence of a help note is shown by a green paper clip next to the heading on the help screen. Clicking on the paper clip lets you view, delete or edit the notes.

Program Manager Summary

Program Manager is an organizer that allows you to sort programs into groups according to your own preference.

Program Manager can display groups as subwindows or as icons.

Group windows have no menu bar—they share the menus and commands of the Program Manager.

Setup will automatically create up to five groups for you as part of the Windows installation.

You must return to the Program Manager to terminate Windows.

Group windows can be arranged as a cascade—stacked one in front of the other—or as tiles, arranged side by side.

On-line help is available at all times.

Keyboard Summary

The following is a list of the keystrokes that can be used within Program Manager and describes what they do.

Alt-F4	Terminate Windows and return to MS-DOS.
Alt-F C	Copy a program from one group to another.
Alt-F D	Delete a selected icon within a group or delete a group if it appears as an icon or an empty window.
Alt-F M	Move a program icon from one group to another.
Alt-F N	Create a new group or add a program item to a group.
Alt-F O	Activate a program. Select the program icon and then use this command to run the program.
Alt-F P	Set or edit the properties of a program item.
Alt-F R	Run a program that is not set up as a Program Manager icon.
Alt-F X	Quit Windows and return to the system prompt.
Alt-H A	Display an information box containing copyright details; within Program Manager only, also provides information about Windows mode and available system resources.
Alt-H B	Describe basic Windows skills.
Alt-H C	Provide help with Program Manager commands.
Alt-H G	Produce a glossary of Windows terms.
Alt-H I	Activate the Help index.
Alt-H K	Supply help with keyboard shortcuts.
Alt-H P	Detail help about Windows procedures.
Alt-H U	Provide help about using the help facility!
Alt-Hyphen C	Reduce group window to an icon.
Alt-Hyphen M	Move group window within Program Manager.
Alt-Hyphen N	Minimize group window—i.e., reduce it to an icon.
Alt-Hyphen R	Restore group window to its former size and position.
Alt-Hyphen S	Change the size of a group window.
Alt-Hyphen T	Make the next group in the list the active window.
Alt-Hyphen X	Maximize group window.

Alt-O A	Turn on the automatic icon arrangement option.
Alt-O M	Toggle the option that allows Program Manager to be reduced to an icon whenever any program is run.
Alt-Spacebar C	Quit Windows and return to the system prompt.
Alt-Spacebar M	Move the Program Manager window.
Alt-Spacebar N	Minimize Program Manager—i.e., reduce it to an icon.
Alt-Spacebar R	Restore Program Manager to a window occupying the same size and position as it occupied before.
Alt-Spacebar S	Change the size of a window.
Alt-Spacebar W	Switch to another program.
Alt-Spacebar X	Maximize a window so that it fills the entire available space of the screen.
Alt-W [number]	Switch to the selected group window.
Alt-W A	Arrange icons within a group window, if one is active; if no group window is active, align the group icons within the Program Manager window.
Alt-W C	Cascade the group windows.
Alt-W T	Tile the group windows.
Ctrl-Tab	Move from one window or icon to another.
Ctrl-Esc	Switch to another program using Task List.
Ctrl-F4	Reduce group window to an icon.
Ctrl-F6	Move from one window or group to another.
Delete	Delete a selected icon, an empty group window or programs within a window.
End	Move directly to the last item in a list box.
Enter	Start the selected program.
Esc	Cancel an operation.
F10	Highlight the first menu on a menu bar. You must press Enter or a command letter to pull down the menu.
Shift-F4	Tile the group windows.
Shift-F5	Cascade the group windows.

CHAPTER 5

Control Panel

Running the Program

The Control Panel (not to be confused with the control menu found on individual windows) is the program that allows you to adjust the way your computer is configured. It also lets you set a number of Windows 3 parameters, including fonts, the Windows color scheme, network connections, and the special properties that apply when running in 386 enhanced mode.

There are a total of twelve system parameters you can reset using the Control Panel. The exact number of options available at any given time depends on the mode in which Windows is running on your system. Here is a complete list of the options that you may see when you start Control Panel:

Color You can change the colors of virtually every Windows screen element. You may choose one of the pre-installed color combinations, or you can create your own palette and use it instead.

Fonts You can add or remove the fonts that Windows 3 uses.

Ports Control Panel lets you assign and configure your PC's serial communication ports without leaving Windows.

Mouse You can modify the way that the mouse behaves under Windows.

Desktop This comprehensive option allows you to change some important Windows background elements.

Network If you are connected to a local area network, you have full control over network connections. (This option is only available if the network is installed and running when you start the Control Panel program.)

Printers Use this option to install and configure printers within the Windows environment.

International You can modify the various national settings—date and currency formats, for example—that will be used by Windows.

Keyboard This option allows you to vary the speed at which the keyboard repeats characters under Windows.

Date/Time You can change the system date and time from within Windows.

Sound If you choose, Windows will notify you of errors with an audible warning.

386 Enhanced You can adjust the way in which Windows behaves when programs are running concurrently. This option appears on the Control Panel only if you are running in 386 enhanced mode.

Each major option is displayed on the Control Panel as an icon. To activate any of them, you simply double click on the icon and a dialog box pops up, overlaying the Control Panel. Each change you make becomes active immediately; there is no need to reboot the computer as there was under Windows/286, although in some cases you have to close the dialog box and return to the Control Panel before you can verify the changes. The changes you make using the Control Panel are saved in a settings file called WIN.INI, located in the Windows subdirectory.

I strongly recommend that you use a mouse if you are going to do anything with the Control Panel. It's possible to run the Control Panel and make most changes using the keyboard, but certain areas of the program really demand a mouse. Changing colors or a desktop pattern, for example, may take you several minutes with the keyboard; the same changes can usually be made in seconds using the mouse.

1. Start Windows as usual by entering WIN from the system prompt.

2. When the Program Manager appears, select the Main window, using **Ctrl-Tab** or **Ctrl-F6** to move between windows if necessary.

3. If you have not already done so, toggle the setting that shrinks Program Manager to an icon by pressing **Alt-O M**. (You'll see a check mark next to the words "Minimize on Use" if this option is turned on.)

4. Using the cursor keys, select the icon labeled Control Panel (it looks like a computer with the letter A displayed on the monitor) and press **Enter**. The Control Panel program will be activated and the Program Manager reduced to an icon at the bottom left-hand corner of the screen.

Control Panel

Control Panel Icon

1. Start Windows as usual by typing **WIN** at the system prompt.

2. When the Program Manager appears, click on **Options** in the menu bar and look for a check mark next to the words "Minimize on Use." If you don't see a check mark, click on the command; otherwise, click anywhere on the screen to clear the menu.

3. In the Main window, double click on the icon labeled Control Panel to start the program.

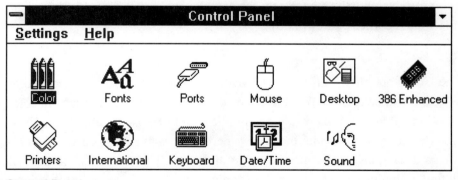

Control Panel

There are only two menus available within the Control Panel. The Settings menu duplicates the options that appear in the Control Panel window as icons, and is therefore useful only if you want to use the keyboard. The Help menu provides detailed on-line assistance for every Control Panel option.

```
┌──────────────────────┐
│ Color...             │
│ Desktop...           │
│ Date/Time...         │
│ Fonts...             │
│ International...      │
│ Keyboard...          │
│ Mouse...          ┌──────────────────────┐
│ Ports...          │ Index                │
│ Printers...       │ Keyboard             │
│ Sound...          │ Commands             │
│ 386 Enhanced...   │ Procedures           │
├──────────────────┤│ Using Help           │
│ Exit             │├──────────────────────┤
└──────────────────┘│ About Control Panel..│
                    └──────────────────────┘
```

Settings and Help Menus

To use either menu, you can click on the key word in the menu bar or press **Alt** and the underlined letter of the menu.

When you have finished with the Control Panel, the easiest and quickest way to close it and return to the Program Manager is to press **Alt-Space C** or **Alt-F4**. If you're more comfortable with the mouse, you can exit by double clicking on the box at the upper left-hand corner of the window.

Color

The Color option within Control Panel allows you to select and edit color schemes that will be used by Windows. You can even create and save custom color combinations. Because Windows is really intended to be used with a color VGA monitor—nothing else provides the same superb colors—the program offers facilities for producing an almost infinite range of colors. (Unfortunately, because of production limitations, this book can show only monochrome versions of Windows screens.)

1. Because the Color option is selected by default, you can just press **Enter** to activate it.

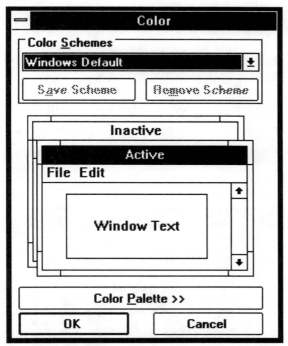

Color Dialog Box, Part 1

 1. Double click on the **Color** icon to activate this section of the program.

The Color dialog box illustrated above includes the following:

a. The **Color Scheme** currently in use. As you have just installed Windows, the program will be using the Windows Default combination. Windows comes complete with eleven pre-defined color schemes—some of them awful.

b. A representation of some (but not all) of the areas in the Windows environment whose colors you can change.

101

c. The **Color Palette** activator. Pushing this button lets you change any of the 64 colors and 13 screen elements under your control.

d. A button labeled **OK**. Clicking here will activate any changes you have made and return you to the Control Panel.

e. A **Cancel** button. Clicking here closes the Color dialog box and returns you to the Control Panel, ignoring any changes you may have made.

 2. Press **Tab** to highlight the Color Palette button (a dark outline will appear around the button), and then press **Enter**. (You can also press **Alt-P** to activate the Color Palette in a single step.)

 2. Click on **Color Palette** and the dialog box doubles in size.

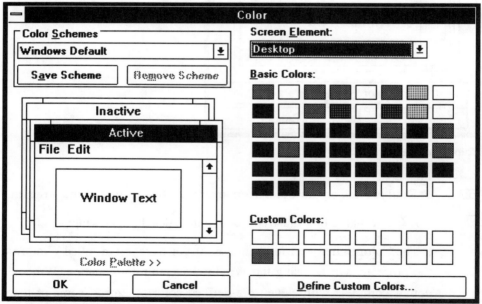

Color Dialog Box, Part 2

The screen display now shows all of the original options plus the following:

f. **Screen Element**, with **Desktop** preselected in the box. This section allows you to change the colors used for individual parts of the Windows environment.

g. A series of 48 little boxes, in six rows of eight, each containing a different color and labeled **Basic Colors**. You can select any one of these colors and apply it to the chosen screen element.

h. A series of 16 boxes, in two rows of eight, labeled **Custom Colors**. Windows allows you to create your own colors, rather than using the predefined ones; when you have done so the created colors will appear in these boxes.

i. A large button labeled **Define Custom Colors**. This activates another dialog box in which you can create your own colors.

Exercise 5.1
Color Schemes

You can select any of the predefined Windows 3 color schemes and apply it to the Windows environment. The color schemes vary from extremely bright to pastel hues. You may decide that you don't like any of these and choose to create your own color scheme. For now, though, we're just going to use the schemes supplied by Microsoft.

1. At the moment, the word **Desktop** is selected in the Screen Element box. Press **Tab** until the phrase **Windows Default** in the Color Schemes box is selected—that is, until the words turn to inverse video. You can also press **Alt-S**.

2. Press **Down** to replace **Windows Default** with **Arizona**. The area immediately below the box will instantly change to give you a preview of how the new scheme will look in the Windows environment.

3. Press **Down** again to move through the list of predefined color schemes one at a time.

1. Click on **Windows Default**; the words will turn to inverse video.

2. Click on the arrow at the right-hand side of the Color Schemes box and a list will drop down. Click on **Arizona**, or any of the other schemes, and preview the colors in the area below the box. You can scroll through the color schemes using the scroll bars at the edge of the list box.

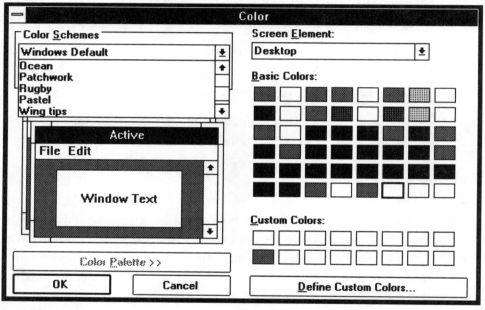

Color Schemes

Take a look at each of the predefined schemes—if one of them is to your liking, it will save you the hassle of creating your own. Personally, I don't like any of the predefined choices, and so I made my own custom scheme.

Exercise 5.2
Design a Scheme

To create your own color scheme you need to allocate a color to each area of the screen display. The quickest way to do this is to select one of the predefined schemes that is closest to what you want and then tweak it by changing selected areas.

1. Having chosen the base scheme, press **Tab** until the Screen Element dialog box is selected (**Desktop** should be highlighted). In the Basic Colors area below, the color that is already assigned to that screen element will be outlined by a thick dark border and surrounded by a box made of gray dotted lines.

2. Press **Tab** to move down to the Basic Colors area.

3. Use the cursor keys to highlight the color you want to use. Press the **Spacebar** to select it and assign it to the screen element. As soon as you do so, the colors in the preview area to the left of the Basic Colors will change to reflect your selection.

4. Press **Alt-E** to move back to the Screen Element box and then press **Down** to select the next element.

5. Repeat steps (2) to (4) until you are satisfied with the combination of colors.

1. Select a base color scheme or the Windows Default, as in the previous exercise.

2. Click on the Screen Element box so that **Desktop** is highlighted.

3. Move the mouse pointer to the Basic Colors area and click on the color that you want to use for the highlighted screen element. As you make your selection, you'll see the changes previewed in the area to the left of the Basic Colors palette. You can click on any other color and instantly see it replace your previous choice. Mouse users have a big advantage when it comes to changing colors!

4. Once you are happy with the color of the Desktop, click on the arrow at the right-hand side of the Screen Element box. A list box will drop down, and you can choose the next area you want to change.

5. Repeat steps (2) to (4) until you are satisfied with the combination of colors.

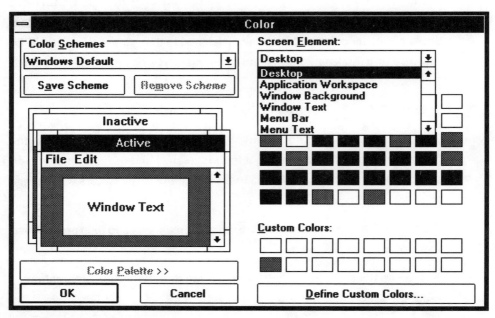

Selecting Screen Elements

Exercise 5.3
Create a Color

The 48 basic colors in the Windows palette should be sufficient for most needs, but Microsoft has provided a facility that allows you to create up to sixteen additional custom colors per palette. This area of the program is far easier to use with a mouse than with the keyboard. In fact, using the keyboard to make custom colors is such a hassle I would not recommend it.

1. Press **Alt-D**, or use **Tab** to select **Define Custom Colors** and then press **Enter**. A new dialog box appears.

1. Click on **Define Custom Colors** and a new dialog box appears.

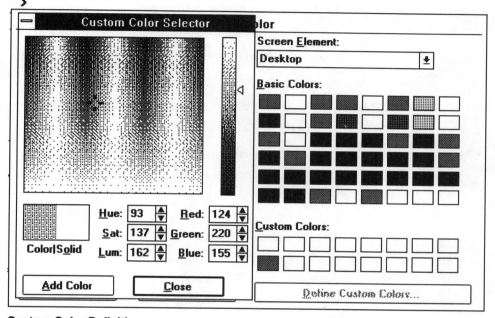

Custom Color Definition

Notice that the Custom Color Selector overlays part of the original dialog box. (You can move it to a different location by clicking on the menu title bar and dragging the box.) The new screen is broadly divided into the following areas.

a. A square that shows all the possible colors and hues. This area contains the color selector cursor, which resembles an open cross.

b. A vertical bar with a triangular sliding pointer, located to the right of the color box. This is used to define the luminosity of any color, from zero, which is black, to the maximum, which is white.

c. A box labeled **Color|Solid**, showing a sample of the color selected in the box above and the solid color closest to it in the spectrum.

d. A series of six boxes in two rows of three. The first set defines the properties of a custom color:

Hue defines the shade of the color. This setting can have any value from 0 to 239.

Sat, short for Saturation, is the density of the color. You can use any value in the range 0 to 240.

Lum, short for Luminosity, sets the brightness of the color. The acceptable range for this property is also 0 to 240.

The second set of boxes defines the color itself. Because your monitor creates colors using three color guns, all colors are made up of relative amounts of red, green and blue. (Each separate color can be in the range 0 to 255.) Note that your monitor can only truly produce solid colors—that is, those with a saturation of 0 or 240; all other colors are simulated by combining different-colored dots. A word of caution: If you make each of the colors the same value, you get gray. Thus, assuming the Hue, Saturation and Luminosity settings are equal, 96 Red/ 96 Green/96 Blue is almost identical to 200 Red/200 Green/200 Blue. (In reality the colors are slightly different, but most monitors are not capable of showing such subtle distinctions.)

 2. Use the **Tab** key to select the Hue box (the value will be shown in inverse video when it is highlighted).

3. Type the new value. Do not press **Enter** until you have redefined all the color settings.

4. Press **Tab** to move down to Saturation. Type the new value.

5. **Tab** to Luminosity and type a new value. Note that as you change Hue and Saturation the color selection cursor moves within the color square; as you change Luminosity, the pointer slides along the vertical bar.

6. **Tab** to Red and type a value; then use **Tab** to move to the other boxes and adjust their values. Your custom color will be shown in the box to the left of the color definition boxes. If you do not like this then go back to step 2 and make changes.

7. Press **Alt-A**; or press **Tab** until **Add Color** is highlighted and then press **Enter**. The customized color will be placed in the first of the 16 boxes in the Custom Colors area.

8. You can define additional colors by repeating steps (2) through (7). Each time you add a color it will be placed in the next empty custom color box, filling the squares from top to bottom and then from left to right. If you try to define more than 16 colors, the new color will overwrite the first box and begin the cycle again.

9. When you are satisfied with the colors you have created, press **Alt-C** or **Escape** to close the Custom Color Selector and return to the main Color area.

 2. Using the mouse, drag the color selector cursor to any part of the color square. As you do so, the values in the six color definition boxes will change and a sample of the color will appear in the preview area labeled **Color|Solid**.

3. Adjust the luminosity of the color by dragging the arrowhead beside the vertical bar.

4. Click on **Add Color** and the color you have designed will appear in the first custom color box.

5. Continue defining colors until you have as many as you want or can have. Each time you add a color it will be placed in the next empty box, filling the squares from top to bottom and then from left to right. (To redefine a custom color, click on the box before clicking on **Add Color**.) If you try to define more than 16 colors, the new color will overwrite the first box and begin the cycle again. Click on **Close** to return to the main screen.

Having designed the custom colors you can now assign them to any of the screen elements.

Exercise 5.4
Save the Scheme

When you are happy with the new color scheme you should save it so that Windows can use it. Note that the changes you have made so far are reflected only in the Color dialog box; they do not appear in the actual Windows environment yet. Once the scheme is saved and the Color option terminated, the scheme becomes active. If you do not save the scheme then Windows will still use it, even if you terminate Windows and then restart it, but your color selections will be wiped out the next time you change color schemes or make any further changes.

1. Press **Alt-A** or click on **Save Scheme**. A dialog box will appear.

Save Scheme Dialog Box

2. Type a name for the scheme. You can use a maximum of 32 characters, including blank spaces.

3. Press **Enter** or click on **OK**. The Color dialog box will disappear and there will be a pause while the changes you have made are implemented. Within a few seconds your new scheme has been applied to the Windows environment and will remain active until you change it.

Fonts

Every Windows application and many areas of the Windows environment itself use text—letters, numerals and symbols—to some degree. Before we get into this Control Panel option, some background about the subject is in order.

Typefaces and Fonts

The design of the characters is called a *typeface*. All typefaces have names, and generally speaking they can be divided into two categories: serif and sans serif. Times Roman, a popular typeface used by newspapers and magazines (so called because it was adapted from a very old typeface called Roman for the Times newspaper in London) is a serif face—that is, there are serifs, or ornamental strokes, at the top and bottom of each character. Helvetica, the typeface used for the captions in this book, is a sans serif typeface—it is drawn with straight lines and no serifs.

There are literally hundreds of different typefaces, and most of them are copyrighted by the designer. Zapf Dingbats, for instance, is a set of characters that produces semi-graphical figures rather than letters and numbers. If your printer is capable of producing Dingbats, then the printer manufacturer has had to license the typeface from the copyright holder, International Typefaces Corporation. (This is one of the overheads that printer manufacturers have to pass on to their customers as part of the purchase price of the machine.)

A *font*, on the other hand, is the set of characters of a typeface in one particular size and style. Thus 12 point Helvetica Italic, 15 point Helvetica, 15 point Helvetica Bold, and 99 point Helvetica are all different fonts in the same typeface.

Pitch and Point

How you refer to the size of the characters you produce depends on the type of printer you are using. Dot matrix and daisy-wheel printers typically use pitch to define character size. Pitch is a measure of the number of characters that can be printed in a one-inch space across the width of the paper. Thus, 10 pitch means you can print ten characters to the inch, 12 pitch is twelve per inch, and so on. The higher the pitch value, the smaller the characters, because you are printing more characters in the same space.

Laser and inkjet printers, on the other hand, typically use points to define character size. The higher the point value, the larger the character. There are 72 points in one inch, and point size refers to the height of the character. The default font for many printers is 12 point—that is, 12/72 or 1/6 of an inch high—which means you can print them 6 lines to an inch down the length of the paper. Does that mean the actual characters are 1/6 of an inch high? Not exactly, although for all intents and purposes you can treat them as if they are. Point sizes are actually a hangover from the days when printers set type using little lead character blocks. The sizes actually refer to these blocks rather than to the symbols they contain. (In some application programs—WordStar and PageMaker, for example—you can define character sizes in tenths of a point, but that can get really confusing. You're better off if you stick to whole sizes.)

Even though two fonts may both be listed as 10 point the actual character sizes can vary. And just to confuse matters further, different typefaces use different amounts of blank space around their characters. Thus, changing from 10 point Courier to 10 point Times Roman can make an enormous difference in your layout. You might expect the characters to stay the same size, but they don't—and all the rest of the text reflows to accommodate the new size.

Screen Fonts

On a PC running in character mode—at the system prompt, let's say—all characters occupy the same area. Depending on the monitor type, the letters and symbols may be designed to fit into a block 9 pixels by 9 pixels or 14 pixels by 9 pixels (a pixel is the smallest area of the screen that can be illuminated independently). In a graphical environment like Windows, you can display multiple fonts side by side; however, the typeface still must be distorted somewhat so that it can be represented onscreen by a collection of pixels. This is why when you look at text on the screen the lines are separated by only a single pixel or two and certain typefaces have jagged edges. But when you print it out the text will normally look just fine, because the printer uses a different resolution and different character blocks.

Fonts in Windows

Windows uses two different kinds of fonts:

Raster fonts are actually bit maps, or collections of dots, that represent the characters. Raster fonts, which are used mainly for displaying text onscreen, display one size only; if you want to see different sized letters on the screen you have to have those sizes installed. Some dot matrix printers use raster fonts but in the normal course of events these fonts are not used for printing.

Vector fonts are scalable outlines of characters that can be stretched or compressed to make different sizes. Using vector fonts reduces the amount of memory needed, as you only have to install one font outline to produce any size you need. Many laser printers, and all PostScript printers, use vector fonts.

Windows includes a number of built-in typefaces and their associated fonts, installed via the Setup routine. (The sizes of the fonts within Windows are always given in points, another indicator that Windows 3 is intended for use with high-quality systems.) These typefaces should be sufficient to cover all of your needs. Some Windows-based programs—Corel Draw, for example—come with extra typefaces.

Windows will automatically substitute one font for another as necessary. For example, suppose you were using Aldus PageMaker with a PostScript printer and you wanted to use the typeface called Palatino. Because this typeface is not installed in Windows, the program will use another typeface of similar style and definition for the purposes of showing the text onscreen. In this case it will probably use Times Roman, because there is not a great deal of difference between the two typefaces. The program "knows" you are using Palatino; thus, all the type attributes, characteristics, spacing and kerning will be handled as if the onscreen typeface were Palatino, which is wider than Roman. When the document is printed on a PostScript printer, the text will appear in Palatino.

Exercise 5.5
Adding and Removing Fonts

You can add extra typefaces and fonts to the Windows environment, but each one will require additional disk and memory space. As a result, unless you have a definite reason for wanting to display the typeface, there is very little point in adding its fonts. To free memory space, you can remove fonts from the Windows environment. The font files themselves remain on the hard disk so that they can be restored to Windows at a later date.

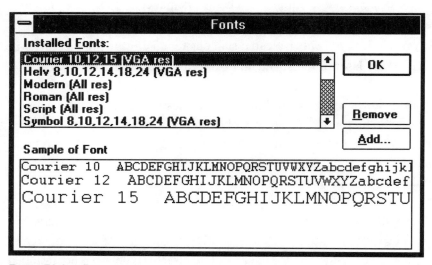

Fonts Dialog Box

 1. Activate the Control Panel and use the cursor keys or the menu to select **Fonts.** Press **Enter** to bring up the Fonts dialog box.

2. You can move through the installed typefaces, and their associated fonts, using the cursor keys. As you do so, the box labeled **Sample of Font** displays the highlighted typeface in the range of sizes that are installed. For a vector font only the base size is shown.

3. To add a font, press **Alt-A**, or use the **Tab** to select **Add** and then press

Enter. The Add Font Files dialog box will appear.

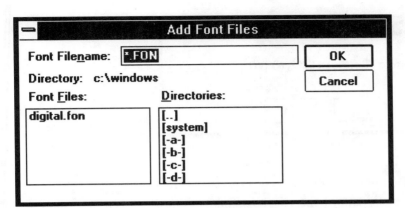

Add Fonts

4. Press **Tab** or **Alt-F** to move to the Font Files list (you may need to **Tab** to the Directories list to change to the drive or directory where the font files are located). Use the cursor keys to select the font you want to install and then press **Enter**. As part of the Setup process, Windows installed a group of fonts in a file called DIGITAL.FON. You cannot reinstall these.

 1. Activate the Control Panel and then double click on the icon labeled **Fonts**. The Fonts dialog box appears.

2. You can click on any of the installed fonts to see what they look like, using the scroll bars if necessary to move through the rest of the list.

3. To add a font, click on **Add** to bring up the Add Font Files dialog box. Change drives or directories if necessary using the Directories list, then click on the name of the font file you want to install. Click on **OK** to add the font to your system.

To remove a font, select it from the Installed Fonts list and then press **Alt-R** or click on **Remove**, which brings up another dialog box. You'll be asked to confirm your choice before the file is actually removed.

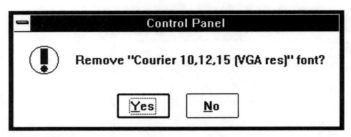

Remove Fonts

Warning: Do not delete the Helvetica fonts! This typeface is used throughout Windows—in menus, dialog boxes, list boxes and the like. If you remove it then you will not be able to read most of the text in the Windows environment.

Ports

The Control Panel allows you to change the settings for any of the four serial ports that may be attached to your computer. These settings affect how information from the computer is transferred to and from peripheral devices connected to the serial ports. Refer to the user's manual for the peripheral device for details as to what these settings should be.

Exercise 5.6
Changing Port Settings

1. From the Control Panel, use the cursor keys or the menu to select **Ports** and then press **Enter**.

2. Use the cursor keys to highlight the port you want to reconfigure and then press **Alt-S** to bring up a new dialog box.

3. Use the **Tab** key to move from area to area and the cursor keys to make changes within each area.

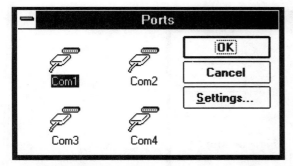

Ports Dialog Box, Part 1

4. Use **Tab** again to select OK and then press **Enter** to save your changes.

5. If you want to make changes to the other ports, repeat steps (2) through (4). When all your changes are complete, press **Enter** to return to the Control Panel.

 1. Double click on the **Ports** icon in the Control Panel.

2. Click on the icon of the port you want to change and then on **Settings**.

3. Click on the various settings to change them. Use the arrow at the right of the Baud Rate box to drop down a list of choices for this setting.

4. Click on **OK** to accept the changes and return to the Ports dialog box.

5. To reconfigure other ports, repeat steps (2) through (4). When your changes are complete, click on **OK** to return to the Control Panel.

Ports - Settings

Settings for Com1

Baud Rate: 9600

OK

Cancel

Data Bits
- ○ 4
- ○ 5
- ○ 6
- ○ 7
- ⦿ 8

Parity
- ○ Even
- ○ Odd
- ⦿ None
- ○ Mark
- ○ Space

Stop Bits
- ⦿ 1
- ○ 1.5
- ○ 2

Flow Control
- ○ Xon / Xoff
- ○ Hardware
- ⦿ None

Ports Dialog Box, Part 2

Mouse

Windows 3 is designed to be used with a mouse. Of course, you can use the program with only the keyboard, but that would be like trying to play football with one arm tied behind your back. It might be possible, but who would want to? As installed, the program is configured to handle input from the mouse in a particular way. However, you can use the Control Panel to change how the mouse responds.

Exercise 5.7
Mouse Work

1. Activate the Control Panel and double click on **Mouse** to bring up the dialog box.

2. The Mouse Tracking Speed setting controls how fast the mouse moves onscreen. Drag the scroll bar all the way to the right (towards **Fast**) or click on the right-hand scroll bar arrow. Now try moving the mouse in a random fashion. Notice how fast it moves.

3. Move the scroll bar all the way to the left-hand side of the box (towards **Slow**). Move the mouse again and the difference is obvious. You should set the Tracking Speed to whatever feels most comfortable for you.

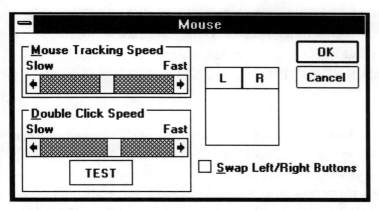

Mouse Settings

4. The Double Click Speed controls how fast you have to press the mouse button for a double click to be recognized. Move the scroll bar all the way to the right (towards **Fast**) and double click on the box labeled **TEST**. Unless you have lightning fingers, the Test box will remain unchanged even after the second click.

5. Now move the indicator all the way to the left (towards **Slow**) and double click on **TEST** again. This time you may find that you're clicking too fast for the command to be recognized. Play with different settings until you find one that works best for you.

6. If you are left-handed you may wish to swap the mouse buttons. By default, Windows assumes that the user will be gripping the mouse with his or her right hand and clicking the left mouse button with the index finger of that hand. If you control the mouse with your left hand, your index finger will naturally sit over the right-hand button. By clicking on **Swap Left/Right**

Buttons you can switch the action of the mouse to accommodate this difference. (Microsoft has always provided this facility in Windows, and they are to be congratulated for thinking of it in the first place.)

7. Once you have finished with the mouse settings, click on **OK** to save them and exit to the Control Panel. Warning: Do not save these settings unless the double click test works or you will be unable to use the mouse for basic Windows functions and will have to use the keyboard instead.

Desktop

While the Color option allows you to set and/or change the color scheme that Windows will use, the onscreen display is more complex than that. The Desktop option allows you to customize the screen even further. It controls a number of settings that affect where and how objects are arranged onscreen. It also allows you to take any bitmap graphic file, such as those generated from Windows Paintbrush, and use it as a background for Windows.

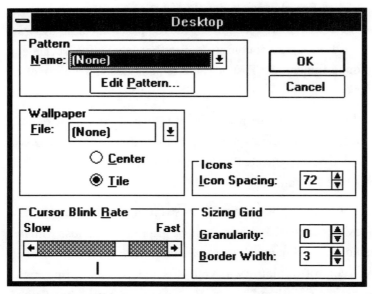

Desktop Dialog Box

The dialog box that appears is divided into five major areas:

a. **Pattern** lets you replace the blank background.

b. **Wallpaper** gives you the option to use a bitmap graphic file as all or part of the Windows background.

c. **Cursor Blink Rate** controls how fast the onscreen cursor flashes within applications.

d. **Icons** allows you to adjust the spacing between icons.

e. **Sizing Grid** creates an invisible grid to align objects on the desktop; it also allows you to set the width of window borders.

Exercise 5.8
Choose a Pattern

The Desktop option allows you to replace the blank screen background with a grid pattern. On a VGA monitor, this pattern is made up of 64 dots arranged in an 8 by 8 grid. Not very much, you might think, but the way that Windows uses them means that you can create quite complex and visually stunning patterns.

When Windows is first installed, there is no pattern used for the background; you simply get a blank screen, with the option to reset its color. However, Windows includes a number of predesigned patterns that you can use instead of the plain backdrop. These patterns all consist of black dots on the Application Workspace background color that you set using the Colors option.

1. From the Control Panel, select **Desktop** using the cursor keys or the pull-down menu. Press **Enter** to activate this option.

2. The Pattern box is selected by default. Use the cursor keys to move through the list; if you press **Alt-Down**, a list box containing the names of the available patterns drops down.

3. Use the cursor keys to select a pattern.

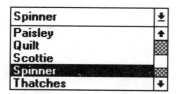

Desktop Patterns List Box

1. From the Control Panel, double click on the **Desktop** icon.

2. Click on the arrow at the right of the Pattern box; a list of available patterns will drop down.

3. Click on the name of the pattern you want to use.

Exercise 5.9
Design a Pattern

After you've selected the pattern, you cannot see what it looks like until you close the Desktop facility. If you don't like the pattern, you have to go back to the Desktop to change it. (I think this is a surprising omission, considering how user-friendly Windows is in other areas.) However, there is a way to get an idea of what the pattern will look like, even though the facility was not intended for this use.

1. Select a pattern name, and then press **Alt-P** to bring up the Edit Pattern dialog box.

1. Select a pattern name and click on **Edit Pattern**.

The dialog box that appears is divided into two parts: The Sample box on the left shows you what the background pattern looks like at its normal size. The large box in the center lets you edit the pattern itself. You can make changes only if you are using a mouse. There is no way to modify the pattern using the keyboard.

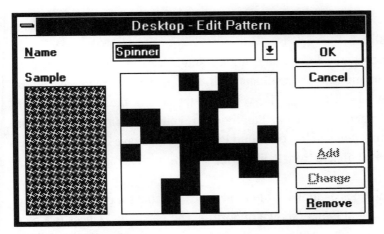

Edit Pattern Dialog Box

2. You can use the cursor keys to cycle through the other predefined patterns and see a sample view of each one. When you find one you like, press **Enter** to return to the Desktop dialog box.

2. Move the pointer over the 8 by 8 grid.

3. If you click on a black square, it will change to the background color, and vice versa. The sample pattern changes instantly as you edit the pattern.

Tip: To edit a block of squares quickly, click and drag the pointer and it will change all the squares it moves over.

4. When you create a new pattern you can save it with the existing ones. Click on **Add Pattern** and type in a name. You don't need to press **Enter** at this stage unless you want to terminate this part of the program.

5. At any time you can remove a pattern by selecting it and then clicking on **Remove**. (You can also remove patterns using the keyboard.)

Exercise 5.10
Internal Decoration

Windows 3 allows you to use any bitmap graphic, even full color ones, as wallpaper on the background. The wallpaper will take precedence over any pattern or color that you have used. To be used as wallpaper the graphic must be in the .BMP file format that is created by Windows Paintbrush. If you have a favorite graphic in .PCX or .MSP format, you can import it into Paintbrush and save it as a .BMP file. Thus you can, with a bit of help from Paintbrush, use almost any graphics file as your wallpaper.

The program includes a number of graphics files suitable for use as wallpaper. My favorite is one called Paper (shown opposite). The one called Chess is a nice example of perspective, but it can only appear if Windows is running in standard or 386 enhanced mode; large graphics files require more memory than is available in real mode. (In fact, if you ever find an application running low on memory, try switching from wallpaper to a simpler background to free up some extra RAM.) When you pull down the list of available wallpaper files, Windows looks only in its own subdirectory—if you want to specify a file from elsewhere on the disk, you'll need to type the complete filename, including the path.

1. Start the Desktop option as usual.

2. Press **Alt-F** and then **Alt-Down** to pull down the Wallpaper list box.

3. Use the cursor keys to select the graphic of your choice. You can elect to have the graphic displayed centrally—that is, as a single image in the middle of the screen—or tiled, with the image repeated as many times as possible and arranged edge to edge so they fill the background. Use **Tab** to switch between the two options.

1. Double click on the Desktop icon to start the Desktop option and then click on the arrow at the right-hand side of the box labeled Wallpaper.

2. Click on the name of the graphics file you want to use.

3. If necessary, click on either **Center** or **Tile** to change the way the graphic display will be arranged.

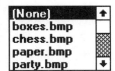

Wallpaper List Box

Remember, your wallpaper selection doesn't take effect until you close the Desktop dialog box and return to the Control Panel.

The PAPER Graphic as Wallpaper

Cursor Blink Rate

This does exactly as it says. In the majority of Windows applications, the cursor flashes to show its position. Use this option to adjust the speed at which the cursor blinks.

Icon Spacing

When you choose the Arrange Icons command from the Program Manager menu, Windows uses the value you specify here to determine the distance between icons. The value is measured in pixels (the smallest area of the screen that can be illuminated). Normally, icons and their accompanying captions can occupy as little as 50 pixels; if your captions are wider than this, you may find them overlapping one another. You can correct the display by increasing the value here. Again, you won't see any effect until you return to the Program Manager and activate one of the two icon arranging commands.

Sizing Grid

Windows can use an invisible grid to align icons and windows. You adjust the grid size using the Granularity option; the value is measured in pixels and must be in the range 0 to 49. Each time you increase the setting by 1, the grid lines move 8 pixels further apart. By default, the granularity is set to 0—in other words, the grid is turned off. With the grid off you can move any icon or window to any position on the screen, and it will remain in that position. Once you increase the granularity value the grid becomes operable and objects align themselves to the grid when you move them.

Border Width

You can change the width of window borders by increasing this value. Here, too, the number is measured in pixels and must be in the range 1 to 49. Increasing the value makes the borders wider.

Network

If you are using Windows on a machine that is part of an active network, then the Control Panel will include a Network icon. Although every network operating system is different, you should be able to perform such common operations as making or breaking network connections, logging onto shared directories, and changing your password. The contents of the associated dialog box will always be specific to the network operating system you are using.

Printers

Windows 3 can be used with almost any printer you're likely to find. The printer driver supplies Windows with essential information about the printer: the fonts it supports, paper sources, page sizes, control characters and so on. The disks supplied with the program contain nearly 200 printer drivers, and Microsoft regularly updates drivers as new printer models are introduced. Even if your printer isn't on the list of supported models, the odds are very good that it emulates one of the popular printers that is supported.

You can install any number of printers when you run the Windows Setup program, and you can add new printers any time via the Control Panel. After you have installed the drivers, you still have to configure the printer for it to work correctly. The steps involved in using a printer with Windows are:

a. Install the printer driver.

b. Assign the printer to a port.

c. Configure the printer to match your preferences.

d. Select an active printer for each port, if necessary.

e. Nominate one of the printers you have installed as the default printer—that is, the one you will use most often.

In the following section we are going to cover all of this ground, using a Hewlett-Packard LaserJet Series II printer as an example. The Series II has two slots for optional font cartridges. By default it uses letter-size ($8^{1}/_{2}$" by 11") paper in portrait orientation—that is, the paper is longer from top to bottom than it is from side to side (as opposed to landscape orientation, where the paper is longer from side to side than it is from top to bottom).

Exercise 5.11
Adding a Printer

As we have seen, you can install printer drivers during the initial Windows Setup; if you later add or change a printer, however, it is much more practical to install the printer driver through the Control Panel.

 1. Activate the Control Panel in the usual way. Then, using the cursor keys or the menu, select **Printers** and press **Enter** to bring up the Printers dialog box.

1. From the Control Panel, double click on the **Printers** icon to open the Printers dialog box.

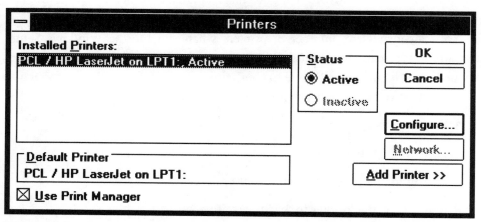

Printer Dialog Box

This is the first of several dialog boxes that you'll use to add a new printer. The initial dialog box is divided into four main areas:

a. **Installed Printers** contains the names of the printer drivers that you have previously installed into the Windows environment.

b. **Default Printer** is the printer that you normally use.

c. **Status** tells you whether the printer highlighted in the Installed Printers list is ready for use.

d. A check box labeled **Use Print Manager** toggles the Windows print spooler on and off.

e. A series of buttons activate additional dialog boxes.

 2. Use the **Tab** key to select **Add Printer** and then press **Enter**, or simply press **Alt-A**. This will expand the dialog box and give you a list of installable printers.

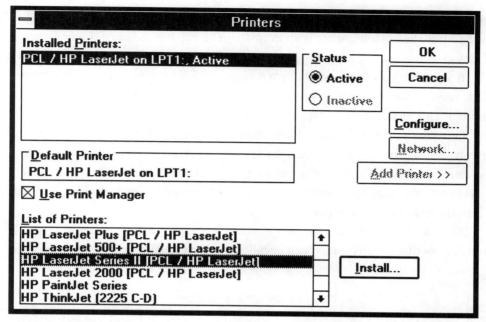

Add Printer Dialog Box

3. Use the cursor keys to move through the list of printers until you find the one you want. (**Tip:** You can jump directly to the appropriate section of the list by typing the first letter of your printer's name.) When the proper name is highlighted, press **Enter** or **Alt-I**.

2. Click on **Add Printer** to expand the dialog box.

3. Use the scroll bars to move through the list of printers; when you find the one you want, highlight the name by clicking on it and then click on the button labeled **Install**.

If your printer is not shown in the list, then you will have to select the name of a printer that it emulates. What happens next depends on the printer drivers that are already installed on your system. If the model you have selected uses the same driver as an installed printer, a message box will pop up telling you so. This gives you the option of using the existing driver, installing a new driver, or canceling the installation. Select whichever is appropriate: You can use the same driver as many times as you wish.

If you have elected to install a new driver, you will be prompted to put the driver disk into drive A: (or another drive you specify) so that Windows can copy the file to your hard disk.

Once the printer driver has been copied or you have elected to use an existing driver, a new printer name appears in the Installed Printers box. Note that the name is generic, not specific. Thus the LaserJet Series II is billed as a PCL/HP LaserJet, as is every other LaserJet model and a number of compatible printers from Toshiba, Kyocera and other manufacturers.

You can install as many printers as necessary at this point—just repeat steps 2 and 3. Now that the driver has been installed, the next step is to configure the printer for use.

4. Press **Alt-C** to bring up the next dialog box.

5. Use the cursor keys to scroll through the list of available ports and select the port to which the printer is attached.

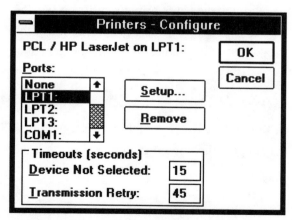

Configure Printer Dialog Box

4. Click on **Configure** to bring up the next dialog box.

5. Use the scroll bars, if necessary, to move though the list of ports, and click on the name of the port to which the printer is attached.

In general, there are four types of ports available:

LPT refers to parallel ports, the type most commonly used for printing.

COM is the designation for serial ports. Some printers can be connected to a serial port, but this configuration tends to be slower than one that uses a parallel port. If you plan to connect your printer to a serial port you will need to check its settings using the Ports option of the Control Panel.

EPT is a special port used by some printers. To use this you must have the necessary add-on board installed in your computer.

FILE allows you to send documents directly to a disk file complete with printer codes.

The other settings in this dialog box, under the heading Timeouts, set the amount of time that Windows will wait before it presents you with an error message that something has gone wrong, and the time that it will wait before trying the printer again. Both values are given in seconds. The defaults should not need to be changed.

At this point, if you wish to remove the highlighted printer from your list of installed printers, you can press **Alt-R** or click on **Remove**. The name will be removed from the list, but the driver remains on your hard disk to allow you to reinstall the printer at a later date.

Once you have assigned the printer port, you have to supply Windows with detailed information about your specific printer configuration.

6. Use the **Tab** key to select Setup and then press **Enter**, or press **Alt-S**, to bring up the next dialog box.

6. Click on **Setup** to continue the configuration.

131

```
┌─────────────────────────────────────────────────────────────────┐
│ ▬        PCL / HP LaserJet on LPT1:                               │
├─────────────────────────────────────────────────────────────────┤
│  Printer:        │HP LaserJet Series II              ▐ ±│  ┌──────────┐ │
│                                                           │    OK    │ │
│  Paper Source:   │Upper Tray                │ ±│         └──────────┘ │
│                                                           ┌──────────┐ │
│  Paper Size:     │Letter 8 ½ x 11 in        │ ±│         │  Cancel  │ │
│                                                           └──────────┘ │
│  Memory:         │512 KB    │ ±│                          ┌──────────┐ │
│                                                           │  Fonts...│ │
│  ┌─Orientation─────────────┐  ┌─Graphics Resolution──┐   └──────────┘ │
│  │                         │  │  ◉ 75  dots per inch │   ┌──────────┐ │
│  │  ┌───┐  ◉ Portrait      │  │                      │   │ Options..│ │
│  │  │ A │                  │  │  ○ 150 dots per inch │   └──────────┘ │
│  │  └───┘  ○ Landscape     │  │                      │   ┌──────────┐ │
│  │                         │  │  ○ 300 dots per inch │   │  Help... │ │
│  └─────────────────────────┘  └──────────────────────┘   └──────────┘ │
│  ┌─Cartridges (2 max)──────┐                              ┌──────────┐ │
│  │ None                 ▲ │   Copies:  │1      │          │  About...│ │
│  │ A: Courier             │                              └──────────┘ │
│  │ B: Tms Proportional 1  │                                           │
│  │ C: International 1     │                                           │
│  │ D: Prestige Elite    ▼ │                                           │
│  └─────────────────────────┘                                         │
└─────────────────────────────────────────────────────────────────┘
```

Printer Name List Box

Note that the types of settings available will vary with the type of printer you have selected. The details shown in the dialog box are the default settings used by the particular printer driver you have installed. They may be correct, in which case you need do nothing to them, but it is more likely that they will need to be changed, especially if you are using a printer emulation. The next step is to select the specific model of printer that you want to use (or emulate).

7. Because the printer name is already highlighted, you can move through the list of printers that use that particular driver by simply using the cursor keys. As you do so, the details in the other boxes will change as well.

7. Click on the arrow at the right of the highlighted printer name and a list of printer names will drop down. Scroll through this box until you find the model you want and then click on it.

```
┌─────────────────────────────────────────────────────────────────────────┐
│ ═                    PCL / HP LaserJet on LPT1:                            │
├─────────────────────────────────────────────────────────────────────────┤
│                                                                           │
│  Printer:        ┌──────────────────────────────┬──┐     ┌───────────┐    │
│                  │ HP LaserJet Series II         │ ↓│     │    OK     │    │
│  Paper Source:   ├──────────────────────────────┼──┤     └───────────┘    │
│                  │ HP LaserJet Series II         │ ↑│     ┌───────────┐    │
│                  │ HP LaserJet IID               │  │     │  Cancel   │    │
│  Paper Size:     │ HP LaserJet IIP               │  │     └───────────┘    │
│                  │ HP LaserJet Plus              │  │     ┌───────────┐    │
│  Memory:         │ HP LaserJet 500+              │ ↓│     │  Fonts... │    │
│                  │ 512 KB          ▼             │  │     └───────────┘    │
│                                                        ┌───────────┐       │
│  ┌─ Orientation ──────────┐  ┌─ Graphics Resolution ─┐│  Options...│       │
│  │                        │  │  ◉ 75  dots per inch   │└───────────┘       │
│  │   ┌───┐  ◉ Portrait     │  │                       │┌───────────┐       │
│  │   │ A │                 │  │  ○ 150 dots per inch  ││   Help... │       │
│  │   └───┘  ○ Landscape    │  │                       │└───────────┘       │
│  │                        │  │  ○ 300 dots per inch   │┌───────────┐       │
│  └────────────────────────┘  └───────────────────────┘│  About... │       │
│                                                        └───────────┘       │
│  ┌─ Cartridges (2 max) ───┐                                                │
│  │ None                 ↑ │   Copies:  ┌──────┐                            │
│  │ A: Courier             │            │ 1    │                            │
│  │ B: Tms Proportional 1  │            └──────┘                            │
│  │ C: International 1      │                                                │
│  │ D: Prestige Elite    ↓ │                                                │
│  └────────────────────────┘                                                │
└───────────────────────────────────────────────────────────────────────────┘
```

Printer Name List Box

Check the settings for paper source, paper size and memory. Paper Source refers to the tray that is normally used to supply paper for the printer. Paper Size sets the default paper size you plan to use. Memory is the amount of RAM installed in the printer. If these details are correct you need do nothing. If any of them are set incorrectly, you'll need to make the necessary changes.

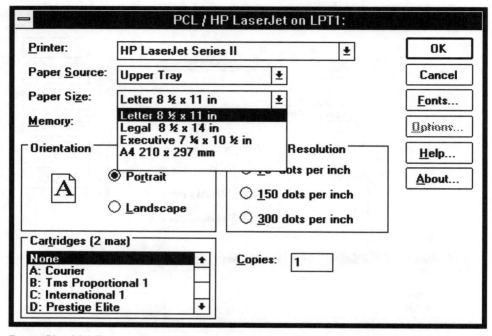

Paper Size List Box

8. Press **Tab** to move to the appropriate line and then use the cursor keys to select the correct entry.

8. Click on the arrowhead at the right of the entry you wish to change and a list box will drop down. Scroll through the list and select the correct entry by clicking on it.

Most letters and business documents are printed using portrait orientation. If you want to print in landscape orientation you must change this setting.

9. Use **Tab** to move to the relevant section of the dialog box and then press **Alt-L** to change the setting to Landscape. Pressing **Alt-R** switches to Portrait. (You may also use any cursor key to switch back and forth between the two modes.)

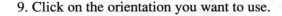

9. Click on the orientation you want to use.

When you install a PCL laser printer, you have the option of selecting which graphics resolution to use. At the default setting of 75 dots per inch (dpi), your output will be very coarse; if your printer has enough memory to handle a higher resolution, you can increase this setting to a maximum of 300 dpi, which produces much sharper images. With a PostScript laser printer you do not have this option because Windows uses the highest resolution it can get. You can, however, select what scaling to use—that is, how much a document or graphic will be shrunk or enlarged when printed. By default this value is set to 100%; I suggest that you leave it at that. It is far better to change the scaling from within an application.

10. **Tab** to the Graphics Resolution box and use the cursor keys to select the desired resolution.

10. Click on the resolution you want to use.

Finally, you'll need to tell Windows which, if any, font cartridges are installed in your system. Using a PostScript printer you set the optional parameters that will be used instead.

11. **Tab** to the Cartridges box and use the cursor keys to scroll through the list of available cartridges. Press the **Spacebar** to mark your choice. If you have more than one cartridge installed, repeat this process until both cartridges are marked.

11. Scroll through the list of available font cartridges and click on the ones you want to use.

```
┌─────────────────────────────────────────────────────────────┐
│ ▬                        Options                              │
├─────────────────────────────────────────────────────────────┤
│ ┌─Print To──────────────────────────┐   ┌─────────────────┐  │
│ │ ◉ Printer                          │   │       OK        │  │
│ │ ○ Encapsulated PostScript File     │   └─────────────────┘  │
│ │   File: [                       ]  │   ┌─────────────────┐  │
│ │                                    │   │     Cancel      │  │
│ └────────────────────────────────────┘   └─────────────────┘  │
│ ┌─Job Timeout────┐ ┌─Margins──────┐      ┌─────────────────┐  │
│ │                │ │ ◉ Default    │      │    Header...    │  │
│ │ [0]   seconds  │ │ ○ None       │      └─────────────────┘  │
│ │                │ │              │      ┌─────────────────┐  │
│ └────────────────┘ └──────────────┘      │   Handshake...  │  │
│ ┌─Header─────────────────────────┐       └─────────────────┘  │
│ │ ◉ Download each job            │                            │
│ │ ○ Already downloaded           │                            │
│ └────────────────────────────────┘                            │
└─────────────────────────────────────────────────────────────┘
```

PostScript Printer Options

When configuring a PostScript printer, you have a number of other options available. The default settings work perfectly with my printer, and so I have never needed to change them. However, this is what they mean:

Print To allows Windows to send the file to an Encapsulated PostScript (EPS) file instead of to the printer. An EPS file can be incorporated into files used in some programs.

Job Timeout refers to the number of seconds that Windows waits before sending you an error message if something goes wrong while printing. I like to know immediately when there's a problem, and so I have left the setting at its default of 0.

Margins controls how close to the edge of the printed page you want the document to be printed. As these are normally set on the printer itself, it is best to leave the setting of **Default**.

Header refers to the PostScript information file that must be sent to the printer before printing can begin. The default setting is **Download each job,** which means that the data will be sent to the printer every time you print a document. This is the best setting to use, because it speeds up the printing by leaving as much of the printer's RAM as possible free. The alternative option is **Already down-loaded,** which allows you to send the information immediately so that it will reside in the printer RAM. This reduces the amount of memory the printer has available and also tends to slow down printing.

The button labeled **Header** allows you to send the header information to the printer or to a file. Clicking on this button brings up another dialog box that will allow you to send the information now or later.

Clicking on the **Handshake** button brings up a dialog box that controls the way the printer communicates with the PC. The proper setting depends on whether the flow of information is controlled by your software or by the printer itself.

Having set the settings you want, you can now return to the main dialog box and determine whether the printer is to be active; you can also select a default printer at this point. You can have only one printer active for each port. If there is only one printer installed for a given port, it will automatically be active. If you have more than one printer assigned to a port, however, you will need to choose which one is active.

 12. Press **Enter** in each dialog box in turn until you get back to the main dialog box.

13. Highlight the printer you wish to activate, and then use the **Tab** key or **Alt-S** to move into the Status box; finally, use any cursor key to make the printer active. Note that any other printers attached to the same port will become inactive as soon as you do this.

14. Press **Enter** to close the main dialog box and return to the Control Panel.

12. In each successive dialog box click on **OK** until you reach the main printer dialog box.

13. Highlight the name of the printer whose status you wish to change. Click either **Active** or **Inactive** as necessary. Note that if you choose **Active**, any other printers attached to the same port will become inactive immediately.

14. Click on **OK** in the main dialog box to return to the Control Panel.

If you have more than one active printer, you will need to tell Windows which is the default printer. This is the printer that certain Windows applications will automatically print to.

15. Highlight the name of a printer in the Installed Printers list and press **Alt-D**.

15. Double click on the name of the printer you wish to set as the default.

International

The International section of the Control Panel allows you to modify how various international characteristics are used, displayed and identified within the Windows environment. If you are using Windows in the United States in English then the default settings should work just fine for you. If you're from anywhere else in the world, however, you will probably need to adjust certain of these settings.

The International section is straightforward and will allow you to make changes very rapidly. The easiest way to reconfigure the system is simply to change the country setting, which automatically changes all related settings at the same time. This section makes extensive use of list boxes and pop-up dialog boxes.

1. From the Control Panel, use the cursor keys or the menu to select **International** before pressing **Enter** to run the program.

1. Run Control Panel as usual and then double click on the **International** icon.

```
┌─────────────────────────────────────────────────────┐
│ ▬              International                          │
├─────────────────────────────────────────────────────┤
│ Country:      ┌─────────────────┬──┐  ┌───────────┐  │
│               │United States    │ ± │  │    OK     │  │
│               └─────────────────┴──┘  └───────────┘  │
│ Language:     ┌─────────────────┬──┐  ┌───────────┐  │
│               │English (American)│ ± │  │  Cancel   │  │
│               └─────────────────┴──┘  └───────────┘  │
│ Keyboard Layout: ┌──────────────┬──┐                 │
│               │US              │ ± │                  │
│               └────────────────┴──┘                  │
│ Measurement:  ┌────────────────┬──┐                  │
│               │English         │ ± │                  │
│               └────────────────┴──┘                  │
│ List Separator: ┌──┐                                 │
│               │ , │                                   │
│               └──┘                                    │
└─────────────────────────────────────────────────────┘
```

International Settings Dialog Box

The dialog box is divided into two main sections:

a. Four lines at the top of the box control the main characteristics; each line uses its own drop-down list to supply choices.

b. The four boxes at the bottom allow you to modify specific format settings through the use of pop-up dialog boxes.

2. Because the Country line is already selected, you can scroll through the list of countries by simply using the cursor keys. Press **Alt-Down** to see the drop-down list. Note how the format settings below change to match the conventions of the highlighted country—in this example, the United Kingdom.

2. Click on the arrow at the right of the Country line and a list box drops down. Page through the list, using the scroll bars if necessary; click on a country name to close the list.

139

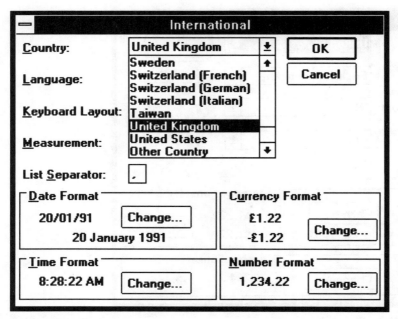

Country List Box

 3. Use **Tab** to move through the next three choices. Select a language, a keyboard layout and a measurement system (English or metric) in the same way you selected a country.

 3. Click on the right-hand arrow to select a language, a keyboard layout and a measurement system (English or metric) from the drop-down lists.

International			
Country:	United States	±	**OK**
Language:	English (American)	±	**Cancel**
Keyboard Layout:	Danish Dutch English (American) English (International) Finnish	↑ ↓	
Measurement:			

List **S**eparator: [,]

Date Format
1/20/91   [Change...]
Sunday, January 20, 1991

Currency Format
$1.22
($1.22)   [Change...]

Time Format
8:28:22 AM   [Change...]

Number Format
1,234.22   [Change...]

Language List Box

The **List Separator** is the character that you want to use for subdividing lists. By default this is a comma, but it can be any character you wish.

The short format for the date depends very much on the national characteristics you are used to. In America the month appears first, followed by the day and the year. In the U.K., on the other hand, the day appears before the month and the year. As you change the country, the format displayed here will change, but you can also modify it directly.

4. Press **Alt-D** to select the option. A new dialog box then appears.

5. Use any cursor keys to select the principal format for the date: Month-Day-Year, Day-Month-Year, or Year-Month-Day.

6. Use **Tab** to move to **Separator** and then type the character you want to use to subdivide the format.

7. **Tab** through the next three elements. Pressing the **Spacebar** will toggle

141

each setting on or off. Setting leading zeros on causes a zero to appear before any single digit—thus July 8th will appear as 07/08 with leading zeros and as 7/8 without one. Change the other elements to your taste.

4. Click on **Change** in the Date Format box and the dialog box pops up.

5. Click on the date layout you want to use.

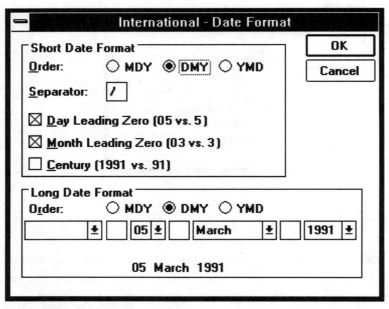

Date Format Dialog Box

6. Click once in the **Separator** box if you wish to change the character shown. Delete the default character and replace it with your own choice.

7. Each of the next three elements is a toggle. Click on any of them to turn the toggle on or off.

The final section of this dialog box lets you reset the long format of the date. You have the option of displaying the day, date, month and year in a variety of ways.

8. Press **Tab** or **Alt-R** to move down to this section. One of the three-letter options will be highlighted. Use any cursor keys to reset the order in which the month, day and year appear.

9. Press **Tab** again to move to the box beneath the word Order. Press **Down** or **Up** to page through the possible selections for displaying the day of the week: a blank line (no day displayed); a short format (e.g., Sun); or the full name (e.g., Sunday). Use the **Tab** key to move through the remaining elements and select the format using the drop-down lists.

10. Finally, press **Tab** until **OK** is selected and then press **Enter** to return to the International main dialog box.

8. Click on the long date format you prefer. The sample date in the box below will change to reflect your choice.

9. Click on an arrow to reveal the drop-down list box for each sub-element and then click on the one you want.

10. Click on **OK** to close the dialog box.

Currency Format allows you to set the currency symbol and define how it will appear. The dialog box contains four selections:

Placement determines whether the currency symbol appears before or after the amount.

Negative establishes how a negative value is shown—for example, preceded by a minus sign or enclosed in brackets.

Symbol is exactly that. The default value here is set when you select a country.

Decimal Digits controls the number of digits you want to appear after a decimal point. The default setting is 2.

11. Press **Alt-U** and a new dialog box appears.

12. You change these settings exactly as you did the elements in the Date Format dialog box. When you have finished, press **Enter** to return to the main screen.

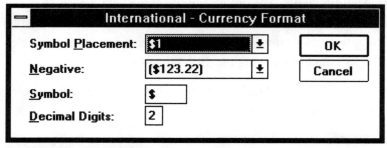

Currency Format Dialog Box

11. Click on **Change** in the Currency Format box to bring up the new dialog box.

12. Make your changes as before. When done click on **OK** to return to the main screen.

The **Time Format** controls how the time will be displayed in applications and in the Clock. You can select either a 24-hour display or a 12-hour format. If you use the latter, then you can select whether you want an AM or PM suffix to appear. You can also toggle the leading zero setting.

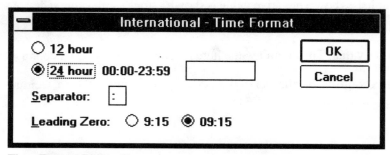

Time Format Dialog Box

Number Format controls the display of numbers. The dialog box allows you to change the separator used for thousands and for decimals. It also permits you to fix the number of decimal places that will be used and whether or not to use leading zeros.

```
┌─────────────────────────────────────────────────────────┐
│ ▬        International - Number Format                    │
├─────────────────────────────────────────────────────────┤
│  1000 Separator:    ┌───┐          ┌──────────┐          │
│                     │ ! │          │    OK    │          │
│  Decimal Separator: ┌───┐          └──────────┘          │
│                     │ . │          ┌──────────┐          │
│  Decimal Digits:    ┌───┐          │  Cancel  │          │
│                     │ 2 │          └──────────┘          │
│                                                          │
│  Leading Zero:   ○ .7      ⦿ 0.7                         │
└─────────────────────────────────────────────────────────┘
```

Number Format Dialog Box

Once you have finished making changes and have returned to the International dialog box, press **Enter** or click on **OK** to return to the Control Panel. To implement some changes, Windows may now ask you to supply one of the original Windows disks. Insert the specified disk in the drive and press **Enter**. The necessary file or files will be copied to your hard disk, which then works like fury as Windows updates its internal files.

Keyboard

This option simply allows you to adjust the speed at which the keyboard processes input. It provides a test strip so you can experiment before you make changes.

Date/Time

Selecting this section brings up a two-line dialog box that allows you to set the system time and date. These changes have the same effect as if you had executed the DATE and TIME commands from the system prompt.

Sound

This setting allows you to turn the audible warning on or off—and that's all.

386 Enhanced

When you are using Windows in 386 enhanced mode, the Control Panel contains an additional icon specific to that mode. The options available here allow you to set the parameters by which non-Windows programs will run concurrently with Windows applications. Under these circumstances, it is possible that two programs might try to use the same device (a printer, for example) at the same time. To avoid potential problems, you have to specify how such conflicts will be resolved. These settings only need to be changed if one of the applications being used is an MS-DOS program. If you are using Windows programs exclusively then you need do nothing— Windows automatically arbitrates concurrent device requests from its own programs.

The dialog box is divided into two parts, Device Contention and Scheduling. The first section offers the following options for each port where a potential for conflict exists:

Always Warn will cause an error message to appear whenever a program tries to use the device connected to that port, if the device is already assigned to another program. At that point you will have to tell Windows which program gets priority. In other words, you are likely to be continually interrupted with error messages overlaying whatever else you are doing.

Never Warn specifies that any program may use any device attached to the port at any time, without producing an error message. This selection keeps you from being interrupted, but it can cause other problems: For example, if two or more programs try to use the same printer at the same time, all you will get is a load of gibberish.

```
┌─────────────────────────────────────────────────────────┐
│ ▬              386 Enhanced                                │
├─────────────────────────────────────────────────────────┤
│ ┌─ Device Contention ──────────────┐   ┌──────────────┐   │
│ │ ┌──────────┐                     │   │      OK      │   │
│ │ │ Com1     │   ○ Always Warn     │   └──────────────┘   │
│ │ │ Com2     │                     │   ┌──────────────┐   │
│ │ │ LPT1     │   ○ Never Warn      │   │   Cancel     │   │
│ │ │          │                     │   └──────────────┘   │
│ │ └──────────┘   ● Idle (in sec.)  │ 2  ▲▼            │   │
│ └──────────────────────────────────┘                     │
│ ┌─ Scheduling ─────────────────────────────┐             │
│ │ Windows in Foreground:        │ 100 │ ▲▼  │             │
│ │ Windows in Background:        │  50 │ ▲▼  │             │
│ │ ☐ Exclusive in Foreground                 │             │
│ └───────────────────────────────────────────┘             │
│   Minimum Timeslice (in msec):   │ 20 │ ▲▼                │
└─────────────────────────────────────────────────────────┘
```

386 Enhanced Mode Settings

Idle allows you to set a period of time during which a device must be unused before another program can use it. The delay value is set in seconds and must be in the range 1 to 999. If the device is idle for that period of time, then the second program can take over use of the device without any problems. The default value is 2 seconds, which is generally more than enough.

The Scheduling section of the dialog box controls the actual multitasking of programs and how Windows behaves when doing so.

Windows in Foreground is used in conjunction with the next setting to specify the relative amount of processor time that all Windows applications share when a Windows program is active. The value must be in the range 1 to 10,000. However, the most important factor is not the absolute value but the ratio of this number to the background setting.

Windows in Background is the amount of processing time shared by all Windows applications when an MS-DOS program is running in the foreground.

The range is the same as for the previous setting.

Exclusive in Foreground, which is a toggle switch, means that whenever a Windows application is active, Windows gets 100% of the processing time available. In other words, MS-DOS programs will be temporarily suspended while a Windows program is running.

Minimum Timeslice sets the number of milliseconds that any program runs before the processor control is given to another program. All Windows applications share a single timeslice automatically, while each MS-DOS program gets its own.

In general, the default values that are given for the 386 enhanced option should be perfectly adequate for any program running concurrently. You are unlikely to need to change them.

Summary

Control Panel is the program that allows you to change the way in which Windows operates.

The program is subdivided into a number of elements so that you can customize only those areas of Windows that you wish to.

Any changes made with the Control Panel will be recorded in the WIN.INI file.

CHAPTER 6

Setup

What Is It?

As part of the Windows 3 installation, a version of the Setup program was copied to your hard disk. When you installed Windows the first time, Setup created a source file that contains information about your system and how it has been configured for Windows. The Setup program that runs within Windows lets you change some (but not all) aspects of the Windows environment. To reinstall Windows or to add device drivers that were not originally included with Windows, you must start Setup from the system prompt.

The Windows Setup program can be used to add programs so they will run in the Windows environment. However, the number of programs you can install in this way is limited. Windows looks only for programs that are included in a list of popular applications. If you wish to include a program that isn't on this list, you'll have to use the File Manager (covered in Chapter 7) or the PIF Editor (see Chapter 15).

When you installed Windows, the Setup program was added to the Main group. Double clicking on the Windows Setup icon pops up a list of basic settings currently in effect. The Setup window cannot be maximized or resized.

Windows Setup	
Options **Help**	
Display:	VGA
Keyboard:	Enhanced 101 or 102 key US and Non US
Mouse:	Microsoft, or IBM PS/2
Network:	Network not installed
Swap file:	Permanent (7506 K bytes on Drive C:)

Windows Setup Main Screen

1. Start Windows as usual. From the Program Manager, move into the Main window, using **Ctrl-Tab** or **Ctrl-F6** if necessary, and then select **Windows Setup** using the cursor keys. Press **Enter** to start the program.

1. Run Windows as usual. Click in the Main group to make it the active window, and then double click on **Windows Setup**.

Note that in the bottom of the box, Setup tells you what type and size of swap file Windows is using. You cannot change this setting from here; this line is for information only.

Changing the Settings

Setup lets you change four types of hardware without having to reinstall Windows. There are four specific types of hardware that you can change in this way:

Display lets you specify the type of monitor and video card you are using.

Keyboard installs a driver for a special keyboard; these are mainly intended to handle unusual models supplied by specific manufacturers.

Mouse adds a mouse driver; here, too, the choices generally reflect models from specific manufacturers.

Network lets you specify a new network or delete support for an existing one.

2. Press **Alt-O** to open the Options menu and then press **Enter** to select **Change System Settings**.

2. Click on **Options** in the menu bar and then select **Change System Settings** from the pull-down menu.

Change System Settings

D**isplay**:	VGA ▼
K**eyboard**:	Enhanced 101 or 102 key US and Non US keyboards ▼
M**ouse**:	Microsoft, or IBM PS/2 ▼
N**etwork**:	▼

| OK | Cancel |

Change Settings Dialog Box

The dialog box lets you change the four settings shown in the previous display.

3. The Display option is already highlighted. To change monitor type, use the cursor keys to page through the list of available choices. To view the list box press **Alt-Down**.

3. Click on the arrowhead at the right of the Display text box to drop down a list of supported monitors. Click on your selection to remove the list box.

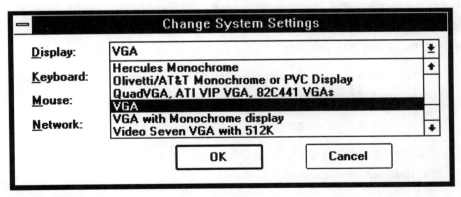

Display List Box

4. To specify a new keyboard type, press **Tab** to move to the second line. Use the cursor keys to run through the list of available models.

4. Open the Keyboard list box and select the appropriate model.

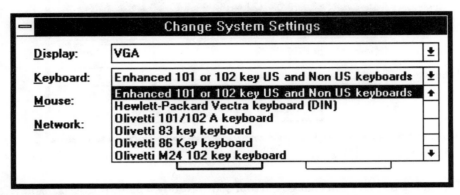

Keyboard List Box

 5. To change mouse drivers, press **Alt-M** to select the correct line and then use the cursor keys to page through the list of supported mice.

 5. Open the Mouse list box and make your selection.

If you are connected to a local area network you need to configure Windows for the network to be fully supported. The network drivers must be installed and running before you make any changes here.

 6. Press **Alt-N** to select the Network line. Use the cursor keys to page through the supported networks one at a time.

7. Having made your changes press **Enter** to close the dialog box.

 6. Open the Network list box and select your network operating system from the 10 available choices.

7. Finally, click on **OK** to save the changes.

```
┌──────────────────────────────────────────────────────────────┐
│ ═      │         Change System Settings                       │
├──────────────────────────────────────────────────────────────┤
│ Display:    │ VGA                                        │ ± │ │
│                                                                │
│ Keyboard:   │ Enhanced 101 or 102 key US and Non US keyboards │ ± │
│                                                                │
│ Mouse:      │ Microsoft, or IBM PS/2                     │ ± │ │
│                                                                │
│ Network:    │                                            │ ± │ │
│             │ 3Com 3+Open LAN Manager (XNS only)         │ ↑ │ │
│             │ 3Com 3+Share                               │   │ │
│             │ Banyan VINES 4.0                           │   │ │
│             │ IBM PC LAN Program                         │   │ │
│             │ LAN Manager 1.x (or 100% compatible)       │   │ │
│             │ LAN Manager 2.0 Basic (or 100% compatible) │ ↓ │ │
└──────────────────────────────────────────────────────────────┘
```

Network List Box

Depending on what type of changes you have made, you may be asked to supply one of the original Setup disks so that certain files can be copied. This will certainly be the case if you have specified a new network or monitor type. Once the files have been copied to your Windows directory, you will be given the choice of rebooting Windows or returning to DOS. Personally, I always choose the latter so that I can compress the hard disk before rebooting the PC—but you don't have to.

Adding Programs

Besides allowing you to change hardware configurations, Setup can be used to add program items to Program Manager. For certain non-Windows programs that Windows knows about, the program creates a Program Information File (or PIF) and runs each one in a separate MS-DOS window. Windows programs don't require PIF data.

Setup can also install Windows programs, including those that were developed for earlier versions of Windows, so that they will run under Windows 3. Remember, however, that any program that was designed to run in an earlier version of Windows can be used only in real mode under Windows 3. Trying to run older programs in standard or 386 enhanced mode may result in corrupted screen displays and may even cause the computer to hang.

The best way to add programs is to use the Program Manager or the File

Manager. The advantage of using Windows Setup is that it lets you quickly and painlessly add a number of programs at one time.

 1. From the Windows Setup screen, press **Alt-O S** to begin the Set Up Applications procedure.

1. Click on **Options** in the Windows Setup menu bar and then select **Set Up Applications** from the pull-down menu.

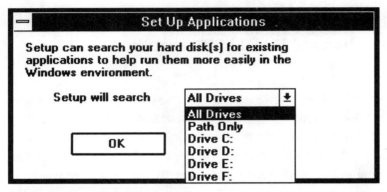

Set Up Applications Main Screen

As the first step in the process, the Setup program searches your hard disk for programs to install. Your hard disk may be set up as a single drive, or it may be partitioned into multiple logical volumes. You specify which areas of the hard disk should be searched. There are three possible selections.

All Drives Windows looks for programs in every logical partition on your hard disk. Floppy disks are ignored. That means you cannot use Setup to install new software; it can only be used to set up programs that already exist on your hard disk.

Path Only If you select this option, Setup looks only in those directories and subdirectories that are included in your PATH statement. Using this option presupposes that you have set a PATH in the first place.

Specific Drives The program can be told to look for programs only on a single logical drive. This option is especially useful if you devote one logical drive exclusively to programs and another to data.

Double click on your choice, or page through the available alternatives using the cursor keys and then press **Enter.** When the program has finished its search it displays the results in a dialog box. You can select which of the found programs will be added to the Windows environment.

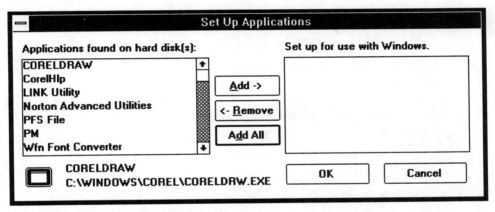

Set Up Applications—Programs Found

The dialog box is divided into three parts:

On the left is a box labeled **Applications found on hard disk(s).** This section contains a list of the programs that Setup found on the designated drive(s).

On the right is a blank box headed **Set up for use with Windows.** Only the programs that you move into this box will be added to Program Manager.

Between the two boxes are three buttons: **Add** and **Remove** let you move files between the left and right windows; **Add All** allows you to select all of the found programs with a single click.

2. Use the **Tab** key to move the selector into the list of found programs. The selector—a gray, dotted box—may be hard to see when it is on the buttons, but it is fairly clear in the list box.

3. You can move through the list of programs using the cursor keys. With the highlighter on the name of a program you want to add, press **Spacebar**. You can select any number of programs in the list before moving on to the next step.

4. Press **Alt-A** and the filenames will be instantly transferred to the box on the right-hand side of the screen. You can use **Tab** to move the selector to the button marked **Add ->** and then press **Enter** to achieve the same result. If you make a mistake or change your mind, select the names in the right-hand box and then press **Alt-R** to remove them from the list.

2. Select each program you want to add by clicking on its name in the left-hand box.

3. When your selections are complete, click on **Add ->** and the filenames are transferred to the other box. If you make a mistake or change your mind, select the names in the right-hand box and click on **Remove**.

Having selected the files you want to add, press **Enter** or click on **OK** and the process begins. The Program Manager will appear as a full window (even if it had been shrunk to an icon), and Setup adds the found programs to existing group windows. Unfortunately, Setup is not very intelligent about where it puts the new icons. Windows programs go into the Windows Applications group; MS-DOS programs are added to the Non-Windows Applications group. If you have renamed or deleted either of those groups, Setup will create a new group with the old name. In that case, you'll have to move the items into the group where you'd really like them.

After all the programs have been added to Program Manager, the Windows Setup screen reappears. To remove it, double click on the Control menu box, or press **Alt-F4** or **Alt-Space C**.

Problems with Setup

Running Setup under Windows lets you make minor changes in the existing system configuration, as outlined above. However, there may be occasions when the changes you want to make are so fundamental that you effectively need to reinstall Windows, or large parts of it. If the drivers for the devices you want to add were not originally supplied with Windows, you will have no choice but to rerun Setup from the system prompt.

You can run Setup directly from MS-DOS by simply entering **SETUP** at the DOS prompt. Do *not* run the Setup program inside an MS-DOS window under Windows 3 or the program is likely to fail with catastrophic results.

Whenever you run Setup from MS-DOS the program examines your hardware and lists the components that the system is using. To do so, Setup has to perform hardware checks on your system. In rare circumstances—most often with unusual hardware configurations—this might cause the entire system to hang. If this happens, don't panic—there is a cure.

Reboot the machine, either by turning it off and then on again or by pressing the reset button. From the DOS prompt, enter SETUP /I. The /I switch prevents Setup from examining the hardware and so the program will display the default settings for the system. You will then have to change these manually as you go along.

Summary

Setup allows you to add drivers for video displays, mice, keyboards and networks.

Setup can also be used to add some programs to the Windows environment.

Setup can be run from MS-DOS to reinstall Windows if necessary.

During the Setup process, Windows checks the components of your system. If the system hangs during this process, start the program by typing SETUP /I at the DOS prompt.

Keyboard Summary

Alt-F4	Quit Setup and return to Program Manager.
Alt-H	Activate help.
Alt-O A	Set up applications for use by the Program Manager.
Alt-O C	Change the system settings.
Alt-O X	Quit Setup.
Alt-Spacebar C	Quit Setup.
Alt-Spacebar M	Move Setup window.
Alt-Spacebar N	Reduce Setup window to an icon.
Alt-Spacebar R	Restore Setup icon to previous size and position.
Alt-Spacebar W	Activate Task List to switch to another application.
Ctrl-Esc	Activate Task List to switch to another application.

CHAPTER 7

File Manager

What Is It?

As the name implies, File Manager allows you to organize your program and data files and maintain directories. You can move, copy, delete and rename files; create and delete directories; change the attributes of files; format and label diskettes; and search for files anywhere on your hard disk. File Manager is not merely a disk utility, however; as the replacement for the MS-DOS Executive found in earlier versions of Windows, it can also be used in place of the Program Manager to launch applications. This program, more than any other except Paintbrush, almost demands that you use a mouse. With a mouse, File Manager lets you manipulate files quickly and accurately; using the keyboard alone slows things down considerably.

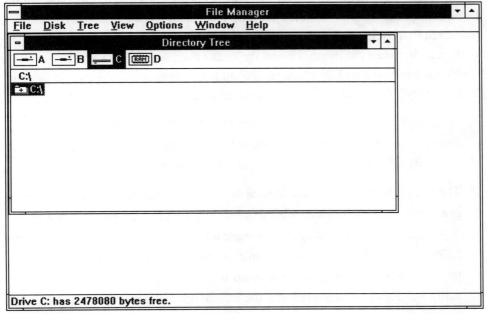

File Manager

159

To run File Manager simply double click on the icon, or select the icon and press **Enter**.

File Manager initially contains only the Directory Tree window, which gives you a graphical representation of the directories on the current drive. The Directory Tree window shows only directories—not files—and lets you navigate around your hard disk rapidly and smoothly. (It is much faster and easier to use than the MS-DOS Executive used to be!) Each directory is represented by a folder icon with the directory name beside it. If the directory contains subdirectories, the folder will have a plus sign on it. Double clicking on the plus sign (or highlighting the icon and then pressing +) will expand the tree to reveal the subdirectories, changing the symbol on the icon to a minus sign in the process. To close the display, double click on the minus sign, or select the icon and then press -. You may use the plus and minus keys on the top row of the keyboard or the ones on the numeric keypad—either set has the same effect.

Like most Windows programs, File Manager contains a Control menu, a title bar, and Minimize and Maximize buttons. The menu bar contains seven keywords. Along the bottom of the window, a status bar tells you which is the current drive and how much free space remains on that drive. Directory windows appear in the application workspace between the menu bar and the status bar.

When you first start File Manager it displays the contents of the current drive in the Directory Tree window. This window contains the following elements:

A line of disk icons appears just below the title bar, beginning with Drive A:, a floppy disk drive. If you have a second floppy drive installed it will appear as Drive B:. The next icon is the first hard disk, Drive C:.

The hard disk icons represent logical drives, not physical ones. A logical drive is a partition on the physical disk that MS-DOS recognizes as a separate entity. A physical drive may contain one or more logical drives. If you are running MS-DOS version 3.3 or earlier, each partition will be no larger than 32 MB, unless the drive has been specially formatted using third-party software. If you are using MS-DOS version 4 or later, the logical drive can be as large as the entire hard disk.

After the hard disk icons come icons for any RAM disks that are installed. These bear the label RAM and have the drive designator letter beside them. Finally, any network drives that are available are labeled NET.

A line of information immediately below the drive icons contains the volume label (if any) of the selected drive, in brackets, and the current directory path.

The balance of the window contains a tree structure representing the contents of the current drive. The example shown here consists of a single folder, over-printed with a plus sign and labeled C:\. This tells you that you are logged onto the root directory of Drive C:. If you press + the tree will expand to reveal a list of the first-level directories on the drive. If the tree is too deep to fit in the window, a scroll bar may appear at the right.

Basic Actions
To Switch to Another Drive:

Either press **Ctrl-[drive letter]** or click on the appropriate drive icon. As you do so, the status line at the bottom of the main window changes accordingly.

To Move or Resize the Directory Tree Window:

Because the window behaves like any document window, you can use the mouse, the Control menu commands or the Maximize and Minimize buttons to adjust its size and position. When the Directory Tree is the only open window, you can expand it to fill the entire available space by pressing **Shift-F4**. This command normally tiles all the directory windows; when there is only one window open it expands to fill the entire area. To return it to its normal size, press **Shift-F5**. (By default, directory windows are always cascaded.)

To Page Through the Directory Listing:

1. Use **Tab**, if necessary, to move from the row of drive icons into the Directory Tree window and then use the cursor keys to move the highlighter within the window. The **Up** and **Down** keys move from top to bottom in the

tree, regardless of their level; **Ctrl-Up** and **Ctrl-Down** move through directories at the same level only. **Left** selects the parent of the current directory, while **Right** highlights the first available subdirectory of the current directory, if any. Pressing **PgUp** or **PgDn** moves the highlighter through the tree one window at a time. **Home** selects the root directory of the current drive, and **End** goes to the last listing in the window. Pressing a letter moves to the next directory that begins with that letter.

1. Use the scroll bars to page the display. Clicking on an arrowhead will move the display up or down one line at a time. Clicking on the scroll bar itself will move the display up or down one window at a time, depending on whether you click above or below the button on the scroll bar. If you want to page rapidly through the listing drag the scroll bar button up and down.

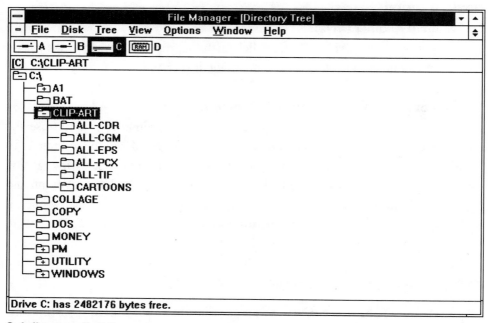

Subdirectory Detail

To Display Subdirectories Under a Directory:

1. Use the cursor keys to select the directory you want to expand. Any directory that contains subdirectories will have a plus sign inside its folder icon.

2. Press + and the tree expands to reveal the subdirectories. The plus sign changes to a minus sign. To collapse the directory again, press -.

3. To expand an entire branch of the tree—every subdirectory under a given directory, including sub-subdirectories—press *.

4. To expand the directory tree completely, revealing every subdirectory at every level, press **Ctrl-***. To quickly collapse the full display again, press **Home** to return to the root directory, and then press -.

1. Click on the icon of any directory with a plus sign inside it to expand the tree listing. Don't double click on the icon or the directory name itself—if you do, you will bring up another window listing the contents of the directory. To close a directory click on the icon again.

To Display the Contents of a Directory:

1. Use the cursor keys or the letter keys to highlight the name of a directory.

2. Press **Enter** and a new window appears, listing the contents of the directory. By default, the new window is cascaded from the Directory Tree window.

1. Double click on the directory name, and a new window listing the contents of that directory appears. If you double click on the folder icon, the directory tree will expand before the directory window pops up.

To Close a Window:

 1. Select the window you want to close using **Ctrl-Tab** or **Ctrl-F6**, and then press **Ctrl-F4** or **Alt-Hyphen C**.

 1. Double click on the Control menu box at the top left of the directory window, or click on the Control menu box and then click on **Close**. Note: You can never close the Directory Tree window; it can be reduced to an icon at any time, but it cannot be closed.

To Reduce a Window to an Icon:

 1. Select the window you want to minimize using **Ctrl-Tab** or **Ctrl-F6**.

2. Press **Alt-Hyphen N** and the window shrinks to an icon within the File Manager window.

 1. Click on the **Minimize** button at the top right corner of the window you want iconized.

There is no limit on the number of windows and icons you can have onscreen at any one time; however, the more windows you have open, or the more icons you have, the slower File Manager works. (In real mode on the Samsung 80286, if I have more than a dozen windows open at one time and try to open another one, I can go away and have a cup of coffee while I'm waiting for it to appear!)

To Move Between Windows:

 1. Press **Alt-W** to pull down the Window menu; then select a directory window by pressing the number next to the name in the list.

2. Or, use **Ctrl-Tab** or **Ctrl-F6** to switch from window to window in turn.

3. Or, press **Alt-Hyphen T** to switch to the next window in the sequence.

1. Click anywhere within the window you want to move to and it becomes the active window. Double click on a directory icon to restore it to its previous position and make it the active window.

2. If the window or icon is not visible, click on **Window** in the menu bar, and then click on the name of the directory in the pull-down menu.

To Select Multiple Fles:

1. To select a continuous range of names, highlight the first name in the range, and then hold down the **Shift** key and use the movement keys—the cursor keys, **Home**, **End**, **PgUp** and **PgDn**—to extend the selection.

2. To select a group of files that are not contiguous, highlight the first file and then press **Shift-F8**. The selector box begins to flash and can be moved, leaving the previous file selected. Use the cursor keys to move the selector to the next file and press **Spacebar**. Repeat this process until you have selected all the files you want. Press **Shift-F8** to stop extending the selection.

1. Click on the first file to highlight it.

2. If the remaining files you want to select are contiguous, press **Shift** and then click on the last file in the sequence. All the intervening files will be highlighted.

3. If the files you want to select are not contiguous, press **Ctrl** and click on another file. You can select as many files as you wish in this way as long as you continue to hold down **Ctrl**.

File Manager Menus

File Manager has seven menus plus the Control menu. Each subwindow also has its own Control menu. Certain commands are operable only in specific circumstances. Any command that is not currently available is shown in gray on the pull-down menu.

File Menu

Several of the commands within this menu are available only if the active window contains files. If the Directory Tree window is the active window, about half of the commands will not be available. Most of the commands in this menu call up dialog boxes.

Open	Enter
Run...	
Print...	
Associate...	
Searc**h**...	
Move...	F7
Copy...	F8
Delete...	Del
Re**n**ame...	
Chan**g**e Attributes...	
Cr**e**ate Directory...	
Select All	Ctrl+/
Dese**l**ect All	Ctrl+\
E**x**it	

File Manager File Menu

Open has the same effect as pressing **Enter** or double clicking on a highlighted item. If the item is a file, Windows will try to run the program associated with it. If the item is a directory name, a directory window will pop up.

Run is used to start a program just as you would from the system prompt. Invoking this command calls up a dialog box in which you can enter a program's name—including, if necessary, the full path to the program. Pressing **Enter** or clicking on **OK** then runs the program.

Print allows you to send a text file directly to the printer. This option is particularly useful if you own a PostScript printer, because it allows you to print a pure ASCII file—something that is not possible from MS-DOS. However, unless you want to see a load of gibberish and waste countless sheets of paper, don't use this command to print graphics or other non-text files!

Associate is used to tell Windows that files with certain extensions are linked with specific programs. Once a file extension has been associated, you can run the program by double clicking on a filename with that extension and pressing **Enter**, or by simply double clicking on the filename. You might, for example, associate all files that carry the .DOC extension with Windows Write. If you have a file called ALPHA.DOC, you can run Windows Write and load the file by double clicking on the name, as if it were a program. The effect is the same as combining a program and filename in the Program Manager.

Search is an extremely useful command, especially if you have a large hard disk and a complex directory structure. With the help of this command you can search anywhere in the current directory for a file or a group of files. If you desire, you can tell File Manager to search throughout the current drive. You can use wild-card characters in the search—for example, ***.TXT** would find every file with an extension of .TXT.

Move allows you to move a file, or group of files, from one directory to another, as if you had copied the files and then deleted the originals. The keyboard shortcut is **F7**.

Copy lets you copy one or more files to another directory, leaving the originals intact. Use **F8** as the shortcut.

Delete allows you to delete selected files, directories and subdirectories. This command is much more powerful than its MS-DOS counterpart: Within MS-DOS you can delete a directory only when it is empty; File Manager, however, can remove a directory and its contents in a single operation. This can have disastrous consequences if you're not careful!

Rename is used to change the name of any file or directory. (The MS-DOS equivalent doesn't allow you to rename directories.) In the dialog box that appears simply enter the new name. A tip: When renaming a directory, do not type the path with the new name, even though the **From** line in the Rename dialog box does. If you do, you will get an error message.

Change Attributes allows you to modify the attributes of any file. This command is more powerful than the MS-DOS **ATTRIB** command, because it allows you to change the System and Hidden attributes.

Create Directory is the equivalent of the MS-DOS **MKDIR** command and lets you add a directory within the current directory. It is theoretically possible to create a directory elsewhere in the directory structure by including the full path; however, the Create Directory dialog box accepts only 12 characters, which limits the possibilities tremendously.

Select All provides a shortcut for selecting every file in a directory. To use the command directly from the keyboard press **Ctrl-/**.

Deselect All cancels any selections you have made in the current directory window. The keyboard shortcut is **Ctrl-**.

Exit closes File Manager. When you invoke this command you are given the opportunity to save any changes you have made so that they become the default settings for the program.

Disk Menu

```
┌────────────────────────────┐
│ Copy Diskette...           │
│ Label Disk...              │
├────────────────────────────┤
│ Format Diskette...         │
│ Make System Diskette...    │
├────────────────────────────┤
│ Connect Net Drive...       │
│ Disconnect Net Drive...    │
└────────────────────────────┘
```

File Manager Disk Menu

The commands available on the Disk menu let you perform some common disk activities. The first four commands are available at all times and are intended, with one exception, for use only with floppy diskettes. The final two menu choices will only be available if you are using a network. Each of the commands brings up its own dialog box.

Copy Diskette is the equivalent of the MS-DOS **DISKCOPY** command. To use this command, the Directory Tree window must be logged onto a floppy disk drive; otherwise you will see an error message. The dialog box asks you to select a destination drive and then prompts you to swap source and target disks as the operation is carried out. (The floppy disk formats must match as well, or you will see an error message.) One annoying quirk with this command is that it does not tell you when it has finished—the disk simply stops spinning and the dialog box vanishes without giving you the opportunity to copy another disk.

Label Disk, equivalent to the MS-DOS **LABEL** command, is the only choice on this menu that can be used with a hard disk or a floppy disk. The command allows you to add a volume label to the drive that is selected in the Directory Tree window. The standard MS-DOS rules about disk labels apply: the label must be no more than 11 characters, and you cannot use the reserved characters.

Format Diskette can be used only with floppy disks; you cannot use this command to format a hard disk. Like the MS-DOS **FORMAT**, this command asks if you want to format another diskette when you have finished. Using a series of dialog boxes, you tell File Manager which drive you want formatted, whether the disk is a high-capacity diskette, and whether you want to create a system diskette.

Make System Diskette allows you to copy the system files to a floppy, just as the MS-DOS **SYS** command does.

Connect Net Drive is only available on networked systems. The command pops up a dialog box that allows you to assign a drive letter to a network drive, giving you the opportunity to enter a password if one is required.

Disconnect Net Drive allows you to cancel a network drive assignment.

Tree Menu

```
┌─────────────────────────────────┐
│ Expand One Level  +             │
│ Expand Branch     *             │
│ Expand All        Ctrl+*        │
│ Collapse Branch   -             │
└─────────────────────────────────┘
```

File Manager Tree Menu

The Tree menu is used with the Directory Tree window only. The choices on this menu are also available directly from the keyboard.

Expand One Level allows you to view the subdirectories contained within any individual directory. (A directory that contains subdirectories is shown by a plus sign [+] on the folder icon.) Selecting the directory and then pressing + performs the same operation.

Expand Branch displays the complete directory tree under a given directory. To use the keyboard shortcut for this command, select a directory and then press *.

Expand All displays the complete directory structure for the entire disk. You can activate this command from anywhere in the directory tree. The direct keyboard shortcut is **Ctrl-*.**

Collapse Branch hides the entire tree structure under the selected directory. To use the keyboard shortcut, select a directory and press -.

View Menu

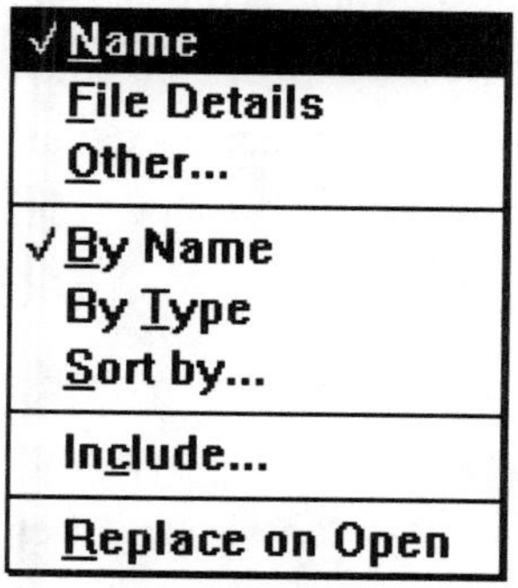

```
√ Name
  File Details
  Other...
─────────────
√ By Name
  By Type
  Sort by...
─────────────
  Include...
─────────────
  Replace on Open
```

File Manager View Menu

The View menu controls how files are displayed in directory windows; it has no effect on the Directory Tree window. The menu is divided into four parts, each of which controls a different aspect of the display. The first part sets the type of information that is supplied for each file; the second changes the way in which the file list is sorted; the third lets you restrict the type of files that are included in the display; and the final part affects the display itself.

The first three choices define the contents of the file list. A check mark is shown next to the currently selected option.

Name is the default option. With this option selected, the display shows only the names of the various files contained within each directory.

File Details allows you to display not only the filename but also the file's size, date and time stamp, and file attributes.

Other lets you select which of the file details will be displayed in addition to the filename. For example, you can turn off the display of the date and time stamp but leave the other details.

You can choose how the contents of the file list will be sorted. Here, too, a check mark shows which option is active.

By Name is the default option. The files shown in directory windows are sorted on the basis of the filenames, in normal alphabetical order. You cannot, unfortunately, choose reverse order. In alphabetical sort order, symbols come before numbers, which are in turn followed by letters. Subdirectory names appear at the beginning of the list, before all filenames, sorted in the same order as the files.

By Type sorts the files and subdirectories according to file extensions. With this option selected, subdirectories are shown first, in alphabetical order; all files are sorted in ascending alphabetical order based first on the file extension, and then on the names of the files within each group of extensions.

Sort By allows you to choose whether to sort the display by name, type, file size, or date and time stamp. This menu choice offers you the option to set a new default sort order for directory windows.

The final two menu choices give you broad control over the contents and display of directory windows.

Include allows you to select which files are included in the display. You can use wild cards to filter the listing, and check boxes to display or hide directories, programs, documents and other files. Additional check boxes lets you set whether hidden and system files are displayed and set system defaults.

Replace on Open reduces the number of windows onscreen at any time. Instead of opening a new window for every directory, when this option is checked you use only two windows, one for the Directory Tree and one to display the contents of a directory. When you open a new directory its contents replace those in the second window.

Options Menu

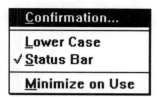

File Manager Options Menu

This menu sets some File Manager defaults.

Confirmation lets you preset whether certain actions must be validated with a confirmation dialog box before they are carried out. The actions affected are deletions, subtree deletions, replacements and direct mouse manipulations of files. For example, if you have the Confirm on Delete option set, you will be doubly prompted before any file or directory is deleted. By default all four options within the dialog box are turned on.

Lower Case causes the names of all files and directories to appear in lower case letters. (By default, Windows uses capital letters for all windows.) You cannot mix upper and lower case letters in File Manager displays.

Status Bar is a toggle switch that determines whether the status line along the bottom of the File Manager window is visible or not.

Minimize on Use is also a toggle switch; if this option is selected, File Manager is shrunk to an icon whenever you run a program from within it.

Window Menu

The Window menu controls the display of windows within File Manager.

<u>C</u>ascade	Shift+F5
<u>T</u>ile	Shift+F4
<u>R</u>efresh	F5
Close <u>A</u>ll Directories	
√<u>1</u> Directory Tree	

File Manager Window Menu

Cascade, the default, arranges all windows in overlapping fashion with the title bars visible.

Tile organizes the directory windows so that they are all visible side by side within the main window.

Refresh is unnecessary most of the time. When you create or modify a file in another application, the File Manager display should be refreshed immediately. In some situations, however, particularly with older Windows applications and networked drives, the window is not properly updated. Selecting this command updates the active directory window.

Close All Directories closes every directory window, leaving only the Directory Tree open.

Exercise 7.1
Copying Files

Because your disk and its directories are different from mine, we will use a single directory—the Windows directory—for all of the following exercises. However, the principles of the exercise apply to all files, directories and subdirectories. If you want to use another directory, by all means do so; just substitute the appropriate directory name every time WINDOWS appears in this chapter.

First, we'll create a new subdirectory within the main Windows directory.

1. Run the File Manager from the Program Manager by selecting the icon and then pressing **Enter**. Be sure the Program Manager's **Minimize on Use** toggle is set on, so that only the File Manager is onscreen as a window.

2. If the only entry in the Directory Tree window is **C:**, then you are logged onto the root directory of the drive. The folder beside the label will have a plus sign on it. Press + to open the folder and display the first-level directory tree of your disk.

3. Press **Down** until the WINDOWS subdirectory is highlighted, or press **W** to jump directly to the directory, and then press **Enter**. A second window appears.

4. Press **Alt-F E** to bring up the Create Directory dialog box. Type ALPHA-1 and then press **Enter**. The new subdirectory will appear at the top of the directory window.

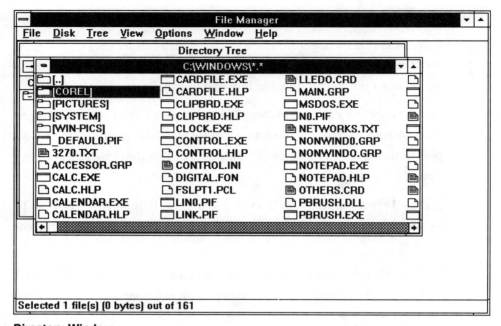

Directory Window

 1. From the Program Manager, double click on the File Manager icon.

2. When you use File Manager for the first time it automatically logs onto the root directory of Drive C:, with the directory structure collapsed. Click on the folder icon beside the C:\ label and the directory tree appears.

3. Double click on the word WINDOWS (use the scroll bars to move through the list, if necessary). A directory window listing the subdirectories and files within the Windows directory appears.

4. Click on **File** and then on **Create Directory**. The Create Directory dialog box appears. Type ALPHA-1 and press **Enter** or click on **OK**. The new subdirectory will appear at the top of the directory window.

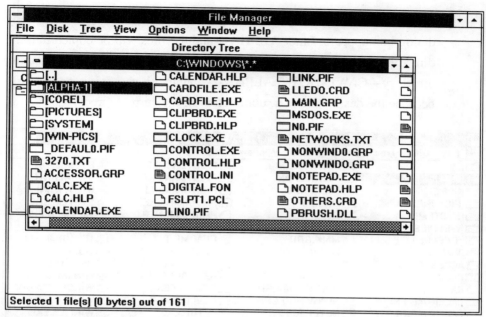

New Directory Created

Exercise 7.2
Copying Files in One Window

Copying files within Windows is easy: You simply select the files you want to copy and then tell Windows where to put them. With a mouse, you can drag the files directly into their new location. In this exercise we're going to copy all the files with an extension of .BMP into the subdirectory we previously created.

1. Because there are so many files in the Windows directory it would be handy if we expanded it to fill the entire available area. Press **Alt-Hyphen X** to maximize the window.

2. Press **Alt-V T** to sort the files by extension.

3. Use the cursor keys to highlight the first file with a .BMP extension. Hold down **Shift** and press **Down** until you have selected all the files with a .BMP extension.

177

4. Press **F8** (or **Alt-F C** if you want to use the pull-down menu), and the Copy dialog box appears. Enter **ALPHA-1** and the files will be copied into the directory. If you wish you can include the full path to the destination directory—C:\WINDOWS\ALPHA-1—but in this case it is not necessary, because the destination is a subdirectory of the current directory.

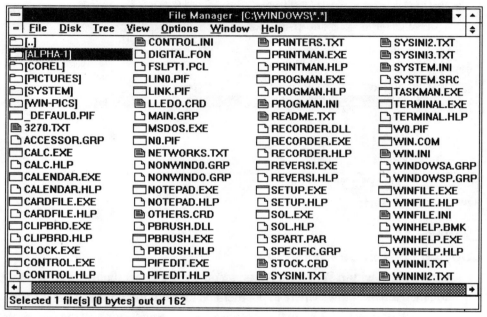

File Manager - [C:\WINDOWS*.*]

| File | Disk | Tree | View | Options | Window | Help |

🗀[..]	📄 CONTROL.INI	📄 PRINTERS.TXT	📄 SYSINI2.TXT
🗀[ALPHA-1]	🗋 DIGITAL.FON	▢PRINTMAN.EXE	📄 SYSINI3.TXT
🗀[COREL]	🗋 FSLPT1.PCL	🗋 PRINTMAN.HLP	📄 SYSTEM.INI
🗀[PICTURES]	▢LIN0.PIF	▢PROGMAN.EXE	🗋 SYSTEM.SRC
🗀[SYSTEM]	▢LINK.PIF	🗋 PROGMAN.HLP	▢TASKMAN.EXE
🗀[WIN-PICS]	📄 LLEDO.CRD	📄 PROGMAN.INI	▢TERMINAL.EXE
▢_DEFAUL0.PIF	🗋 MAIN.GRP	📄 README.TXT	🗋 TERMINAL.HLP
📄 3270.TXT	▢MSDOS.EXE	🗋 RECORDER.DLL	▢W0.PIF
🗋 ACCESSOR.GRP	▢N0.PIF	▢RECORDER.EXE	▢WIN.COM
▢CALC.EXE	📄 NETWORKS.TXT	🗋 RECORDER.HLP	📄 WIN.INI
🗋 CALC.HLP	🗋 NONWIND0.GRP	▢REVERSI.EXE	🗋 WINDOWSA.GRP
▢CALENDAR.EXE	🗋 NONWIND0.GRP	🗋 REVERSI.HLP	🗋 WINDOWSP.GRP
🗋 CALENDAR.HLP	▢NOTEPAD.EXE	▢SETUP.EXE	▢WINFILE.EXE
▢CARDFILE.EXE	🗋 NOTEPAD.HLP	🗋 SETUP.HLP	🗋 WINFILE.HLP
🗋 CARDFILE.HLP	📄 OTHERS.CRD	▢SOL.EXE	📄 WINFILE.INI
▢CLIPBRD.EXE	🗋 PBRUSH.DLL	🗋 SOL.HLP	🗋 WINHELP.BMK
🗋 CLIPBRD.HLP	▢PBRUSH.EXE	🗋 SPART.PAR	▢WINHELP.EXE
▢CLOCK.EXE	🗋 PBRUSH.HLP	🗋 SPECIFIC.GRP	🗋 WINHELP.HLP
▢CONTROL.EXE	▢PIFEDIT.EXE	📄 STOCK.CRD	📄 WININI.TXT
🗋 CONTROL.HLP	🗋 PIFEDIT.HLP	📄 SYSINI.TXT	📄 WININI2.TXT

Selected 1 file[s] [0 bytes] out of 162

Maximized Directory Window

1. Click on the **Maximize** button at the top right-hand corner of the directory window.

2. Click on **View** in the menu bar and then on **By Type**. The display is sorted by file extension.

3. Click on the first file with a .BMP extension. Then hold down the **Shift** key and click on the last file with that extension. All the intervening files will be selected. Release the **Shift** key.

4. Point anywhere in the highlighted area, hold down the **Ctrl** key, and then click the mouse button. The cursor will change into a graphic that looks like a stack of cards. While still pressing **Ctrl**, drag this graphic until it sits atop the directory name ALPHA-1. Release the mouse button and **Ctrl**. A dialog box asks you to confirm that you want to copy the files into the directory. Click on **OK**.

Warning: Make sure you press **Ctrl** while dragging the group of selected files; otherwise, the files will be moved and not copied.

Exercise 7.3
Copying Files Using Search

Instead of rearranging the display, you can use the Search command to select a number of files and act on them en masse. Search produces a new window containing the files it finds.

1. Press **Alt-F H** to bring up the Search dialog box.

2. The default entry in the text box is *.*; type ***.BMP** instead. **Tab** down to the next line and press **Space** to deselect the Search Entire Disk option. Press **Enter** to begin the search. After a brief delay, the Search Results window containing all the .BMP files appears. A new window appears bearing the title Search Results. Note that this window contains not only those files within the Windows directory but also the .BMP files in the ALPHA-1 subdirectory. The reason is that the Search command considers any subdirectory to be part of the current directory.

3. Tile the windows using **Shift-F4** and then use **Ctrl-Tab** or **Ctrl-F6** to make the Search Results window active. Highlight the files as you did in the previous exercise; if you prefer, you can press **Ctrl-/** to highlight all the files in the window. Finally, press **F8**, type **ALPHA-1** in the dialog box and press **Enter**.

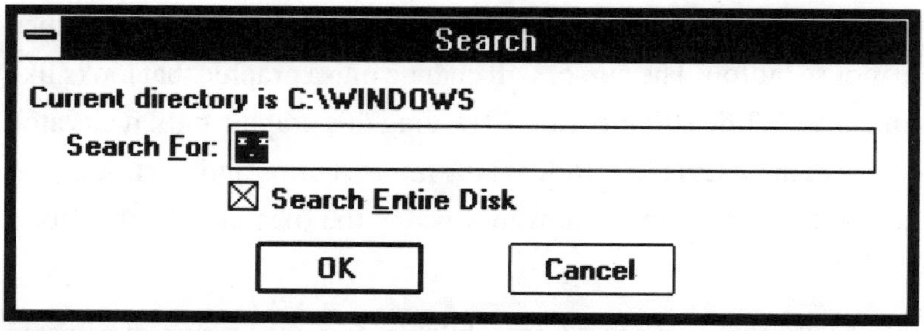

Search Dialog Box

4. Because the files already exist in the target directory, each time Windows tries to copy a file it will pop up a dialog box saying the file already exists and asking if you want to overwrite it. Press **Y** to overwrite the file, **N** to skip to the next file, or **Esc** to cancel the Copy operation. Finally, close the Search Results window by pressing **Ctrl-F4** and cascade the remaining windows by pressing **Shift-F5**.

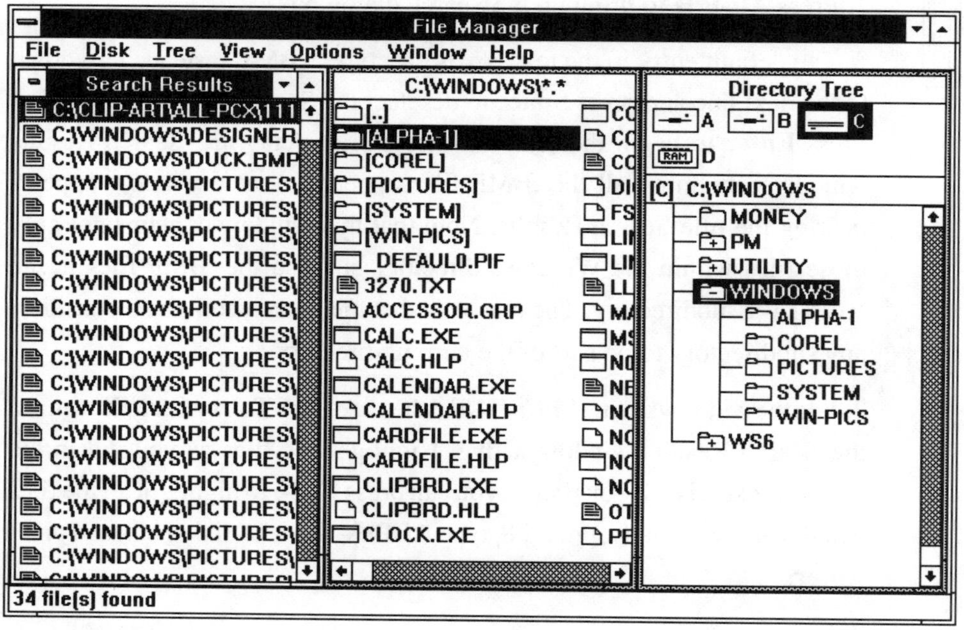

Three Windows Tiled

1. Click on **File** in the menu bar and then on **Search** to bring up the Search dialog box.

2. Type ***.BMP** and then click on **Search Entire Disk** to turn off the toggle. Click on **OK** to begin the search. A new window appears bearing the title Search Results. Note that this window contains not only those files within the Windows directory but also the .BMP files in the ALPHA-1 subdirectory. The reason is that the Search command considers any subdirectory to be part of the current directory.

3. Select the files as in the previous exercise. You can now copy them directly by pointing anywhere in the highlighted area, holding down **Ctrl** and holding the mouse button. Drag the files into the Windows directory window and position the files icon over the ALPHA-1 directory. Release the mouse button, but do not release the **Ctrl** key until the confirming dialog box appears.

4. A dialog box will pop up, asking you to confirm that you want to copy the selected files into the new location. Click on **Yes** to continue. Then, because the files already exist in the target directory, Windows will pop up a dialog box as you try to copy each file, asking if you want to overwrite the existing file. Click on **Yes** to overwrite the file, **No** to skip to the next file, or **Cancel** to end the Copy operation. Finally, close the Search Results window by double clicking on the Control menu box and cascade the remaining windows by clicking on **Window** and then on **Cascade**.

Exercise 7.4
Deleting Files

Windows allows you to delete one file or a large group of files in a single action. We'll use this exercise to delete all the files in the ALPHA-1 directory. As part of the exercise, we'll speed things up by telling File Manager to delete files without confirming dialog boxes.

1. Press **Alt-O C** to bring up the Confirmation dialog box. Touch the **Spacebar** to turn off the Confirm on Delete option. Press **Enter** to accept the new setting.

2. With the C:\WINDOWS directory window active, select the ALPHA-1 subdirectory and press **Enter**. The contents of the subdirectory will appear in a new active window.

3. Press **Ctrl-/** to select all the files.

4. Press **Delete** to delete the selected files.

1. Click on **Options** in the menu bar, then on **Confirmation** to bring up the Confirmation dialog box. Click on the check box next to Confirm on Delete to turn off this option. Select **OK** to accept the new setting.

2. Double click on the name ALPHA-1 and a new directory window appears.

3. Click on the first filename in this window; then press **Shift** and click on the last filename. (Use the scroll bars if necessary to move to the bottom of the list.) All the files in the window will be highlighted.

4. Click on **File** and then on **Delete** to erase the files.

As the files are being deleted you will notice one of the quirks of Windows 3. As each file is deleted the screen display is correspondingly refreshed. These constant screen updates slow down the deletion process, but that's the way Windows works and there's no way to change it. You can, however, circumvent this annoying feature: Before deleting the files, reduce the ALPHA-1 window to an icon. Then, with the icon highlighted, press **Delete**. The files will be deleted rapidly without any refreshing. Finally you get a message asking if the sub-directory should be deleted. If you answer negatively then the sub-directory remains in place but all the files are gone. If you answer yes then the sub-directory will be deleted. (You will need the ALPHA-1 sub-directory later.)

Exercise 7.5
Renaming Files

File Manager allows you to rename files just as the MS-DOS command does, but it also lets you rename directories, which is something you cannot do in DOS.

Warning: Do not change the names of any of the files that are supplied with Windows 3.

1. Select the ALPHA-1 directory in the C:\WINDOWS directory window.

2. Press **Alt-F N** to bring up the Rename dialog box. The name of the selected directory appears on the first line.

3. Type a new name—**ALPHA-2**—on the second line. Do not include any path details; if you do you will receive an error message. Press **Enter**. The dialog box vanishes and the directory has been renamed.

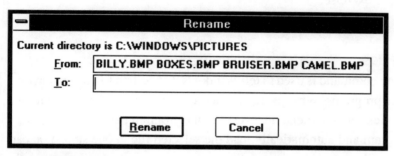

Rename Dialog Box

4. You can also rename a number of files at once. Select all the files with a .BMP extension as in Exercise 7.1. Press **Alt-F N** to bring up the Rename dialog box. Believe it or not, the first text box contains the names of all the selected files, although you cannot see them all.

5. On the second line type ***.ABA** and then press **Enter**. The extensions of all the selected files will be changed. Now change them all back to *.BMP in the same way. Change the name of the ALPHA-2 directory back to ALPHA-1, and don't delete it; we'll use it in a later exercise.

1. Click on ALPHA-1 to select it.

2. Click on **File** in the menu bar and then on **Rename**.

3. Type the new name—**ALPHA-2**—on the second line and then click on **OK**.

4. You can also use this command to rename multiple files. Select all the .BMP files as in the first exercise and then open the Rename dialog box as above.

5. Type ***.ABA** on the second line of the dialog box and click on **OK**. As each file is renamed the display in the window will be refreshed. Make sure you change the extensions back to .BMP when you are done. Change the name of the ALPHA-2 directory back to ALPHA-1, and don't delete it; we'll use it in a later exercise.

Exercise 7.6
Associating Files

The Associate command is used to tell Windows that certain file extensions are related to specific programs. Why? Because once an association exists you can start the program by clicking on a filename instead of the program name. Windows will then run the program and automatically load the selected file in one step. You can associate as many file extensions as you like with any program, but you can only associate one program with each extension.

1. Select a filename that contains the extension you want to associate with a specific program.

2. Press **Alt-F A** to bring up the Associate dialog box.

3. Type the name of the program—including its extension—in the dialog box and then press **Enter**. That's it. The changes are added to your WIN.INI file and will be available any time you run Windows.

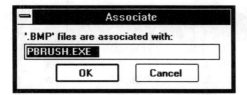

Associate Dialog Box

1. Click on a file that contains the extension you want to link to a program.

2. Click on **File** in the menu bar and then on **Associate**.

3. Enter the program name the extension is to be associated with. Click on **OK** to save the changes in the WIN.INI file.

Exercise 7.7
File Attributes

When you create or modify a file, DOS stores its name, a date and time stamp, and information about four attributes. These are:

Archive Whenever a file is backed up, either by DOS or by third-party software, this attribute is turned on. When a file is modified, the attribute is turned off. The purpose is to allow you to quickly select files that have been modified since they were last backed up.

Read Only If this attribute is turned on, the file can be read—that is, loaded into an application program—but it cannot be modified unless it is renamed.

Hidden Normally, under MS-DOS, you cannot see any file that has this attribute turned on; it will not show up when you enter **DIR**. Within File Manager, however, you can choose to see all files on your disk—even if they are set as hidden files.

System A number of special files used by the operating system have this attribute turned on. They should never be changed, or your computer is almost certain to hang in glorious fashion.

C:\WINDOWS*.*				
WEAVE.BMP	190	5/01/90	03:00:00	——A
FIG-098.CLP	33787	10/19/90	17:36:40	——A
FIG-099.CLP	33787	10/19/90	17:38:00	——A
FIG-100.CLP	33787	10/19/90	17:38:18	——A
FIG-101.CLP	7107	10/19/90	17:38:46	——A
FIG-102.CLP	33787	10/19/90	17:38:20	——A
FIG-103.CLP	8693	10/19/90	17:40:58	——A
FIG-104.CLP	8693	10/19/90	17:40:44	——A
WIN.COM	19358	6/07/90	18:28:40	——A
DATA1.CRD	72	12/07/90	16:28:58	——A
PBRUSH.DLL	7724	5/01/90	03:00:00	——A
RECORDER.DLL	11774	5/01/90	03:00:00	——A

Change Attributes Dialog Box

The MS-DOS **ATTRIB** command lets you change only the first two attributes. There are a number of programs—both commercial and shareware—that allow you to modify the Hidden and System attributes of a file. Windows 3 now includes this ability as well. From File Manager, you can change the attributes of any file or directory—if you'd like, you can even hide directories.

1. With the C:\WINDOWS directory window active, press **Alt-V F**. The directory window now displays the name, size, date, time and attributes of the files. Note that only the Archive attribute (shown by the letter A) is turned on for each file.

2. Select all the .BMP files as before.

3. Press **Alt-F G** to bring up the Change Attributes dialog box. Use **Tab** and **Spacebar** to place an X next to the **Archive**, **Read Only** and **Hidden** boxes. Press **Enter**. The display changes so that the listings for the selected files now say RH-A; in other words, the Read Only, Hidden and Archive attributes are turned on.

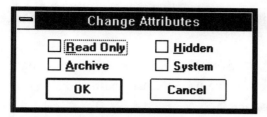

Change Attributes Dialog Box

1. With the C:\WINDOWS directory window active, click on **View** and then on **File Details**. The display now includes the file attributes. Note that only the Archive attribute (shown by the letter A) is turned on for each of the files in the list.

2. Select all the .BMP files as before.

3. Click on **File** in the menu bar and then on **Change Attributes**. In the dialog box that appears, click on **Read Only**, **Hidden** and **Archive**. Click on **OK**. The display will be updated to show the changed attributes.

To see the effect of the changes you have just made, select **View Include**. Click on the box that says **Show Hidden/System Files**. With this option turned on, the files are visible. When the option is turned off, the display behaves just as it would under the DOS **DIR** command; the hidden files cannot be seen. I suggest that you change the attributes on the files again so that only the Archive attribute is switched on.

You can also use this command to change the attributes of directories--something that can't be done under MS-DOS. Using this trick, you can create a directory, store files in it and set its Hidden attribute to make it disappear from view.

Exercise 7.8
Formatting Floppy Disks

Windows 3 can be used as a shell in place of MS-DOS if you want to. The File Manager is more colorful, more intuitive and easier to use than the system prompt. It also provides most of the major functions you would expect to use from MS-DOS, including the ability to handle floppy disks. Before any disk can be used it must first be formatted.

 1. Place a floppy disk into the disk drive. This exercise will destroy any data that may be on the disk. For safety's sake, use either a brand-new disk or one that does not contain any important data.

2. Press **Alt-D F**. Select the drive that contains the disk to be formatted. Windows will not allow you to format the hard disk.

3. A dialog box warns you that formatting a floppy disk will erase all data on the disk. Press **Enter** if you're ready to continue.

Format Diskette Warning Message

4. The next dialog box allows you to choose between standard and high-capacity diskettes. (Don't format a standard disk to high capacity or vice versa; the results are likely to be unpleasant in either case.) You also have the choice of making a system disk—a bootable disk that contains the hidden system files. Use **Tab** and **Spacebar** to select the options you want, and press **Enter** to begin formatting.

 1. Place the disk to be formatted in the appropriate drive.

2. Click on **Disk** in the menu bar and then on **Format Diskette**. Select the proper drive and click on **OK**. Note that File Manager will not let you format a hard disk.

3. The next dialog box allows you to choose between standard and high-capacity diskettes. (Don't format a standard disk to high capacity or vice versa.) You also have the choice of making a system disk—a bootable disk that contains the hidden system files. Click on the options you want, and then click on **OK** to begin formatting.

As the disk is being formatted, File Manager supplies a continuous report showing, in percentage terms, how far the process has run. Once the operation is complete you will be asked if you want to format another disk or not.

Exercise 7.9
Adding to the Program Manager

If you wish, you can run programs directly from the File Manager instead of using the Program Manager. Simply double click on the program name in a directory window, or select the program name and press **Enter**.

One of the most useful features of File Manager is its ability to add programs directly to Program Manager. This is the only set of circumstances under which you can move an item outside the Program Manager window or a file outside the File Manager window. You must use a mouse; there is no way to accomplish this bit of wizardry with the keyboard alone.

1. Start Windows as usual; make sure the Program Manager is active.

2. Double click on **File Manager**.

3. Arrange the Program Manager and File Manager windows so they are side by side on the screen. The easiest way to do this is to press **Ctrl-Esc**, or double click on the background and bring up the Task List. Click on **Tile** to tile the two windows. Then press **Shift-F4** to tile all the open windows within the Program Manager.

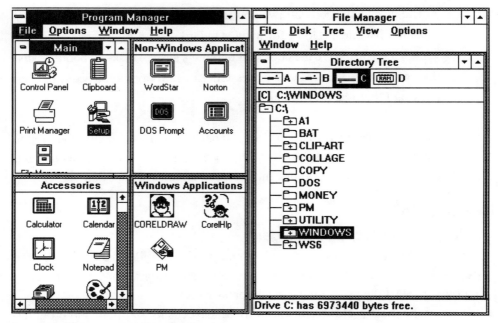

Program Manager and File Manager

4. Within the File Manager, open a directory window that contains the program or programs you want to add.

5. Select the programs as if you were going to copy them—in a sense, that is what you're going to do.

6. Drag the selected file into the appropriate group window in Program Manager. A new icon will appear bearing a label that matches the program name. Continue doing this until you've created Program Manager icons for all the programs you selected.

7. Reduce the File Manager to an icon by clicking on the **Minimize** button. Resize and reposition the Program Manager window, retile the group windows and arrange the contents of the group windows to your satisfaction. Finally, reduce Program Manager to an icon.

Exercise 7.10
Pruning and Grafting

Windows 3 allows you to prune and graft directories—to move a whole section of the directory tree from one place to another in a single operation. This feat just wasn't possible using previous versions of Windows. In fact, there is no simple way to do this under MS-DOS, either. Until now, pruning and grafting directories required a special utility like PC Tools. Here, too, you really need a mouse; the keyboard alone won't get the job done.

1. Double click on the Control menu to close the C:\WINDOWS directory window and return to the Directory Tree window.

2. Close all the branches of the directory structure except the Windows directory. (You might find this easier if you maximize the Directory Tree window first.)

3. Select the ALPHA-1 directory (assuming you haven't deleted it), and drag it up until it sits directly over C:\ at the top of the window. Release the mouse button and you'll see a message asking if you want to move all the files to this point. Click on **OK**. The subdirectory and all the files it contains will be grafted onto the root directory of Drive C:.

4. You will then be asked if you want to remove the subtree C:\WINDOWS\ALPHA-1. Click on **OK**. The original subdirectory will be removed. If you select **Cancel**, the original subdirectory remains in place and you have simply copied it, and its contents, into the root directory.

Exercise 7.11
Closing File Manager

To close the File Manager and return to Program Manager, press **Alt-F4**. A dialog box appears, asking you to confirm that you really want to quit. If you click on **Save Changes**, the settings you have changed—sort order, file details, and the like—will be restored the next time you run File Manager. Otherwise it will default to the prior setting.

Summary

File Manager is a utility program that allows you to manage the files and directories on your disks quickly and easily.

The program can be used with the keyboard but is much easier to use if you combine both keyboard and mouse actions.

Using a mouse, you can create a program icon by dragging a filename from the File Manager into the Program Manager.

Certain File Manager functions—including the ability to set System and Hidden attributes and to prune and graft directories—have no MS-DOS equivalents.

Keyboard Summary

Alt-D C	Copy the contents of one floppy disk to another.
Alt-D D	Disconnect from a network drive.
Alt-D F	Format a floppy disk.
Alt-D L	Create or change a drive's volume label.
Alt-D M	Copy system files to a formatted floppy disk.
Alt-D N	Connect to a network drive.
Alt-F A	Associate a file extension with a program.
Alt-F C	Copy selected files to another directory or disk.
Alt-F D	Delete selected files, subdirectories or icons.
Alt-F E	Create a directory.
Alt-F G	Change file and directory attributes.
Alt-F H	Search the disk to find a file or group of files.
Alt-F L	Deselect all the files in a directory.
Alt-F M	Move selected files to another directory or disk.
Alt-F N	Rename selected files or directories.
Alt-F O	Run the program associated with the selected file.
Alt-F P	Send the selected file directly to the printer.
Alt-F R	Run a program by typing a filename in a dialog box.
Alt-F S	Select all the files in a directory.
Alt-F X	Quit File Manager.

Alt-F4	Quit File Manager.
Alt-Hyphen C	Close directory window. Not available when Directory Tree window is active.
Alt-Hyphen M	Move directory window.
Alt-Hyphen N	Shrink directory window to an icon.
Alt-Hyphen R	Restore icon to window.
Alt-Hyphen S	Resize directory window.
Alt-Hyphen T	Select next directory window or icon in sequence.
Alt-Hyphen X	Maximize directory window.
Alt-O C	Select whether specific File Manager operations will require confirming dialog boxes.
Alt-O L	Change display to lower-case letters.
Alt-O M	Minimize File Manager when running other programs.
Alt-O S	Toggle display of status bar.
Alt-Spacebar C	Quit File Manager.
Alt-Spacebar M	Move File Manager application window.
Alt-Spacebar N	Reduce File Manager application window to an icon.
Alt-Spacebar R	Restore File Manager application window.
Alt-Spacebar S	Resize File Manager application window.
Alt-Spacebar W	Switch to another program using Task List.
Alt-Spacebar X	Maximize File Manager application window.
Alt-T A	Show entire directory structure of selected drive.
Alt-T B	Display complete directory tree for a selected directory.
Alt-T C	Collapse display of directory structure for a selected directory.
Alt-T X	Display first-level subdirectories for a selected directory.
Alt-V B	Sort file display alphabetically by filename.
Alt-V C	Select types of files and directories to be shown.
Alt-V F	Show full file details for directory window.
Alt-V N	Show filenames only.
Alt-V O	Show selected file details.
Alt-V R	Limit the number of directory windows to one.
Alt-V S	Sort file display by selected criteria.

Alt-V T	Sort file display by extension.
Alt-W [number]	Switch to selected window.
Alt-W A	Close all windows except Directory Tree.
Alt-W C	Cascade open windows within File Manager.
Alt-W R	Refresh window display.
Alt-W T	Tile open windows within File Manager.
Ctrl-[letter]	Display contents of selected drive in Directory Tree window.
Ctrl-Esc	Switch to another program using Task List.
Ctrl-F4	Close directory window.
Ctrl-F6	Switch to next directory window in sequence.
Ctrl-Tab	Switch to next directory window in sequence.
Ctrl-*	Show entire directory structure of selected drive.
Ctrl-/	Select all the files in a directory.
Ctrl-	Deselect all the files in a directory.
Delete	Delete selected files, directories and icons.
F5	Refresh window display.
F7	Move selected files to another directory or disk.
F8	Copy selected files to another directory or disk.
Shift-F4	Tile open windows within File Manager.
Shift-F5	Cascade open windows within File Manager.
Shift-F8	Extend selection to include files that are not contiguous.
*	Show complete directory structure for selected directory.
+	Display first-level subdirectories for a selected directory.
-	Collapse directory tree for selected directory.

CHAPTER 8

Print Manager

Behind the Scenes

Normally, when you want to print a document or a graphic image, you simply choose the appropriate command from within the application program you used to create the document. When you send a document to the printer, however, it does not go straight down the printer cable and into the printer, as you might expect. A fairly complex sequence of events happens before the printed pages begin to appear. These steps use up processor time and memory. In fact, depending on the program, you may find that your machine is effectively tied up until the print job is done.

Printing is a memory-hungry task. The application program first has to add the printer commands to the document, and in some cases it has to prepare the printer itself. For example, suppose you are printing a document from WordStar to a Hewlett-Packard LaserJet Series II. The document uses three downloadable fonts, all of the same typeface, in three different sizes. When the document is being prepared for the printer, the application has to find the fonts on your hard disk, download them to the printer, and then send the details of the pages themselves. All this activity takes time; more importantly, it requires the full attention of the processor, and thus you are unable to use the PC for anything else until the print job is complete.

If you are using a PostScript printer, there is a lengthy delay while the application generates the PostScript code. (PostScript is actually a specialized computer language that is used to describe the contents of an entire page.) A PostScript printer includes a generous selection of built-in vector fonts, but if you choose one of the thousands of additional PostScript fonts it will need to be downloaded to the printer as well. Even using internal fonts, the process takes time and processor power.

Regardless of what type of printer you're using, the printer has a cache of memory called a *buffer*. With a large document, it's easy to fill the buffer faster than the printer can produce pages. When that happens, the application has to pause and wait for the buffer to clear before continuing to print.

One of the most powerful advantages of Windows is its ability to run a number of applications concurrently and to perform routine jobs like printing in the background. So how does Windows keep from being bogged down by big print jobs? It cheats. When you issue the **Print** command from within any Windows application, the program actually bypasses the printer and instead sends the output to a print file. That file is in turn sent to a program called Print Manager, which handles the actual printing. Because the printing is now being controlled by a Windows program that has been designed to work in the background, you can continue to use other applications as if you were not printing anything.

Actually, that's not quite true. Using Print Manager slows down everything else to some extent. The file to be printed has to be stored somewhere—on a RAM disk, if you have one, or on the hard disk. If you use the hard disk as temporary storage you'll notice a delay whenever an application accesses the disk at the same time the Print Manager is spooling a print job. The extent of the slowdown depends on the type of machine you are using and the system resources you have available.

On the Samsung 80286, for example, I used Print Manager once and never bothered trying after that first time. There just isn't enough memory or processor muscle available on that machine to make background printing a viable proposition. I found instead that the best thing to do is to leave the printing until I have nothing else to do, and then do all the print jobs at one time. If I increased the amount of RAM on the 80286 to at least 4 MB, I suspect I could get the machine to print far more effectively.

Printing from the 80386SX, on the other hand, is no problem at all because of its ample system resources. Windows uses the RAM disk for temporary storage, and printing fairly flies along without any noticeable slowdown in other Windows programs.

Printing from DOS

The Print Manager handles printing from all Windows-based applications, but it can't control printing from MS-DOS programs running within Windows. When you run an MS-DOS program like WordStar inside the Windows environment, any print jobs will use the program's own printer drivers. In some cases, you may experience problems with printing. This is typically the result of inadequate system resources and has nothing to do with Print Manager. On several of the machines I use, for example, there is enough memory to create and edit documents using WordStar, but there's not enough memory to let me print documents.

I can play around with the various settings and free enough memory so that I can print from within Windows, or I can run the program from MS-DOS whenever I want to print. An even better solution might be to change to another word processor. WordStar, an old, text-based application, is beginning to show its age. I just got a copy of Amí Professional from Samna, and I'll be using that from now on. Using the new word processor, I know I'll be able to print without any hassle—after all, the program is designed to run under Windows 3!

Printing from Windows

When you select **Print** from any Windows application the program captures the output in a file and sends it to the Print Manager. You can use the Control Panel to disable Print Manager, in which case the document will be sent directly to the printer. With Print Manager shut down, printing takes priority over everything else: You will be unable to use any program—Windows or MS-DOS— until the printing is finished. Enabling Print Manager again provides the strongest possible evidence of its benefit: It allows you to continue working while the printing goes on in the background.

As soon as you issue the command to print a document, the Print Manager icon appears at the bottom of the screen. You can continue to send files to be printed, even while the first one is still being processed. The list of files waiting to be printed is called the *print queue*. You can view the list of files waiting to be printed and check their order in the queue by selecting the Print Manager icon from the Main group in Program Manager.

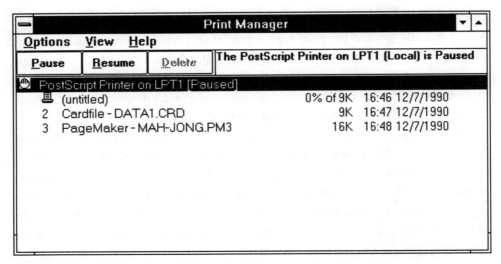

Print Manager

Print Manager resembles other Windows applications. Its application window contains a Control menu, a title bar, and Minimize and Maximize buttons, along with a menu bar containing three keywords. Below the menu bar are three buttons and a message box. The buttons allow you to control any jobs that are still in the print queue.

Pause lets you temporarily suspend the printing of the highlighted file.

Resume restarts a print job that has been suspended. You may also need to use this button if the printer has gone off line for some reason—for example, if it runs out of paper.

Delete allows you to eliminate a file from the print queue.

The message box tells you the name of the active printer and provides an indicator of its status: idle, paused, or printing.

Immediately below these three buttons is a list of files waiting to be printed. Each entry also includes the following associated information:

The position of the file within the print queue. A small printer appears next to the file that is currently being printed. The other entries in the list are numbered according to their position in the queue. You can change the priority of any file that has not yet been printed by clicking on the filename and dragging it to a new position within the queue. To move a queued file using the keyboard, highlight the filename and press **Ctrl-Up** or **Ctrl-Down**.

The originating program—Write or Notepad, for example—followed by the filename itself.

The size of the file, in kilobytes, followed by the time and date the file was sent to the queue. The entry for the file that is currently being printed will show, in percentage terms, how much of the file has been sent to the printer. These last details are optional; you can choose not to display them, if you wish.

Print Manager Menus

The Print Manager menu bar consists of three keywords: Options, View and Help. Help provides the detailed and extensive on-line reference facilities that are typical of Windows 3 applications.

Options Menu

```
Low Priority
√ Medium Priority
  High Priority

  Alert Always
√ Flash if Inactive
  Ignore if Inactive

  Network...

  Exit
```

Print Manager Options Menu

The **Options** menu controls print speed and lets you choose how to handle printer status messages. The menu is divided into four parts.

You may choose one of the first three lines to set the speed at which data is fed to the printer. A check mark appears next to the selected speed.

When you first installed Windows 3, the Print Manager speed was set to its default value, **Medium Priority**. The Print Manager and any application that is running simultaneously share the processor time equally. This speed produces printed output fairly quickly, but not as fast as it would if you were printing directly from an MS-DOS application.

Low Priority allocates more of the processor's time to applications. On my PostScript printer, this setting will very effectively slow down printing to roughly half the normal speed.

High Priority gives extra processor time to Print Manager, at the direct expense of other applications running at the same time. At this setting, the printer functions at nearly normal speed, although performance varies depending on which other applications are running at the time.

The next three lines govern the display of warning messages that require user action—for example, when the printer has run out of paper. These commands do not affect the display of system messages, such as a notice that the printer is off-line; they are only concerned with Print Manager messages.

Always Alert will cause Print Manager messages to interrupt any other active application.

Flash if Inactive, the default setting, causes the Print Manager icon or title bar to flash and also produces a beep to draw your attention to it. The flashing continues until you switch to the Print Manager window, at which time the error message will be displayed.

Ignore if Inactive suppresses the display of warning messages if the Print Manager is an inactive window or is shrunk to an icon. You will see any messages only when you switch to the Print Manager window.

Network gives you the option to bypass Print Manager when printing to a network print queue and lets you decide whether to update network queue displays continuously.

Exit quits Print Manager. If there are documents waiting in the print queue, you will be warned that closing the Print Manager window will delete all the pending jobs. The dialog box lets you decide whether to cancel the request and continue printing, or to go ahead and quit.

View Menu

The **View** menu allows you to turn off the display of date and time and size information about each file in the list. It also gives you additional options for viewing network queues.

```
√ Time/Date Sent
√ Print File Size

  Update Net Queues

  Selected Net Queue...
  Other Net Queue...
```

Print Manager View Menu

By default the first two options are checked, allowing you to see the time and date that the file was sent and the size of the file being printed. Having the file size visible is particularly useful, because it helps you get a feel for how much longer a given print job will take.

The network options under this menu give you an expanded view of network print queues. **Update Net Queues** lets you manually refresh the display if your network operating system does not automatically update the queue status. **Selected Net Queue** shows you all jobs pending in a network queue instead of just the ones you have sent. **Other Net Queues** calls up a dialog box that lets you view the contents of queues for networked printers that you are not connected to; this facility can help you find a lightly used printer on a busy network.

Problems with Printing

Print Manager is a very effective utility, but it can't install a printer or turn it on for you. If you encounter printing problems, the odds are that the difficulty has nothing to do with Print Manager but is instead caused by a faulty printer installation.

When I first installed Windows 3 I configured my StarScript printer using the Apple LaserWriter NTX driver. After all, this is the printer emulation I used under Windows/286 with no problems whatsoever. But the first time I tried to print from Windows 3 using this emulation the printer itself gave me an error message. After playing around with different emulations, I found that the printer would work just fine if I installed an Apple LaserWriter Plus driver. (Oddly enough, that emulation wouldn't work at all in Windows/286!) The moral? If you run into printer problems, check the printer configuration before you do anything else.

Of course, before you try to do any printing make sure the printer is turned on. It sounds silly, but it *does* happen. A consultant friend of mine once earned a rather nice fee for simply turning on a printer. His client was having trouble printing a document and called him for help. When he wasn't available, they called another consultant, who turned everything off, rebooted the system and managed to produce a printout. He got his fee and the client was happy. The next morning the system wouldn't print again. The guy in charge had a minor fit and called my friend, who was available this time. He turned everything off and then asked the operator to boot up the system. The operator carefully switched everything on except the printer! That's how to earn a nice fat bonus in one easy lesson.

Whenever anything goes wrong with a computer system and its peripherals check the obvious problem areas first.

Is the printer plugged in? Is the power switch on? Is the on-line switch turned on?

Are the cables connected to the right ports? Are the connections secure?

Have you configured the printer properly for the application software?

Is there paper in the printer?

Is there toner (or ink, or a ribbon) in the printer?

If the hardware checks out, make sure that the printer is properly configured. Installing a printer simply copies a device driver into your Windows directory; you'll need to go into the Control Panel to configure the driver for the specific model you're using. (See Chapter 5 for details.) Double check the options and the port assignments. If you are using a serial port make sure the settings are right. If the printer still doesn't print, exit from Windows and try printing from an MS-DOS application. If the printer works outside Windows, then there's probably a problem with the Windows configuration. If it doesn't work here, then the fault probably lies with the printer itself.

If you have more than one printer installed, be sure the correct printer is selected as the default. If you have a PostScript printer set as the default but used a PCL (LaserJet-compatible) printer for a document, you will almost certainly see gibberish.

Any fonts you are using must be available to the printer. Have you created the fonts you are trying to use, and are they in the correct directory? If the printer cannot find the fonts you specify, the resulting printout, if any, will be wrong.

Summary

Print Manager intercepts print output from Windows applications and manages printing as a background process. Non-Windows applications cannot use Print Manager.

You can set the relative amount of processor time allotted to printing in comparison to other applications.

The Print Manager allows you to change the position of files in the queue, delete files and pause the printer.

Keyboard Summary

Alt-D	Delete file from print queue.
Alt-F4	Quit Print Manager.
Alt-O A	Allow Print Manager error messages to interrupt applications.
Alt-O F	Flash inactive Print Manager window in case of error messages.

Alt-O H	Set High Priority printing.
Alt-O I	Ignore error messages when Print Manager is inactive.
Alt-O L	Set Low Priority printing.
Alt-O M	Set Medium Priority printing.
Alt-O N	Set network queue display options.
Alt-O X	Quit Print Manager and cancel all print jobs in queue.
Alt-P	Pause printing.
Alt-R	Resume printing.
Alt-Spacebar C	Quit Print Manager and cancel all print jobs in queue.
Alt-Spacebar M	Move Print Manager window.
Alt-Spacebar N	Reduce Print Manager window to icon.
Alt-Spacebar R	Restore Print Manager to window.
Alt-Spacebar S	Resize Print Manager window.
Alt-Spacebar X	Maximize Print Manager window.
Alt-V O	Choose alternate network print queue.
Alt-V P	Display file size of queued print jobs.
Alt-V S	View complete contents of network print queue.
Alt-V T	Display date and time jobs were added to queue.
Alt-V U	Manually update network print queue.
Ctrl-Esc	Switch to another program using Task List.
Ctrl-Down	Move print job to lower priority in queue.
Ctrl-Up	Move print job to higher priority in queue.
Delete	Delete selected file from print queue.

CHAPTER 9

Odds and Ends

Some of the most useful Windows utilities can't really be called applications at all. The chances are good, though, that you'll use each of these three features every time you run Windows.

Clipboard

The Clipboard is a fundamental part of the Windows environment. This powerful feature makes it easy to share data between different programs running under Windows. Using the Clipboard, you can cut text or graphics from one program and paste it into another with just a few mouse clicks or keystrokes.

Most of the time, you use the Clipboard without even thinking about it. Whenever you choose **Copy** or **Cut** from a Windows application menu, the selected text or graphic is copied to the Clipboard and can be retrieved using the **Paste** command. As in previous versions of Windows, the contents of the Clipboard are replaced every time you cut or copy something new. In Windows 3, however, you can save the contents of the Clipboard to a file and reload it later.

There are other improvements in the Windows 3 Clipboard as well. You can capture the entire screen or an open window and copy it to the Clipboard. (All the illustrations in this book were captured using this facility.) You can even grab a shot of the Clipboard containing a shot of the Clipboard containing a shot of the Clipboard! Clipboard transfers color information as well, as long as your applications and hardware support color.

All in all, the improvements that Microsoft has made in Clipboard are praiseworthy: I just wish they had gone a little bit further. For example, it would be nice if the Clipboard could load a .PCX or .BMP file directly, without having to load it into Paintbrush first. It would also be helpful to have the option to cut or copy a bit of data and append it to the Clipboard without erasing the current contents. Maybe the next version of Windows will include these refinements.

Except for games and some control programs, most Windows applications include an **Edit** menu. The list of commands on this type of menu invariably includes the following:

> **Cut** copies selected data from the application to the Clipboard and then deletes it from the application itself. The data is held in the Clipboard until you change it, clear the Clipboard or exit Windows.

> **Copy** puts a copy of the selected data in the Clipboard without deleting it from the application.

> **Paste** takes the data from the Clipboard and places it into the current application at the cursor location. The data remains in the Clipboard until you change it, allowing you to paste it as often as necessary.

To copy a Windows screen into the Clipboard, press **PrintScrn**. If you press **Alt-PrintScrn** only the active window or dialog box will be copied.

Normally the Clipboard runs in the background; however, you can run it in its own window if you choose. This option lets you view the contents of the Clipboard, although you cannot edit them directly. You must run Clipboard in its own window if you wish to save the Clipboard contents to a file.

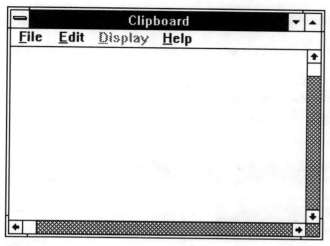

Clipboard

Exercise 9.1
Grab an Image

The Clipboard allows you to grab the entire screen or just the active element, either a window or a dialog box.

1. From the Program Manager, select the **Clipboard** icon in the Accessories group and then press **Enter**. The Clipboard window will appear onscreen. As it first appears the Clipboard window is very small. For the purposes of this exercise, you'll need to use the Control menu to resize the window so that it fills about half of the screen.

2. Press **PrintScrn** and the image of the Windows background, complete with the open Clipboard window, will appear in the Clipboard window.

3. Use the cursor keys to move around the image area. Press **Alt-F A** to bring up the File Save As dialog box. The suggested filename in the text box is **DEFAULT.CLP**. Type **TEST1** (the contents of the box will be replaced as soon as you begin typing) and then press **Enter**. There's no need to type an extension; Clipboard automatically appends .CLP to the filename. The

image on the Clipboard is written to the disk and the dialog box vanishes.

4. Press **Delete** to clear the Clipboard. Press **Enter** in response to the confirming dialog box.

5. Now press **Alt-PrintScrn** to capture the active window to the Clipboard. The new image that appears in the Clipboard window consists only of the Clipboard itself, because that is the active window. Save this as **TEST2**.

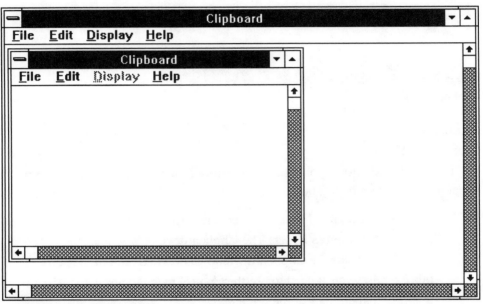

Clipboard in the Clipboard

6. Reload the original file by pressing **Alt-F O** and then entering **TEST1** in the text box; you may also use **Tab** and the cursor keys to select the file from the list. There's no need to add the extension here, either; Clipboard assumes that you want to open a .CLP file. Press **Enter** in response to the dialog box asking if you want to delete the Clipboard contents. The first image reappears, ready to be pasted into any Windows program that can handle graphic files.

1. From the Program Manager, double click on the **Clipboard** icon in the Accessories group. Grab the lower right-hand corner of the window border and resize the window so that it fills about half of the screen.

2. Press **PrintScrn** and the image of the Windows background, complete with the open Clipboard window, will appear in the Clipboard window.

3. Use the scroll bars to move around the image area. Click on **File** in the menu bar, and then on **Save As**. The suggested filename in the text box is **DEFAULT.CLP**. Type **TEST1** (the contents of the box will be replaced as soon as you begin typing) and click on **OK**. There's no need to type an extension; Clipboard automatically appends .CLP to the filename. The image on the Clipboard is written to the disk, and the dialog box vanishes.

4. Click on **Edit** and then **Delete** (or simply press **Delete**) to clear the Clipboard.

5. Now press **Alt-PrintScrn** to capture the active window to the Clipboard. The new image that appears in the Clipboard window consists only of the Clipboard itself, because that is the active window. Save this as **TEST2**.

6. Reload the original file by clicking on **File** and then **Open** and selecting **TEST1** from the file list. Click on **OK** in response to the dialog box asking if you want to delete the Clipboard contents. The first image reappears, ready to be pasted into any Windows program that can handle graphic files.

Exercise 9.2
Pasting to MS-DOS

You can use the Windows Clipboard to do cut-and-paste operations between a Windows application and an MS-DOS program that is running in the Windows environment—or even between two non-Windows applications. The process is not nearly as easy as it is under Windows, however, and there are some severe limitations. Only unformatted text can be transferred to and from an MS-DOS application; formatting information will be lost in the process, and graphics cannot be transferred at all. The technique varies slightly, depending on the mode in which you are running Windows.

For the purposes of this exercise, let's copy some text from the Windows Notepad into an MS-DOS word processor. We'll assume that the MS-DOS program is running in full-screen mode—the only option available in real and standard mode.

1. Start Notepad and load any text file (one of the .TXT files in the Windows directory will work nicely). Highlight a few sentences and press **Ctrl-Ins** to copy the selected material to the Clipboard.

2. Start the MS-DOS word processor from Program Manager; you can start with a new file or load an existing file. Place the cursor at the point where you want the data to be pasted.

3. Press **Alt-Esc** to switch back to Windows and reduce the MS-DOS program to an icon.

4. Click once on the MS-DOS program icon and the Control menu box will pop up. Click on the **Paste** command and the program returns to the foreground.

5. The data will be pasted in where the cursor sits in the MS-DOS application. (With some applications, you may need to press a key before the data appears.) The effect is exactly as though someone were sitting at your keyboard typing in the characters.

Copying data from a full-screen non-Windows application to the Clipboard is trickier. You can only copy text, one screen at a time. While the MS-DOS application is running, press **PrintScrn**. All the text on the screen—probably a great deal more than you wanted—is copied to the Clipboard. You can then paste it into a Windows application and cut what you don't need.

The process is a bit easier if Windows is running in 386 enhanced mode, because you can run an MS-DOS application in a window and issue the **Paste** command with the window visible. To switch between full-screen and windowed operation (in 386 enhanced mode only), press **Alt-Enter.** The application appears in a window with a Control menu, Minimize and Maximize buttons and a title bar. You can click

210

anywhere within the window to define a block of text to be copied to the Clipboard. As soon as you begin marking the text block, the label on the title bar changes to read **Select [application name]**. Click on the Control menu box and choose **Edit** and **Copy** to transfer the text. To paste text into a windowed MS-DOS application, place the application's cursor where you want to paste the text (don't use the mouse to mark this point). Click on the Control menu box and choose **Edit** and **Paste** to begin the transfer.

Task List

In the Control menu of every application window, the final command is **Switch To...** This command pops up the Task List, which allows you to jump immediately to any other program that is already running—whether it is reduced to an icon or sitting in a window. You can even switch instantly to a full-screen MS-DOS application. **Ctrl-Esc** is the keyboard shortcut that activates the Task List; you can also call it to the foreground by double clicking anywhere on the background wallpaper.

When you select the Task List, what happens depends on the type of application that is active. If you are running an MS-DOS program, you return to Windows and the program you were using is reduced to an icon. If you are working with a Windows program, the Task List simply pops into the foreground and becomes the active window. Unlike most windows, the Task List cannot be maximized, resized or shrunk to an icon. The window consists of a list and six buttons.

```
┌─────────────────────────────────────────┐
│ ▬           Task List                    │
├─────────────────────────────────────────┤
│ Clipboard                                │
│ Program Manager                          │
│                                          │
│                                          │
│                                          │
│                                          │
│ ┌───────────┐ ┌───────────┐ ┌──────────┐│
│ │ Switch To │ │ End Task  │ │  Cancel  ││
│ └───────────┘ └───────────┘ └──────────┘│
│ ┌───────────┐ ┌───────────┐ ┌──────────┐│
│ │  Cascade  │ │   Tile    │ │Arrange Icons││
│ └───────────┘ └───────────┘ └──────────┘│
└─────────────────────────────────────────┘
```

Task List

Immediately below the title bar is a list of all the programs that are currently running. You can switch instantly to any of them, either by double clicking on the program name or by clicking on the button labeled **Switch To**. If the selected program has been shrunk to an icon it will be restored to a window in the process.

The Task List also allows you to terminate programs without having to first switch to the application. Select a program name and then click on **End Task**—the program briefly becomes active and then is terminated. If you have modified a file without saving it, you will be given a chance to save the file before the program quits.

Clicking on **Cancel** removes the Task List and leaves you in Windows.

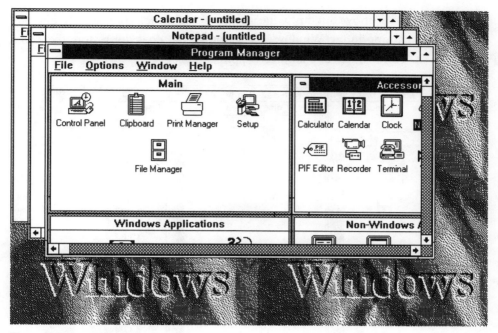

Three Windows Cascaded

The three buttons along the bottom of the dialog box allow you to arrange open windows and/or icons on the screen.

Cascade will neatly overlap all applications that are currently running in a window, just as document windows can be cascaded within application windows like Program Manager or File Manager.

Tile arranges the windows side by side, with the active window in the upper left-hand corner.

The final option, **Arrange Icons**, places the program icons in a neat row along the bottom of the screen.

You can also switch directly from one application to another using **Alt-Tab** and **Alt-Esc**. When you use either of these keyboard shortcuts, the Task List does not

213

appear; instead, you move directly to the next program in line. **Alt-Esc** highlights any icons that are sitting in the Windows background, but does not restore them to a window. **Alt-Tab** restores any iconized applications.

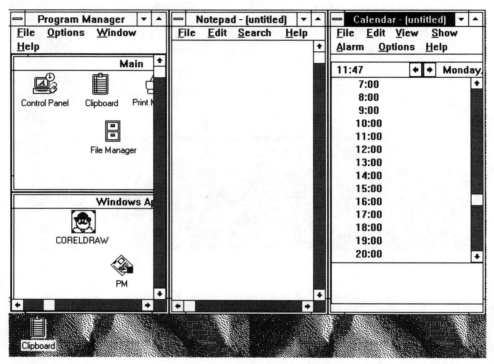

Windows Tiled

DOS Window

As part of the installation routine, Setup automatically creates an icon in the Main group labeled **DOS Prompt**. Selecting this icon runs a copy of COMMAND.COM, effectively giving you a window on the system prompt. From this window you can run any MS-DOS program, although you'll have less memory than you're accustomed to because Windows is using a chunk of RAM. You can leave the DOS window running in the background and switch to it when necessary, just as you would any MS-DOS application, or you can close it by entering **EXIT** at the system prompt.

When using a second copy of MS-DOS in this way you should avoid running any program that directly manipulates your hard disk's File Allocation Tables. A disk compression program like Speed Disk can play havoc with your system if you try to run it while Windows is active in the background.

Summary

Clipboard is a fundamental part of Windows that lets you share text and graphics between applications.

Clipboard normally runs in the background, but you can display it as a window or an icon if you wish to view the Clipboard contents or save them to a file.

When you cut or copy data from an application, the current contents of the Clipboard are replaced.

The Task List is a pop-up window that lets you instantly switch between running applications or close an application.

Task List buttons let you cascade or tile application windows and arrange application icons.

Keyboard Summary

Alt-D A	View Clipboard contents in format of originating application.
Alt-E D	Clear Clipboard.
Alt-Enter	Switch MS-DOS application between windowed and full-screen display (386 enhanced mode only).
Alt-Esc	Switch to next program or icon without using Task List.
Alt-F A	Save Clipboard contents to a file.
Alt-F O	Load a previously saved Clipboard file.
Alt-F X	Close Clipboard window.
Alt-F4	Close Clipboard window.
Alt-H	Activate Help.
Alt-Spacebar C	Close Clipboard window.
Alt-Spacebar M	Move window or icon.
Alt-Spacebar N	Reduce window to an icon.

Alt-Spacebar R	Restore window to its former size and shape.
Alt-Spacebar S	Resize window.
Alt-Spacebar W	Switch programs using Task List.
Alt-Spacebar X	Maximize window or icon.
Alt-Tab	Switch to next program in list, maximizing icon if necessary.
Ctrl-Esc	Switch programs using the Task List.
Ctrl-Ins	Copy highlighted data to Clipboard.
Delete	Clear Clipboard contents.
F1	Activate Help.
Shift-Delete	Cut data from application and place in Clipboard.
Shift-Ins	Paste data from Clipboard at insertion point.

CHAPTER 10

Paintbrush

What Is It?

Windows Paintbrush is a vast improvement over the Paint program that came with Windows/286. Based on ZSoft Corporation's PC Paintbrush, the program allows you to create full color or monochrome graphics in a variety of formats. This is a *paint* program—that is, it produces bitmapped images made out of tiny dots. Bitmaps look fine at the size at which they're created; shrinking or enlarging a bitmapped image can cause it to look distorted and unnatural. *Drawing* programs like Corel Draw are more powerful (and more expensive); they create images by defining objects—curves, lines, boxes, and the like—that can be scaled up and down to produce pleasing results at any size.

Paint programs tend to produce fairly large image files, because every detail of the graphic is stored. Drawing programs, on the other hand, are object oriented. Instead of tracking thousands of individual pixels, the program keeps a list of objects and their characteristics—saying, for example, "There is a square measuring x by y positioned at a,b and its color is black." Object-oriented disk files can be much smaller than comparable bitmap files; because they tend to be used for much more complex graphics, however, they are generally quite large.

Windows Paintbrush is a wonderful introduction to computer graphics, but don't expect to become a da Vinci overnight. Curiously, many skilled artists have a lot of difficulty when it comes to computer art. On the computer screen, the drawing area is limited and by definition flat, making it difficult to generate true perspective. To create pictures in proper perspective, you have to zoom in and create the image almost dot by dot. In other words, if you want to produce a good picture you have to spend a long time doing so, whereas with pen and paper you can do a passable picture in minutes.

The biggest failing of computer graphic programs in general is the inability to produce your colorful graphic as a printed copy. High-quality color printers are rare and expensive, and the printed image rarely matches the screen image. You can print any graphic generated in Windows Paintbrush on a standard printer, of course, but only in black and white. However, you can create wonderfully bright and dynamic pictures and then use them as wallpaper for Windows. And because Windows Paintbrush supports the popular PCX format, there are literally tens of thousands of images available—many of them in the public domain.

Windows Paintbrush is fun. It produces tangible results quickly and easily, and it can be an enjoyable way to learn the basics of Windows. It can also be terribly frustrating. Even when you know what you want to do, actually getting it onscreen can be difficult—but if you persevere, your troubles will be rewarded.

To run the program, double click on the most colorful icon in the Program Manager—the one shaped like a painter's palette. Windows Paintbrush, more than any other Windows program, demands the use of a mouse. Trying to use the program with only the keyboard is utter nonsense. This chapter contains no exercises that are keyboard based. If you want to use Paintbrush and you don't have a mouse, go out and buy one!

Paintbrush Layout

Like most Windows applications, the top line of the window contains the Control menu box, the title bar, and the Minimize and Maximize buttons; beneath the title bar is the menu bar.

Down the left-hand side of the screen is the Toolbox, which contains 18 icons representing the various drawing implements you can use. To select any tool you just click on it.

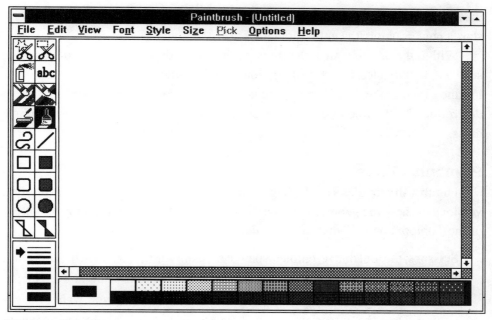

Windows Paintbrush

In a separate box at the lower left-hand corner of the window is the Linesize box, which contains a series of lines in different thicknesses. You select the thickness of the line that will be used for drawing by clicking on one of these lines.

Across the bottom of the window is the Palette—a series of 28 boxes, each of which contains a separate color. Only a few of these colors are pure; the majority are made up of two or three different colors. To the left of the palette is a box containing the current foreground and background colors—by default, these are black on white. The small box in the center is the foreground or ink color; it is surrounded by the background or paper color. To select a new foreground color click on one of the boxes in the palette using the left hand button; to change the background color, click in the palette using the right hand button.

The large space in the center of the window is the drawing area. The size of the drawing area depends on how much memory you have available. If you have only a limited amount of memory, the drawing area will be reduced in size. Whenever you start a new drawing, the foreground and background colors you have set affect how the screen appears. For instance, if you select red as the background color and then start a new drawing, the entire drawing area is colored red.

Within the drawing area, the shape of the cursor depends on the tool you have selected, and to a lesser extent on options like line thickness and brush shape. For instance, using the brush tool produces a small square cursor whose size is determined by the line thickness; the cursor associated with the Scissors tool is a cross.

Paintbrush Tools

Paintbrush provides a total of eighteen tools; some are merely filled and unfilled versions of the same geometric shape. Reading from left to right and top to bottom of the Toolbox; here's what each one does.

Scissors, the tool that resembles a pair of scissors with a star above it, allows you to mark out irregular shapes for use with the Clipboard or with the Pick menu. To use the tool, select it and then click at the point where you want to begin cutting. Drag the cursor around the area you want to cut until you eventually arrive back at your starting point. Release the mouse button and the area you have just delineated will be shown by a dashed line.

Pick, which looks like a pair of scissors under a rectangle, allows you to select rectangular areas only. (The selected area is called a *cutout*.) Click on the tool and then click in the drawing area at a corner of the area you want to select. Drag the cursor to the diagonally opposite corner and release the button; you can now copy the cutout to the Clipboard or choose commands from the Pick menu. You can also move or copy the cutout directly, without using the Clipboard.

Airbrush looks like a spray can and produces a circular scattering of dots in the foreground color. The size of the area covered by these dots depends on the line thickness you have selected. To use the tool, select it and the color you want to spray with. Position the cursor and then click and hold the left mouse button. To "spray" the drawing area, move the cursor; faster movements produce a thinner coat of dots.

The **Text** tool, shown as **abc**, allows you to place text directly into the graphic. The appearance of the text depends on the settings you make in the three text menus. You can make changes to the text only until you click on the scroll bars or on the drawing area. Once you perform either of these actions the text is frozen in place as a graphic and cannot be changed using the Text tool.

Color Eraser, the one below the spray can, allows you to change one color into another. As you move the Color Eraser over the drawing area, any pixels that match the color shown in the foreground box are changed to the color shown in the background box. Thus, to change red pixels into blue, select red as the foreground and blue as the background and then drag the cursor over the area that contains the color you want to change. You can change the size of the cursor by resetting the line thickness. To automatically change every instance of one color to another in a drawing, set the foreground and background colors and then double click on the Color Eraser tool.

Eraser, the tool below the Text tool, changes everything it passes over to the current background color. Its size is adjusted by using the Linesize box.

Paint Roller, shaped like its namesake, lets you flood an enclosed area with the current foreground color. Point to the area to be flooded with the apex of the triangle at the bottom of the roller. The area to be flooded must be enclosed, or bounded, in some way; otherwise the color leaks out into the surrounding area. A bounded area can consist of a single line. When you flood an area, only those parts of the area that are the same color and are touching each other will change color.

Brush allows you to draw freehand lines in the foreground color at the thickness that is set in the Linesize box. To use the tool, drag the cursor across the drawing area.

Curve resembles a backwards S; it allows you to draw a straight line of the current thickness and color and then bend it in one or two directions. To use the tool, click at the starting point of the line and then drag the cursor to the ending point. Release the button to anchor the beginning and end of the line. Move the cursor onto the line and then click and drag; as you do so the line will bend in the direction of the mouse movement. When you are satisfied with the curve, release the mouse button. If you'd like, you can now bend the line in the other direction as well. Click the left mouse button again to fix the curve in its position. This description sounds complex, but using the tool is really quite easy.

Line draws straight lines of the current foreground color and thickness. To use the tool, click at the point where you want the line to begin and drag the cursor to the point where you want the line to end. Releasing the button fixes the line in place.

The final eight tools produce filled and unfilled geometric shapes. In every case, you click on a point in the drawing area and drag the cursor to create the shape. Releasing the left mouse button locks the shape into place; while the left button is held down, you can click the right button to erase the shape and start over. The filled versions of each shape contain a border in the current background color and are filled with the current foreground color. To produce a solid shape, set the foreground and background to the same color.

The **Box** tool will draw an unfilled quadrilateral using the current foreground color and line thickness as the border. To use the tool, click at the point where you want to locate one corner of the box and then drag the cursor to the diagonally opposite corner. Releasing the button fixes the rectangle in place. You can force the tool to draw squares by holding down **Shift** as you drag.

Filled Box produces rectangles that are filled with the current foreground color and bordered with the current background color. You can draw squares with this tool as well by holding down **Shift** while dragging the cursor.

Rounded Box, immediately below the Box tool, draws boxes that have rounded corners. Unfortunately, there is no way to change the aspect of the rounded corners. Hold down **Shift** while dragging to create a square with rounded corners.

Filled Rounded Box works just like the Filled Box tool, but produces squares and rectangles with rounded corners.

Circle/Ellipse, shown as an unfilled circle, produces ellipses or circles drawn in the current foreground color at the currently selected line thickness. To use the tool, click at a point in the drawing area and drag the cursor to stretch the ellipse; release the mouse button to fix the shape in place. You can force the tool to produce circles by holding down **Shift** while you drag the cursor.

Filled Circle/Ellipse produces circles and ellipses that are bordered by the current background color and filled with the current foreground color. Holding **Shift** as you drag produces perfect circles.

Polygon, shown by an icon made of two triangles joined at their apexes, allows you to draw multi-sided shapes. To use the tool, click at the point where you want the shape to start, drag the cursor to the end of the first line—just as if you were using the Line tool—and release the button. Now move the cursor to the end point of the next line and click once to draw a line from the last point to the current position. Repeat this process as often as you like. To complete the polygon, double click the left mouse button— a line will appear from your last position back to the starting point. You can force the tool to produce only straight horizontal, vertical or diagonal lines by holding down **Shift** as you drag the cursor.

Filled Polygon works exactly the same way as the Polygon tool, except that the line is drawn in the background color and the resulting shape is to be filled with the foreground color. When you double click to complete the shape, only those areas that are totally contained are filled.

Exercise 10.1
Changing Colors

With Windows Paintbrush, it's easy to change the ink and paper colors. All you have to do is click on the colors you want.

1. Change the background color to red by pointing to the third box in the top row of the Palette and clicking the right mouse button. The background in the box to the left of the Palette turns red.

2. Change the foreground color to yellow by pointing to the fourth box in the top row of the Palette and clicking the left mouse button. The small box inside the box at the left of the Palette changes to yellow.

3. Now start a new drawing. There are three ways to do this:

Click on **File** in the menu bar and then on **New**.

Double click on the Eraser tool.

Press **Ctrl-N**.

A dialog box appears, asking if you want to save the current image. Click on **No**. The new drawing area appears with a bright red background. If you double clicked on the Eraser tool, the cursor shape has changed to an outlined box.

4. Change back to the default color scheme: Click on white with the right mouse button and on black with the left one. Notice that when you move the cursor onto the palette it changes into an arrow; the tool cursor appears only when the pointer is on the drawing area. Double click on the Eraser again and you're back to the original layout.

Exercise 10.2
Draw a Line

The first thing you want to do is draw something, so let's try just that.

1. Click on the Brush tool and then move the cursor onto the drawing area. The cursor becomes a small solid square.

2. Move down to the Linesize box and click on the top line. The arrowhead within the box moves up to point to the line you have selected.

3. Move the cursor back onto the drawing area. The solid square is now smaller than before.

4. Let's create a squiggle. While holding down the left mouse button, move the mouse in a figure-eight pattern. The cursor leaves a trail along the path you trace.

5. Release the button and move the mouse again. This time the cursor moves but there is no trail. Paintbrush tools become active only when you click the left button; otherwise they are dormant.

6. Click on the fattest line in the Linesize box and draw another figure eight. Try each of the line thicknesses in turn.

7. Double click on the Eraser tool again; click on **No** when the dialog box asks if you want to save the current image. Once the screen has cleared, click on the Line tool and select the thinnest line from the Linesize box. The cursor changes to a thin cross shape.

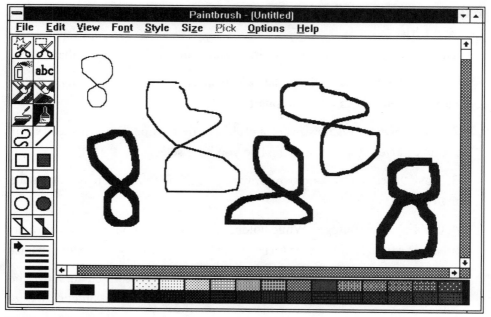

Figures of Eight

8. Move the cursor onto the drawing area, somewhere near the top left-hand corner. Click and hold the left mouse button and then drag the cursor to the right. This time, the trail that follows behind the mouse is not fixed. If you move the mouse up or down, the line follows the pointer but remains anchored on the position where you first clicked. Once the line is straight, release the button. The line now appears on the drawing area.

9. Select the next line thickness and repeat the previous step. Notice as you do so that the line is apparently the same thickness as the previous one. It is not until you release the button that the line assumes the thickness you have selected.

10. Draw a series of lines, one above the other, using all the different thicknesses.

11. Click on the Paint Roller tool (to the left of the Brush) and select another foreground color. The Roller allows you to flood an enclosed area with the

foreground color; the paint comes from the tip of the triangular area at the bottom of the roller shape. Point to the thickest line and click the left mouse button once. The line is flooded with the ink color. If you missed the line, then the drawing area is flooded with the foreground color.

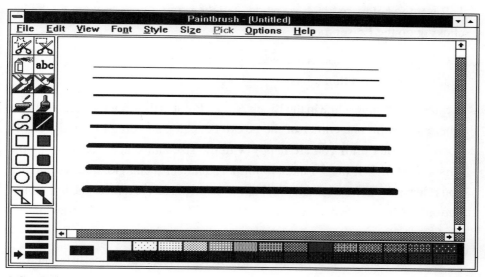

A Stack of Lines

12. Without changing tools, select another foreground color and flood another line. Change all the lines to different colors.

13. Click on **Edit** in the menu bar and then on **Undo**, or use the shortcut **Alt-Backspace**. All the colors you have just flooded vanish and you are back to black lines on a white background. The Undo facility cancels whatever you have done since you last changed tools. (Using the scroll bars, resizing the window or opening another application will also start a new Undo cycle.)

14. Try flooding the lines again, but at some point click on another tool and then select the Paint Roller again. Press **Alt-Backspace** again. Only those lines that have been flooded since you changed tools are returned to black.

Exercise 10.3
Boxes and Circles

Windows Paintbrush provides eight different tools that allow you to draw simple shapes in addition to straight lines.

1. Reset the colors to black on white, and then start a new drawing by double clicking on the Eraser tool.

2. Click on the Box tool. When you move the cursor onto the drawing area it is again shaped like a thin cross.

3. Select the thinnest line in the Linesize box. Point in the drawing area at a point where you want one corner of the box to be. Click and drag to the diagonally opposite corner until you are happy with the size and shape. As you drag the cursor a set of four lines, linked to form a square or rectangle, follows it. Once you release the mouse button the shape is set in place. As long as the left mouse button is still held down, you can press the right button to cancel the drawing and start over.

4. Use the same tool to draw some more boxes, but with different line thicknesses. Notice that when you draw a rectangle that sits on top of another rectangle, you can still see the outline of the first shape.

5. Click on the Filled Box tool and draw some more shapes. Each box has a white border and is filled with black.

6. Change the background color to red and the foreground color to blue and draw some more. The shapes now have a red border and are filled with blue.

Tip: To draw perfect squares, hold down **Shift** and then click and drag.

Try using the other shape tools to see how they work. The Rounded Box tool works just like the Box tool. Holding down **Shift** while using the Circle/Ellipse tools will draw perfect circles. The Polygon tools allow you to draw many-sided shapes; double click the left mouse button at the final position to fix the polygon into position.

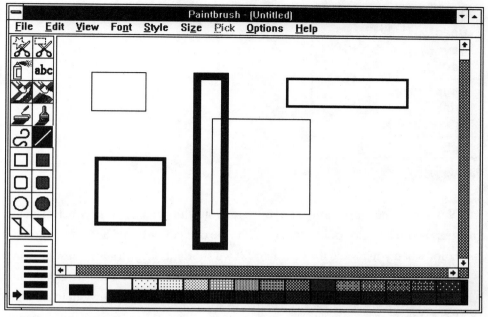

Squares and Rectangles

Paintbrush Menus

In addition to the standard Help menu, Windows Paintbrush offers eight menus, three of them specific to text. The Pick Menu is active only when the Pick tool or the Scissors tool is selected.

File Menu

The File menu lets you load, save and print files; you can also set various printer options. You can open the menu by clicking on **File** or by pressing **Alt-F**. It contains the following commands:

New	Ctrl+N
Open...	
Save	Ctrl+S
Save As...	
Page Setup...	
Print...	
Printer Setup...	
Exit	

File Menu

New clears the drawing area and presents you with a clean area in which to create graphics. The color of the paper will be the one you selected as the background color when you issued the command. Two shortcuts let you start a new drawing quickly; either press **Ctrl-N** or double click on the Eraser tool. If the current graphic has been changed in any way, you will be asked if you want to save the file before the screen is cleared. To save the file, click on **Yes** and supply a filename. To discard the graphic, click on **No**.

Open allows you to load a graphic file into Windows Paintbrush. The command brings up the File Open dialog box and a list of files. To move through your hard disk directory structure, double click on the appropriate entry. For example, to move up to the parent of the Windows directory, double click on [..]. To load a file from a floppy disk, double click on the appropriate drive letter and the dialog box contents will change to show a list of available files. By default, the dialog box will show the file type you have selected—PCX, BMP, or MSP—and only files with the selected extension will appear in the list box.

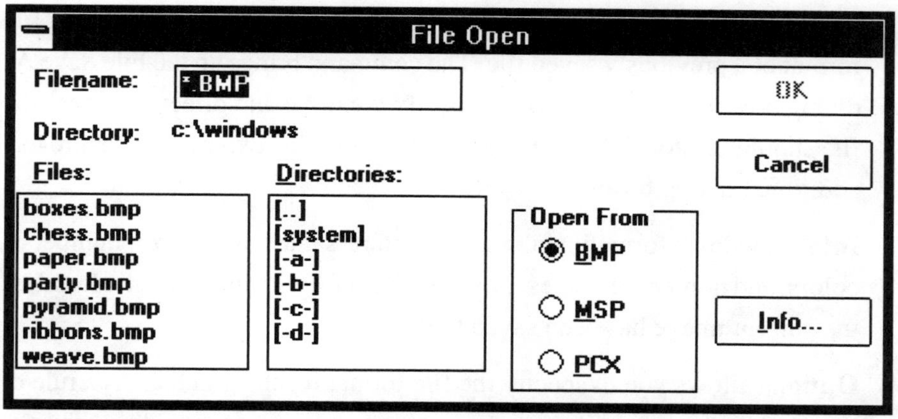

Open Dialog Box

Save writes the current file to disk. The command brings up another dialog box that allows you to specify which directory or disk you want to save the file to. The keyboard shortcut for this command is **Ctrl-S**. You should get into the habit of saving your work often. This applies to any type of document but is especially true with graphics.

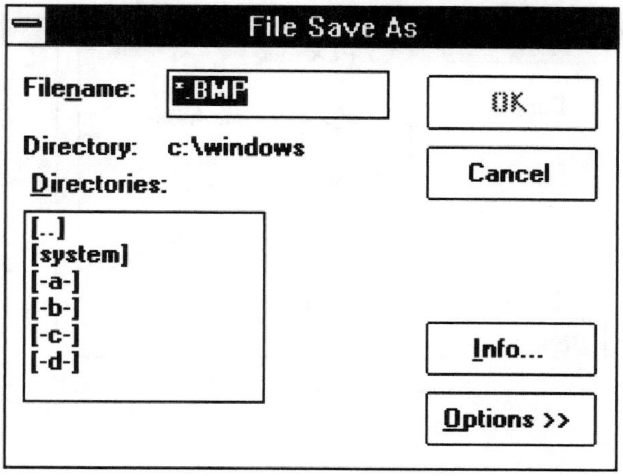

Save As Dialog Box

Save As lets you write a newly created file to disk or change the name or file format of a previously saved file. The command brings up the File Save As dialog box, which allows you to specify the drive and directory where the file should be stored. The dialog box also contains two buttons that reveal additional dialog boxes.

Info provides information about the picture's attributes—size, number of colors, and number of planes. This message box will not be available unless the current image has been saved to disk.

Options allows you to specify the file format for the graphic. As a rule of thumb, never save a file to a format that contains more colors than the picture. For example, if you have created a monochrome image, don't save it as a 256-color bitmap. If you're not sure how many colors the graphic is using, click on **Info**. Type a filename in the appropriate text box and press **Enter**. You need not specify an extension—Paintbrush will apply the proper extension for the file format you have selected.

```
┌────────────────────────────────────────────────────────────────┐
│ ▬                        File Save As                           │
├────────────────────────────────────────────────────────────────┤
│                                              ┌─ Save As ───────┐ │
│  Filename:   *.BMP          ┌──────────┐     │  ○ PCX          │ │
│                             │    OK    │     │                 │ │
│  Directory:   c:\windows    └──────────┘     │  ○ Monochrome   │ │
│  Directories:               ┌──────────┐     │     bitmap      │ │
│  ┌──────────────┐           │  Cancel  │     │                 │ │
│  │ [..]         │           └──────────┘     │  ◉ 16 Color     │ │
│  │ [system]     │                            │     bitmap      │ │
│  │ [-a-]        │                            │                 │ │
│  │ [-b-]        │                            │  ○ 256 Color    │ │
│  │ [-c-]        │           ┌──────────┐     │     bitmap      │ │
│  │ [-d-]        │           │  Info... │     │                 │ │
│  └──────────────┘           └──────────┘     │  ○ 24-bit       │ │
│                             ┌──────────┐     │     bitmap      │ │
│                             │Options >>│     └─────────────────┘ │
│                             └──────────┘                         │
└────────────────────────────────────────────────────────────────┘
```

Options Dialog Box

Page Setup is only necessary if you want to print your graphic. The dialog box allows you to set the page margins and also provides options for formatting headers and footers. The formatting codes must be preceded by an ampersand (&) in the appropriate box. The codes are:

&c Center text between the margins. This is the default.

&d Include the current system date.

&f Print the name of the image file.

&l Left justify following text.

&p Include page numbers.

&r Right justify following text.

&t Include the current system time.

You can include any of these codes, either singly or in combination, as headers or footers or both.

Print sends your graphic to the printer, via the Print Manager if it is active. The command brings up a dialog box that allows you to specify the number of copies, the scaling, the print quality and the section of the image to be printed.

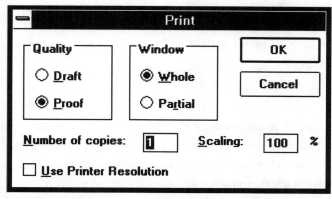

Print Dialog Box

Printer Setup allows you to select the printer to which the image will be sent. You may choose only from those printers you have installed and configured using the Control Panel.

Exit quits Windows Paintbrush. You will be prompted to save a changed image or cancel the command before returning to the Program Manager.

Exercise 10.4
Changing Format

You can use Windows Paintbrush to turn PCX files into BMP files that can then be used as wallpaper for your Windows background. You must have a graphic file saved in PCX format to carry out this exercise.

1. Run Windows Paintbrush and click on **File** and **Open** in the menu bar.

2. Change the setting in the dialog box by clicking on **PCX**. Switch to the correct drive or directory using the list box.

3. Double click on the filename you want; the image is loaded into Paintbrush.

4. Click on **File** and then on **Save As**. Don't press **Ctrl-S**— that will just save the file in PCX format again.

5. Click on the **Options** button to expand the dialog box; select one of the four available bitmap formats.

6. Finally, click on **OK** to save the image in the new format. You can now install it as wallpaper in the Control Panel.

Edit Menu

The Edit menu is used primarily to cut and paste images or parts of images to and from the Clipboard. Unlike most Windows applications, however, Windows Paintbrush allows you to copy graphic information directly to another file; it will also allow you to paste an image from another graphic file directly into the current one. To open the Edit menu, either click on **Edit** in the menu bar or press **Alt-E**.

Undo	Alt+BackSpace
Cu_t	Shift+Del
_C_opy	Ctrl+Ins
_P_aste	Shift+Ins
C_o_py To...	
Paste _F_rom...	

Edit Menu

Undo will cancel any drawing or editing you have done with a specific tool since you last changed tools. (Resizing a window, using the scroll bars or opening another application will also eliminate your ability to undo any changes.) **Undo** is a comforting safeguard against unwanted changes to your graphic. When you're satisfied with a change you've made, it's a good idea to reset this facility by clicking on the current tool in the Toolbox.

There are two keyboard shortcuts for **Undo**. Press **Alt-Backspace** to restore the drawing to its state before you started working with the current tool. If you press **Backspace**, the cursor turns to a box with an X in it; if you hold down the left mouse button, you can selectively erase any work you've done with the current tool.

Cut is only active when the Pick or Scissors tool is selected and a cutout is marked. **Shift-Delete** is the keyboard shortcut. This command deletes the selected image area and places it in the Clipboard. If you use **Undo** to restore the deleted area, the cutout element remains in the Clipboard.

Copy leaves the cutout area in the current image and places a copy in the Clipboard. The keyboard shortcut is **Ctrl-Ins**.

Paste lets you insert the contents of the Clipboard into a graphic. The keyboard shortcut is **Shift-Ins**. If the Clipboard is empty, the command will be grayed out. Whenever you paste data into Paintbrush, it will always appear at the top left corner of the drawing area; drag the pasted section into position and release the left mouse button, then click anywhere outside the cutout to fix the new position.

Copy To is similar to **Save As** except that it copies only the cutout part of the image to a designated file. This command gives you exactly the same options as when you save a new file.

Paste From is similar to **Open**, but it allows you to merge a number of files into a single image. You cannot use this command to select part of another image; it works only on the whole file.

View Menu

As you would expect, the **View** menu controls the image of Paintbrush on the screen. You can click on **View** in the menu bar or press **Alt-V** to open the menu.

Zoom In lets you magnify a portion of the image and edit it one pixel at a time. The keyboard shortcut is **Ctrl-Z**. When you activate the command a small gray box appears onscreen. Place it over the area you want to enlarge and click the left mouse button. The largest part of the drawing area is devoted to a magnified image of the dot pattern in the selected area. The area you have selected appears at normal size in a small box at the upper left corner of the drawing area.

Zoom In	Ctrl+Z
Zoom Out	**Ctrl+O**
View Picture	**Ctrl+C**
√ **Tools and Linesize**	
√ **Palette**	
Cursor Position	

View Menu

When you are working in a magnified area, there are only two tools you can use: the Paint Roller and the Brush. In areas of solid color, the Paint Roller works just as it does with full-size images. The Brush operates in a slightly different way: Clicking the left mouse button changes the pixel under the cursor to the current foreground color, while the right button changes it to the background color.

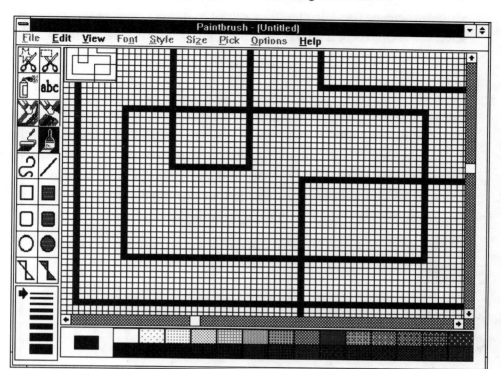

Area Enlarged

Zoom Out is really two different commands. From the magnified image, it will restore the drawing area to its original size. However, if you select this command from the normal-size drawing area, the entire image—regardless of its size—is scaled to fit in the drawing area. You can cut, copy and paste in the zoomed image, but none of the drawing tools will work. This is the only way to paste in a piece of graphic material that is larger than the drawing area. The keyboard shortcut is **Ctrl-O**. To get back to the normal view press **Ctrl-Z** or **Esc**.

View Picture shows the entire image without having the Paintbrush window in the way. The keyboard shortcut is **Ctrl-C**. To return to the Paintbrush window press any key.

Tools and Linesize is a toggle that controls whether or not these elements are visible onscreen. The default setting, shown by a check mark next to the menu selection, is On. There is no way to change tools or reset the line thickness when these elements are hidden.

Palette is also a toggle; it controls whether or not the Palette is visible.

Cursor Position produces a tiny window that displays the coordinates of the cursor. It is very useful if you want to produce images that contain precisely aligned elements. The default setting for this toggle switch is Off. You can move the cursor window anywhere outside the drawing area by dragging it to a new position. To remove the cursor position window, either double click on its Control menu box or click on the toggle in the **View** menu. If it is the active window, you can press **Alt-F4** to close it.

Cursor Position

Text Menus

The next three menus all determine the appearance of text created with the Text tool.

The **Font** menu lets you select any of the typefaces that are installed in Windows. A check mark appears next to the name of the current font. The default selection is always **System**.

The **Style** menu allows you to apply different attributes to the characters you enter. The default selection is **Normal**. You can change this setting to one of the following alternatives:

Bold The shortcut is **Ctrl-B**.

Italic The shortcut is **Ctrl-I**.

Underline The keyboard shortcut is **Ctrl-U**. The underlining appears beneath all characters, including spaces.

These three characteristics can be applied individually or in any combination. To remove all effects click on **Normal**.

Outline produces a border, in the current background color, around the characters you enter. This effect might be hard to see unless your text is fairly large.

Shadow places a thin shadow, in the background color, behind the characters.

Outline and Shadow are mutually exclusive— you can use one but not both. If the currently selected background color is the same as the drawing background, the shadow or outline will not be visible!

The **Size** menu allows you to change the point size of the characters according to the typeface you are using. Some typefaces can be used only in specific sizes. An asterisk appears next to sizes that exist in Windows font files. All other available sizes are created by scaling an existing font—often with unattractive results.

When you select the Text tool, click on the point in the drawing area where you want the text to start. The thin insertion cursor will appear. Then just start typing; the text you enter will appear in whatever typeface, style and size are currently active. As long as the Text tool remains active, you can change the typeface, style, size and colors of the text you have just entered. The text is not fixed in place until you change tools, click on the scroll bars, resize the window, open another application or move the text cursor.

Handling text is certainly not what Windows Paintbrush does best. When you enter text, any text that is not visible in the drawing area is irretrievably lost. In addition, once the text has been fixed in position it becomes part of the painting and can only be edited as a graphic. You can rub it out or flood it with different colors, but you cannot change the size, style or typeface.

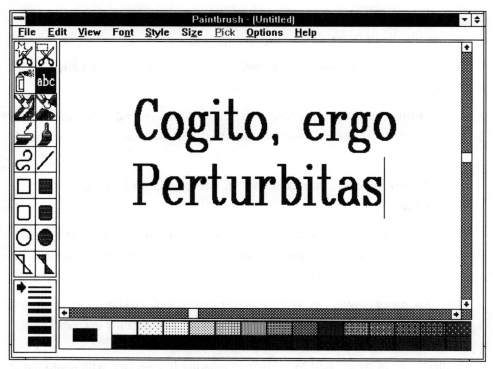

Text (I think, therefore I am confused!)

Pick Menu

This menu is active only if you have already selected and used the Pick or Scissors tool. You use either of these tools to define an area of the image called a *cutout*. Once you have released the button this menu becomes active. You can manipulate the cutout in a variety of ways using the effects in the Pick menu.

Flip Horizontally turns your selected area around a vertical axis so that the left-hand side becomes the right and vice versa.

Flip Vertically rotates the selected area around a horizontal axis so that the top becomes the bottom and the bottom becomes the top.

Inverse changes the colors of the cutout area into their complements. Black becomes white, blue turns to yellow, red to green and so on. In practice, the results are not quite what you would expect. Blue becomes ochre, red changes to a dirty cyan, yellow turns to dull purple and green becomes a dark magenta. It seems that the colors and their brightness are being inverted; thus, dark colors become bright and vice versa.

Shrink + Grow is a toggle that remains active until you deselect it. It allows you to copy the selected item and change its size and shape—as many times as you wish until you deselect the command. You can pick a square, for example, and produce as many distorted quadrilaterals as you want. The original cutout remains in place unless you select the **Clear** command as well.

Tilt allows you to move the selected object to a new position and angle it in any direction you choose. When you use this command, either the top or bottom of the cutout stays in place and the remainder of the object is tilted according to how you move the mouse, producing a parallelogram shape. This command is also a toggle and remains active until it is deselected.

Clear applies to the original selected area and is used in combination with the other commands on this menu. If you select this command the original picked area is erased when you manipulate the cutout. Otherwise, the original remains in position and a copy of the cutout is changed.

Options Menu

The Options menu provides a range of controls over the images you produce using Windows Paintbrush.

Image Attributes allows you to control the size of the default drawing area and choose whether to work in color or monochrome. The default image size is based on the memory available in your system and the type of monitor you have. You can adjust this size up or down, within limits. You can also choose to display the size in one of three units of measurement: inches, centimeters or pixels. As you select each option, the values in the Width and Height boxes are adjusted. The settings you make here become the new defaults, although they do not take effect until you start a new graphic or restart Paintbrush.

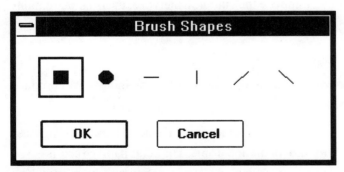

Image Attributes Dialog Box

Brush Shapes brings up a dialog box from which you can select the shape of the brush you will use. You can bypass the menu and bring up the Brush Shapes dialog box immediately by double clicking on the Brush tool. The brush shape has an effect on most of the drawing tools.

Brush Shapes Dialog Box

Edit Colors allows you to create custom colors, although the choice of colors is very dependent on the type of monitor you are using. You can change the three basic colors—red, green and blue—in single steps from 0 to 255. In theory this means you could have 16,777,216 different colors—of course, there isn't a monitor available that is capable of showing these variations, and even if there were, the human eye couldn't distinguish them. The color you change is the one that is currently selected as the foreground color. Paintbrush remembers the default color scheme, making it possible for you to change a custom color to its original setting at any time.

Edit Colors Dialog Box

Get Colors allows you to load a palette of previously saved colors. Until you create such a thing there isn't one!

Save Colors lets you save the current palette to the disk so that it can be loaded later. It is worth spending some time designing a number of custom palettes and saving them, because you can use any number of different palettes in a single graphic.

Exercise 10.5
Pick a Piece

The Pick tool can do much more than just cut and paste or flip the cutout. You can use the tool to create special effects that can produce very interesting images. The figures used in this exercise are all taken from a library of shareware clip art, because I can't draw!

1. Create a drawing of something—it doesn't matter what. Then select the Pick

tool and mark out an area. I've used a picture of an elephant because it's a good size and shape to work with. The entire animal is enclosed in the cutout box. If you drag the cutout at this point, it will move around the screen, stopping when you release the left mouse button. Hold down the **Shift** key as you drag to create a copy of the cutout and move it into a new position.

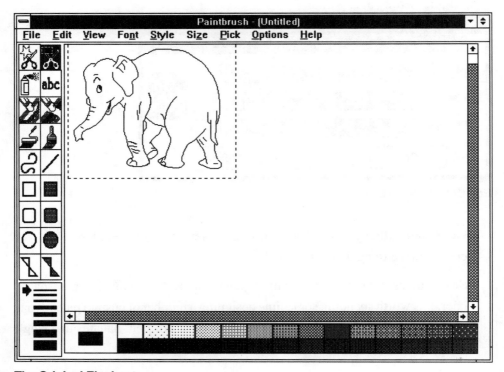

The Original Elephant

2. Copy the cutout into the Clipboard by pressing **Ctrl-Ins**.

3. Click on **Pick** in the menu bar and then on **Shrink + Grow**. The box around the cutout vanishes but the cursor remains the same.

4. Click on another point in the drawing area and drag to create a box that is smaller or larger than the original image. When you release the button the cutout

image appears in a new size within the area you drew. Because the **Shrink + Grow** command remains active until you deselect it, you can resize and reproduce as many copies of your original area as you want.

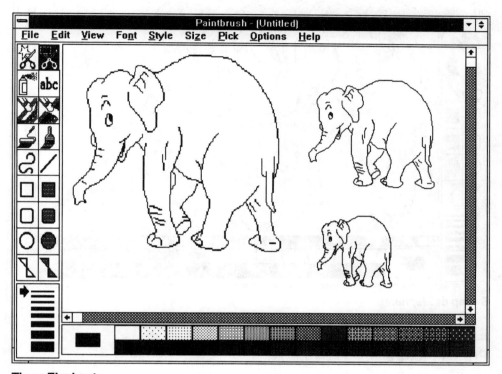

Three Elephants

5. One fascinating effect that is available when the Pick tool is selected is the ability to "sweep" an object through the drawing area. Outline an object with the Pick tool or import one via the **Paste From** command in the **Edit** menu.

6. Hold down **Ctrl** and click on a point inside the boxed area, then drag the cursor around the screen. The selected image area now acts as a giant brush that uses the colors and shape of the area you have selected. This technique can be useful for creating the illusion of movement in a drawing.

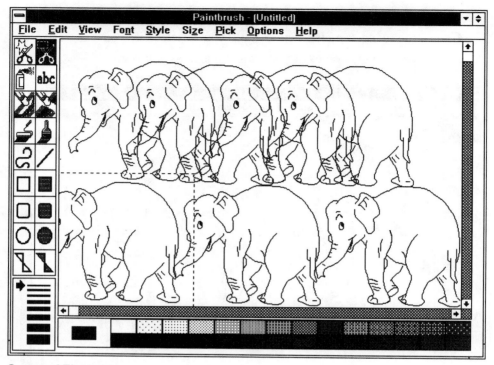

Sweep of Elephants

Exercise 10.6
Print a Picture

Windows Paintbrush will allow you to print graphic files, although the quality of the hard copy depends very much on the type of printer you are using.

1. Create or import an image.

2. Save the current graphic you have just created by pressing **Alt-F A** or by clicking on **File** in the menu bar and then on **Save As**. You can use any format you like.

3. Press **Alt-F P** to bring up the Print dialog box.

```
  ┌─────────────────────────────────────────────┐
  │ ─                  Print                      │
  │ ┌─Quality──┐ ┌─Window────┐  ┌──────────────┐ │
  │ │          │ │           │  │      OK       │ │
  │ │ ○ Draft  │ │ ◉ Whole   │  └──────────────┘ │
  │ │          │ │           │  ┌──────────────┐ │
  │ │ ◉ Proof  │ │ ○ Partial │  │    Cancel     │ │
  │ └──────────┘ └───────────┘  └──────────────┘ │
  │                                               │
  │ Number of copies:  [1]   Scaling: [100]  %    │
  │ ☐ Use Printer Resolution                      │
  └─────────────────────────────────────────────┘
```

Print Dialog Box

This dialog box asks you to make a number of decisions about the appearance of the printed image. Your first choice is print quality: **Draft** produces blocky pictures very quickly; **Proof**, the default setting, is slower but produces images of much higher quality.

The Window option box allows you to print the whole image or to select a portion of the image for printing. The default setting is **Whole**. If you choose **Partial**, the display zooms out to show you the entire image; you select a rectangle for printing using the mouse pointer.

How many copies do you want? The default setting is 1, but you can print as many as you wish. And how large do you want the image to be? By default the scaling is set to 100%, which means that the printed image will be roughly the same size as it is on the screen. You can reduce or enlarge your pictures by changing this value.

The final check box is **Use Printer Resolution**. Selecting this option will cause the image to be stretched or shrunk, if necessary, to match the size of pixels on the printer.

Once you have set these parameters, press **Enter** or click on **OK** to send the picture to the printer. If the picture is too large to fit on the page, you will receive an error message.

Summary

Windows Paintbrush is a paint program that produces bitmapped images. Although you can use the keyboard to create and edit images, the program really demands the use of a mouse.

Paintbrush can be used to produce or modify images that are then usable as Windows wallpaper.

Only by playing with the program will you discover its capabilities—and you might be surprised at your own artistic ability! Examine the BMP files that come as part of Windows to see just what the program is capable of.

Keyboard Summary

Alt-Backspace	Undo last action.
Alt-E C	Copy cutout to Clipboard.
Alt-E F	Paste existing file into current painting.
Alt-E O	Copy cutout to a disk file.
Alt-E P	Paste Clipboard contents into painting.
Alt-E T	Cut selection into Clipboard.
Alt-E U	Undo last action.
Alt-Esc	Switch to next program without using Task List.
Alt-F A	Save image to new filename.
Alt-F N	Start a new painting.
Alt-F O	Load an image file from disk.
Alt-F P	Activate print dialog box.
Alt-F S	Save current image to existing filename.
Alt-F T	Change page setup.
Alt-F X	Quit Paintbrush and return to Program Manager.
Alt-F4	Quit Paintbrush and return to Program Manager.
Alt-H	Open Help menu.
Alt-O B	Select new brush shape.
Alt-O E	Customize colors.
Alt-O G	Load previously saved color palette from disk.

Alt-O I	Open Image Attributes dialog box.
Alt-O S	Save existing color palette to disk.
Alt-P C	Select original picked area.
Alt-P H	Flip picked area around vertical axis.
Alt-P I	Invert colors in picked area.
Alt-P R	Select a printer.
Alt-P S	Toggle Shrink + Grow.
Alt-P T	Toggle Tilt command.
Alt-P V	Flip picked area around horizontal axis.
Alt-S B	Turn on bold text.
Alt-S I	Turn on italic text.
Alt-S N	Set text to normal.
Alt-S O	Turn on outline text.
Alt-S S	Turn on shadow text.
Alt-S U	Turn on underlined text.
Alt-Spacebar C	Quit Windows Paintbrush.
Alt-Spacebar M	Move application window.
Alt-Spacebar N	Reduce window to an icon.
Alt-Spacebar R	Restore window to its former size and shape.
Alt-Spacebar S	Resize window.
Alt-Spacebar W	Switch programs using Task List.
Alt-Spacebar X	Maximize window.
Alt-V C	Display cursor position in small window.
Alt-V I	Zoom in to selected area.
Alt-V O	Zoom out to normal screen or view whole page.
Alt-V P	Toggle Palette display.
Alt-V T	Toggle appearance of Toolbox and Linesize box display.
Alt-V V	Remove main window elements to view whole picture.
Alt-V Z	Open Size menu.
Ctrl-B	Turn on bold text.
Ctrl-C	View entire picture area.
Ctrl-Esc	Switch programs using Task List.
Ctrl-I	Turn on italic text.

Ctrl-Ins	Copy picked area to Clipboard.
Ctrl-N	Clear current image and start a new one.
Ctrl-O	Zoom out.
Ctrl-S	Save image.
Ctrl-U	Turn on underlined text.
Ctrl-Z	Zoom in to selected area.
Delete	Click right mouse button.
F1	Activate Paintbrush Help.
F9-Delete	Double click right mouse button.
F9-Ins	Double click left mouse button.
Ins	Click left mouse button.
Shift-Delete	Cut selection into Clipboard.
Shift-Ins	Paste Clipboard contents.

CHAPTER 11

Write

What Is It?

Windows Write is a practical tool for editing and formatting text. The program is perfectly suitable for producing short documents of less than a dozen pages or so, but it's not quite powerful enough to compete with today's top word processors. For instance, it has no spell checker or thesaurus and no built-in macro capabilities; it uses its own quirky file format; and it can't handle files from any other word processing formats except Microsoft Word. Given those flaws, I certainly would not recommend it for use in a business capacity; but if your needs are modest it is easy to learn and can be quite useful.

The version of Write that comes with Windows 3 is virtually identical to the one in Windows/286. The program works with any printer that Windows supports and provides a full range of formatting options. It allows you to insert graphics into your documents, and you can paste graphics or text from other programs via the Clipboard.

When you install Windows, the Setup program places Windows Write in the Accessories group. To run the program, just double click on the icon (it looks like a pen drawing the letter A) or select the icon and press **Enter**. As with all Windows applications, you can easily resize or maximize the window.

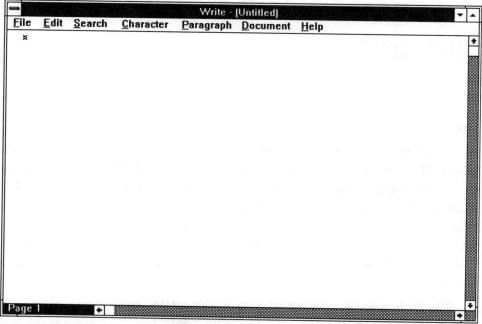

Windows Write

The application window includes the familiar Control menu box, title bar, Minimize and Maximize buttons, and menu bar. The main part of the window is blank except for a thin flashing cursor and the star-shaped end-of-document marker. The mouse pointer appears as an I-shaped insertion cursor when it is in the editing window. In the lower left corner, next to the scroll bar, is a page status area that displays the current page number.

Exercise 11.1
Setting the Format

One of the first things you'll want to do after you start Windows Write is to adjust its initial format settings to match your preferences. By default, Write displays all measurements in inches, and sets the top and bottom margins to 1 inch and the left and right margins to 1.25 inches. Changing these settings is easy—although it can take a bit of time. Here's how it's done.

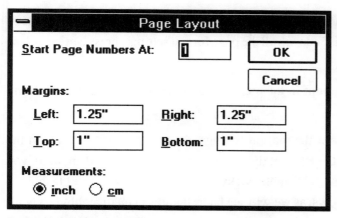

Page Layout Dialog Box

1. Press **Alt-D P** to bring up the Page Layout dialog box.

2. The first text box, which lets you set the starting value for page numbers, is highlighted. As there's no reason at this stage to change the numbering, press **Tab** to move to the next box. If you want to change the starting page number, type a value and then press **Tab**. Don't press **Enter** or you will close the dialog box.

3. The text box that is now highlighted, **Left**, contains a value in inches. You can change the left margin to any number that will work with the paper size that is specified in your printer configuration. If you try to enter a number that is too large or too small, Write will give you an error message. Because the default measurement system is inches, there's no need to enter "; you can enter a value in centimeters, if you wish, by typing **cm** after the number. (It's perfectly acceptable to mix measurement systems in this dialog box.) Do the same for the right, top and bottom margins and then press **Tab** to move on to the Measurements option box.

4. To change from inches to centimeters press **C**, or use the cursor keys to switch between the two choices. As you change this option, note that the

values in the margin settings are translated to the new measurement system. When you are satisfied with all the page format settings, press **Enter** to close the dialog box.

1. Click on **Document** in the menu bar and then on **Page Layout** to bring up the dialog box.

2. To change any of the margin settings, double click on the value in the appropriate box; the entry in the box will be highlighted and anything you type will overprint it. (Double clicking like this is a very useful technique throughout Windows, as we will see later. It allows you to highlight a word in one quick motion and then edit it if necessary.) Change any or all of the margin settings to values that are appropriate for the current paper size. Because the default measurement system is inches, there's no need to enter "; you can enter a value in centimeters, if you wish, by typing **cm** after the number. (It's perfectly acceptable to mix measurement systems here.)

3. To change the default measurement system, click on **cm** in the option box at the bottom of the screen. Notice as you change the default measurement system that the values in this dialog box are automatically translated.

The new page layout settings apply to the current document only. If you open a new document or restart Write, the settings return to their original values. Although the program has no way to store new defaults, there is a trick you can use to achieve the same end: Change the page layout to suit your preferences, but don't enter any text. Next, save the empty document as **DEFAULT.WRI** in the directory where you store your word processing files. Finally, change the properties of the Write icon in Program Manager (see Chapter 4 for details) so the empty formatted file is loaded every time you start Write. If you're ambitious, you can even create different templates for letters, reports and other types of documents.

Exercise 11.2
Ruler and Tabs

As it stands, the Write window is extremely plain: You can enter text, but you can only see it in the standard font, and the screen provides no information about what your page will look like. Let's make the display more informative by showing the Ruler onscreen. Then we can set some tabs.

1. Press **Alt-D R**. The ruler line appears along the top of the editing workspace.

1. To bring up the ruler click on **Document** in the menu bar and then click on **Ruler On** in the pull-down menu. The ruler appears across the top of the page.

Ruler

Actually, the Ruler consists of three lines, although you may not realize it at first glance. Along the top are three groups of icons. The two icons in the first group can be used to choose between left-aligned and decimal tabs if you are using a mouse. The next group of icons gives you three options to control line spacing. The final set of icons let you set the text alignment for a paragraph to one of four choices: left aligned (the default), centered, right aligned or fully justified.

The middle line contains a series of markers in the default measurement system. The scale begins with 0 at the document's left margin and is numbered at every whole point—i.e., every inch or centimeter.

At either end of the third line, just below the measurement scale, are the left and right indent markers, which are depicted by triangular shapes. The first-line indent marker, a very small dot, sits on top of the left indent marker. This line is also where tab settings are shown. You can set a maximum of 12 tab positions and choose whether they are left-aligned or decimal tabs. (Decimal tabs align text on a period and are useful for arranging numbers into neat columns.) Let's set some tabs for the current document.

2. Press **Alt-D T** to bring up the Tabs dialog box. There are 12 empty boxes, each of which has a check box underneath. The flashing cursor is sitting in the first text box.

Positions:						
Decimal:	☐ .	☐ .	☐ .	☐ .	☐ .	☐ .
Positions:						
Decimal:	☐ .	☐ .	☐ .	☐ .	☐ .	☐ .

Tabs

[OK]   [Cancel]   [Clear All]

Tabs Dialog Box

3. The value in the box defines the distance of the tab from the left margin. Enter a value for the first tab position and press **Tab**; press the **Spacebar** if you want to create a decimal tab. Press **Tab** again to move on to the next box. Repeat this process until you have defined as many tab positions as you want. Press **Enter** to save the tab settings and close the dialog box. Notice that the tab positions you have just entered in the dialog box now appear on the third line of the ruler.

2. To set a tab, just click on the third line of the Ruler, using the measurement scale to locate the distance of the tab from the left margin. A tab marker will appear. If you want to change the type from left-aligned to decimal (or vice versa), click on the appropriate icon before setting the tab position. If you make a mistake, just delete the tab marker by dragging it down off the Ruler.

By default, Write does not include any tabs and the Ruler is always turned off.

Tab settings apply only to the current document. Having formatted the page and set the tab positions, you can now begin to create a document.

Exercise 11.3
Entering, Saving and Formatting Text

Write handles text justification automatically; all you need do is type away. Your text will fill as many lines as necessary based on the page format and font size you are currently using. Because this exercise uses both the mouse and the keyboard, it does not distinguish between the two as usual.

1. Type enough text to fill more than a single screen. Don't worry about spelling and formatting for now; just type away until the text begins to scroll off the editing screen.

2. Once all your text is entered, press **Ctrl-Home** to return to the top of the document. Don't use the scroll bars; if you do, the text will scroll through the window, but the cursor will remain in its current position.

3. Click on **File** in the menu bar and then on **Save As** in the pull-down menu. The File Save As dialog box allows you to choose where and how the file will be saved.

File Save As Dialog Box

The first text box allows you to enter a filename for your document, Choose a legal filename (the standard MS-DOS rules apply) and type it in the box; don't include an extension. You can change the target directory by navigating through the Directories list box.

The three check boxes to the right of the Directories list allow you to determine what format the file will be saved in. You can select any of these toggles directly from the keyboard, but it's much easier to simply click with the mouse.

When the **Make Backup** switch is selected, Write creates a copy of the previous version of the file anytime you save a document. The extension for the backup file is .BKP, if the file is in Write format, or .BAK if the file is in Word format. The keyboard shortcut is **Alt-M**.

The second switch, **Text Only**, saves the document in Windows ANSI format. This is different from a pure-text ASCII file. Most Windows text files follow the ANSI format; files created in non-Windows programs typically do not. Press **Alt-T** to choose this option from the keyboard.

The final switch allows you to save the file in **Microsoft Word Format**. This file format can be loaded directly into Microsoft's MS-DOS word processing program; other applications, including Aldus PageMaker, can also interpret files in this format. If your Write document includes graphics, you should not use Word format or the pictures will vanish. **Alt-W** is the keyboard shortcut.

If you click on both **Text Only** and **Microsoft Word Format**, the document will be saved as an unformatted Word file, the equivalent of an ASCII text file.

Once you have typed the filename and chosen the format, press **Enter** to write the file to disk. As the file is being saved, Write counts the number of characters in the file and displays the total in the page status area. Now that the file is saved, you can make changes to it with impunity. Let's change the typeface and font of the first paragraph.

4. Move the mouse pointer into the selection area—the white space just to the left of the text. The pointer changes to an arrowhead shape. Double click and the entire paragraph is highlighted. (If you click just once, only the line beside the cursor is selected.)

5. Click on **Character** and then on **Fonts** (or press **Alt-C F**) and up pops the Fonts dialog box. The list of available typefaces will be determined by the default printer and any additional fonts you have installed. Click on the name of a typeface to select it and then double click on a point size. The dialog box vanishes and the highlighted text is now shown in the typeface and size you have selected. (If there is no corresponding screen font for the selected font, Windows substitutes the closest available match.)

Fonts Dialog Box

6. To change the appearance of the text you can use the Character menu directly. With the paragraph still selected, pull down the menu again. Click on any of the character attributes—**Bold**, **Italic**, **Underline**, **Superscript** or **Subscript**—and the selected effect is applied to the paragraph.

Normal	F5
Bold	**Ctrl+B**
Italic	**Ctrl+I**
Underline	**Ctrl+U**
Superscript	
Subscript	
√ 1. AvantGarde	
2. Helv	
3. Helvetica-Narrow	
Reduce Font	
Enlarge Font	
Fonts...	

Character Menu

A Windows Write document can contain many fonts. The Character menu contains a list of the three typefaces you've used most recently; clicking on any of the names applies that typeface to the selected text. You can also change the size of the font by selecting **Enlarge** or **Reduce**. The text will be adjusted to the next available size. If there is no smaller or larger size, the command has no effect.

Fonts and character attributes can be applied to any text selection, from a single character to an entire document. Line spacing, justification and indents, on the other hand, are applied only to blocks of a paragraph or more. You can use the Paragraph menu to make these formatting changes, but it's much easier to use the Ruler and the mouse. Let's change the justification and indents in our sample document.

7. With the paragraph still selected, click on the last icon shown on the Ruler line, the one that contains four equal lines. The selected paragraph is instantly fully justified—that is, each line is filled out so that the left and right margins are in straight lines. Click on the penultimate icon and the text is aligned to the right margin, leaving a ragged left margin. Try clicking on each of the justification and line-spacing icons to see what kind of paragraph options are available.

8. Now for some indentation. Move the mouse cursor up to the third line of the Ruler. Point to the first-line indent marker—the tiny dot over the left indent marker—and drag it to the right. When you release the button, the first line of the highlighted paragraph will be indented.

```
┌─────────────────────────────────────────┐
│ ▬          Indents                       │
├─────────────────────────────────────────┤
│ Left Indent:    [0"]      ┌──────────┐   │
│                           │    OK    │   │
│ First Line:     [0"]      └──────────┘   │
│                           ┌──────────┐   │
│ Right Indent:   [0"]      │  Cancel  │   │
│                           └──────────┘   │
└─────────────────────────────────────────┘
```

Indent Dialog Box

Let's indent the entire paragraph, rather than just the first line. You can set indentations from the left or right margins by dragging the triangular markers along the Ruler. For this exercise, though, we'll use the Paragraph menu. Be sure the cursor is sitting anywhere in the paragraph you want to change; the entire paragraph need not be selected.

9. Press **Alt-P I** to bring up the Indents dialog box. Notice that the text box in the middle shows the first-line indent you set in the last step. Enter **3** in the Left Indent text box and then press **Enter**. The entire paragraph will be shoved three inches (or centimeters, if you selected that as the default measurement) to the right. You can create a *hanging indent* by setting the first-line indent to be less than the left indent. To remove an indent, you can call up the dialog box again or use the mouse to drag the triangular indent markers back to their original positions on the Ruler.

Cursor Keys

You can use the mouse or the keyboard to move through text; when entering text, the keyboard is usually faster. Most people will probably find a combination of the two most effective. If you try an action that is not allowed, the computer will beep at you, providing you haven't used the Control Panel to turn off the Warning Beep.

Write uses one special key—the 5 on the numeric keypad, called the **Goto** key—to trigger a number of shortcuts.

Ctrl-Right	Next word.
Ctrl-Left	Previous word.
Goto-Right	Next sentence.
Goto-Left	Previous sentence.
Home	Beginning of current line.
End	End of current line.
Goto-Up	Beginning of current paragraph.
Goto-Down	Beginning of next paragraph.
Ctrl-PgUp	First line in the window (the cursor remains in the same column).
Ctrl-PgDn	Last line in the window (the cursor remains in the same column).
Ctrl-Home	Beginning of file.
Ctrl-End	End of file.
Goto-PgDn	Next page.
Goto-PgUp	Previous page.

Holding down a key combination will force the command to repeat until you release the keys or the program reaches a point where it cannot continue. For example, if you press **Ctrl-End** to move to the bottom of the document, and then press **Goto-Up**, the cursor will move up a paragraph at a time until it reaches the top of the document, at which time the computer will beep. It will continue beeping until you release the keys.

Highlighting Text

Write also provides a wide array of shortcuts that let you quickly highlight blocks of text with the keyboard or the mouse. To select a block of text using the keyboard, hold down the **Shift** key and move the cursor using any of the key combinations listed above.

To highlight text with the mouse, you can use any of the following shortcuts:

To highlight a section of a document, click on a point in the text and drag the mouse pointer to the end of the block. You may also point to the beginning of the block, hold down the **Shift** key and then point to the end of the block.

Double click on a word to select it.

Hold down the **Ctrl** key and click once to select an entire sentence.

Click once in the selection area in the left margin to mark one line.

Double click in the selection area to highlight a paragraph. Hold down the **Shift** key and click on one or more succeeding paragraphs to continue the selection.

Hold down the **Ctrl** key and click once in the selection area to choose the entire document.

Changing Text

Write makes it easy to find and/or change a character, a word or a phrase of up to 255 characters. You can stipulate that Write search for whole words only; you can even specify that it search for words that match the case you enter. The program can change all occurrences of a word or phrase or only selected instances.

Find Dialog Box

To start a text search, press **Alt-S F** or click on **Search** in the menu bar and then click on **Find**. When the Find dialog box appears, type the word or phrase you want to find, click on the options you want to set, and then click on **Find Next**. The program will highlight the specified word or phrase whenever it finds a match. You can click on **Find Next** or press **Alt-N** to continue the search to the end of the file. To switch from the editing screen to the Find dialog box and back again, simply click in the appropriate location, or press **Alt-F6**. To remove the dialog box, press **Esc** or **Alt-F4**, or double click on the Control box menu. You can repeat the last Find operation by pressing **F3**.

Write also provides a facility for finding and replacing words. Click on **Search** and then click on **Change**. The resulting dialog box resembles the Find box, except that it allows you to specify what the word or phrase should be changed to.

```
┌─────────────────────────────────────────────────────────┐
│ ▬                          Change                         │
├─────────────────────────────────────────────────────────┤
│ Find What:   │                                          │ │
│                                                           │
│ Change To:   │                                          │ │
│                                                           │
│ ☐ Whole Word              ☐ Match Upper/Lowercase        │
│  ┌──────────┐ ┌────────────────┐ ┌────────┐ ┌──────────┐ │
│  │ Find Next│ │ Change, then Find│ │ Change │ │ Change All│ │
│  └──────────┘ └────────────────┘ └────────┘ └──────────┘ │
└─────────────────────────────────────────────────────────┘
```

Change Dialog Box

The dialog box provides four options when it has found the target word or phrase:

Find Next does nothing, but instead searches for the next occurrence.

Change, then Find changes the highlighted words and then searches for the next occurrence.

Change replaces the currently highlighted words only and waits for your next request.

Change All tells Write to change all occurrences of the target words automatically. If a block of text is highlighted when you issue the Change command, this button will read **Change Selection**.

As with the Find dialog box, you can close the Change box by double clicking on the Control menu box or pressing **Alt-F4** or **Esc**.

Exercise 11.4
Adding Graphics to Write

Write allows you to incorporate graphic images into a document. The graphic must be transferred from an application to the Clipboard before being pasted into Write.

1. Copy a graphic image into the Clipboard from an application like Windows Paintbrush.

2. Click on the point in the Write document where you want to place the graphic, usually a blank line. Press **Shift-Ins** to paste the image from the Clipboard. The picture is pasted in, probably at the wrong size. No problem—Write lets you resize a picture.

3. Click on the graphic and press **Alt-E S**, or click on **Size Picture** in the Edit menu. The cursor changes into a dual-box shape. Use the mouse or the cursor keys to change the border positions—the gray outlines around the graphic. When you are happy with the size, click once to fix the picture at the new size.

4. You can also move the graphic to another position within the page. Click on the graphic to select it again and press **Alt-E M** or click on **Move Picture** in the Edit menu. The cursor changes to the same shape as in the previous step, and the image's gray borders appear. Unfortunately, you can only move the graphic from side to side; you cannot move it up or down the page. When you are satisfied with the position, click once and the image will be fixed into place. (You can use the paragraph formatting commands and icons to center an image or align it to the left or right.)

Exercise 11.5
Printing Your Document

Write uses the Print Manager, if it is turned on, to handle all printing. After you issue the print command, you can get on with using Write while the printing is handled in the background.

1. Before you print the document you should paginate it so that you know how many pages there are.

2. Press **Alt-F E** or click on **Repagination** in the File menu. The Repaginate Document dialog box asks if you want to confirm page breaks. You should accept this option, which lets you avoid awkward-looking pages. Click on the option box and then click on **OK** to begin the pagination process.

3. Before a page break is placed, Write will prompt you to approve or adjust the position of the page break. Click on **Up** or **Down** to move the page break to a suitable location, and then click on **Confirm** to set the page break. The program moves on to the next until all the page breaks are in position.

Tip: Always move page breaks up—if you move them down, you may find that lines run off the page.

4. After the pagination is finished, press **Ctrl-Home** to go back to the beginning of the document. Press **Alt-F P** or click on **Print** in the File menu to bring up the Print dialog box.

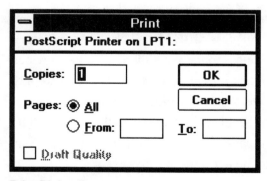

Print Dialog Box

5. Within the dialog box, you can select the number of copies you want to produce, which pages you want printed and, depending on your printer, whether to speed up printing by using draft quality.

6. After you have selected the print options, click on **OK** to send the document to the printer.

Summary

Windows Write is a useful word processor, although it lacks the advanced features of today's top word processing programs.

The program offers a variety of mouse and keyboard shortcuts to quickly select and edit text.

Write lets you paste graphics into your documents via the Clipboard.

Keyboard Summary

Alt-Backspace	Undo last action.
Alt-C B	Turn on bold text.
Alt-C C	Create subscript text.
Alt-C E	Enlarge point size of selected font.
Alt-C F	Select font.
Alt-C I	Turn on italic text.
Alt-C N	Set normal character attributes.
Alt-C P	Create superscript text.
Alt-C R	Reduce point size of selected font.
Alt-C U	Create underlined text.
Alt-C [number]	Select specified typeface.
Alt-D F	Create or edit footer.
Alt-D H	Create or edit header.
Alt-D P	Set page layout options.
Alt-D R	Display or hide Ruler.
Alt-D T	Set tab positions.
Alt-E C	Copy selected block to Clipboard.
Alt-E M	Move selected graphic laterally.
Alt-E P	Paste Clipboard contents into document at cursor position.
Alt-E S	Resize graphic.

Alt-E T	Cut selected block to Clipboard.
Alt-E U	Undo last action.
Alt-Esc	Switch directly to another program.
Alt-F A	Save the document to a new filename or format.
Alt-F E	Repaginate the document.
Alt-F N	Begin a new document.
Alt-F O	Load a previously saved document from disk.
Alt-F P	Print document.
Alt-F R	Change or modify printer setup or select an alternate printer.
Alt-F S	Save the current document to existing filename.
Alt-F X	Quit Windows Write.
Alt-F4	Quit Windows Write.
Alt-F6	Switch from Find or Change dialog box to document.
Alt-H	Activate Help menu.
Alt-O S	Save the current document to existing filename.
Alt-P 1	Set 1" line spacing.
Alt-P C	Center text.
Alt-P D	Set double line spacing.
Alt-P I	Set indents using dialog box.
Alt-P J	Justify text.
Alt-P L	Left-align text.
Alt-P N	Set normal paragraph style.
Alt-P R	Right-align text.
Alt-P S	Set single line spacing.
Alt-S C	Find and change specified text.
Alt-S F	Find specified text.
Alt-S G	Jump directly to specific page (available only after document has been paginated or printed).
Alt-S R	Repeat last Find operation.
Alt-Spacebar C	Quit Write and return to Program Manager.
Alt-Spacebar M	Move application window.
Alt-Spacebar N	Reduce window to an icon.

Alt-Spacebar R	Restore window to previous size and shape.
Alt-Spacebar S	Resize application window.
Alt-Spacebar W	Switch programs using Task List.
Alt-Spacebar X	Maximize application window.
Ctrl-B	Turn on bold text.
Ctrl-End	Move to end of file.
Ctrl-Esc	Switch programs using Task List.
Ctrl-Home	Move to beginning of file.
Ctrl-I	Turn on italic text.
Ctrl-Ins	Copy selected block to Clipboard.
Ctrl-Left	Move to previous word.
Ctrl-PgDn	Move to last line in window (the cursor remains in the same column).
Ctrl-PgUp	Move to first line in window (the cursor remains in the same column).
Ctrl-Right	Move to next word.
Ctrl-Shift-Hyphen	Insert optional hyphen.
Ctrl-U	Create underlined text.
End	Move to end of current line.
F1	Activate Windows Write Help.
F3	Repeat last Find operation.
F4	Jump directly to specific page (available only after document has been paginated or printed).
Goto-Down	Move to beginning of next paragraph.
Goto-Left	Move to previous sentence.
Goto-PgDn	Move to next page.
Goto-PgUp	Move to previous page.
Goto-Right	Move to next sentence.
Goto-Up	Move to beginning of current paragraph.
Home	Move to beginning of current line.
Shift-Delete	Cut selected block to Clipboard.
Shift-Ins	Paste Clipboard contents into document at current cursor position.

CHAPTER 12

All the C's

Rather than deal with each of the remaining accessories individually—which would produce some very small chapters—we can group them together. The Calculator, Calendar and Cardfile are handy replacements for their desktop counterparts.

Calculator

Windows Calculator is a utility that can be popped up over any Windows application. It can be used in conjunction with an MS-DOS program only if you are using 386 enhanced mode and running the MS-DOS program in a window. To run the Calculator, double click on its icon, or select the icon and then press **Enter**.

The first time you use the Calculator it will appear as a standard, short-function pocket calculator. The application window contains a Control menu box, a title bar and a Minimize button, but there is no Maximize button—the size of the Calculator window cannot be changed.

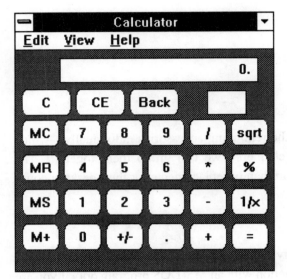

Standard Calculator

Calculator can be used with the keyboard or with the mouse. The numeric keypad will function very much like a standard 10-key calculator if **Num Lock** is turned on. The cursor, when it appears within the Calculator window, remains a white arrowhead.

The Standard Calculator includes a number of other functions besides the basic arithmetic operators shown on the numeric keypad. The complete list of operators, their corresponding keystrokes and the calculated results is as follows:

+	+	Add.
-	-	Subtract.
*	*	Multiply.
/	/	Divide.
sqrt	@	Compute the square root of the displayed number.
%	%	Compute percentages.
1/x	r	Compute the reciprocal of the displayed number.
+/-	**F9**	Change the sign of the displayed number—negative to positive and vice versa.

272

CE	**Delete**	Clear the displayed number.
C	**Esc**	Clear the current calculation.
MC	**Ctrl-C**	Memory clear—clear the value stored in memory.
MR	**Ctrl-R**	Memory recall—display value stored in memory.
MS	**Ctrl-M**	Memory store—place displayed number in memory.
M+	**Ctrl-P**	Add the displayed number to the value stored in memory.
=	**= or Enter**	Carry out the operation or repeat last operation.

Exercise 12.1
Simple Sums

The best way to learn the Calculator is to use it. The following exercise employs all of the basic operators. Because most people find the Calculator easier to use with the mouse than the keyboard, this exercise is built around the mouse. Keyboard equivalents are included in parentheses. Be sure **Num Lock** is turned on before beginning.

1. Run Calculator from the Program Manager.

2. Enter the value **1024** and store it in the memory. (**1024, Ctrl-M**)

3. Divide the displayed number by 64 (**/, 64, Enter**). The result should be 16. (If you press = again, the result of the previous calculation will be divided by 64 again. The previous calculation remains active until you change it.)

4. Multiply the previous result by 2 (***, 2, Enter**). The result should be 32.

5. Add -32. Click on + **32** and then on +/- before clicking on = (**+, 32, F9, Enter**). The displayed result should now be 0.

6. Clear the calculation by clicking on **C** (**Esc**), and then retrieve the original number from the memory by clicking on **MR** (**Ctrl-R**).

7. Find 50% of the original number. The fastest way to do this is to simply multiply by .5 (***, .5, Enter**). Or you can use the percentage button (***, 50, %**). Don't press **Enter** or click on = after executing a percentage operation or the original number will be multiplied by your result.

8. Click on **C** (**Esc**) to clear the display, and then recall the original number from memory (**Ctrl-R**). Click on **1/x** (**r**). The result is 0.0009765625.

9. Finally, clear the display again by clicking on **C** (**Esc**) and then click on **MR** to retrieve the original number again (**Ctrl-R**). Click on **sqrt** (**@**) and you get the answer 32. Multiply this by itself by clicking on *** =** (*** Enter**) and you should get 1024 again. Add this to the memory by clicking on **M+** (**Ctrl-P**). Click on **MR** (**Ctrl-R**) and the result should change to 2048. Finally, click on **MC** (**Ctrl-C**) to clear the memory and then on **C** (**Esc**) to clear the Calculator.

You can cut or copy the contents of the Calculator into the Clipboard. When you use the Clipboard to paste data from another application into the Calculator, you can include codes that actually cause the Calculator to perform specific actions on the imported numbers. The characters that have an effect are:

C Clear the memory.

E Enter numbers in scientific notation (Decimal mode); specify value **E** (Hexadecimal mode).

M Store the current displayed value in memory.

P Add the displayed number to the value stored in memory.

Q Clear current calculation.

R Display the value stored in memory.

: Interpret next letter as part of a control sequence—e.g., **:C** is the equivalent of **Ctrl-C**.

In Scientific mode, the Calculator can perform a dizzying array of trigonometric, statistical and other advanced calculations. To switch to the Scientific display click on **View** in the menu bar and then click on **Scientific**, or simply press **Alt-V S**.

It's beyond the scope of this book to delve into the higher mathematics of the Scientific Calculator. (Besides, I have trouble enough with algebra, much less trigonometry and statistics, so I'd have a hard time designing a suitable exercise for this section!) There are literally dozens of keyboard shortcuts available in this mode as well, too many to include in the summary at the end of this chapter. If you're familiar with this type of calculator, feel free to play with it on your own. The functions, their meanings and all the available keystrokes are detailed in the excellent on-line Help facility.

When you quit the Calculator, it remembers what mode you were using and saves that setting as the default mode for the next time you start the program. Thus, if you close the program in Scientific mode, the next time you run the program it will appear in that mode.

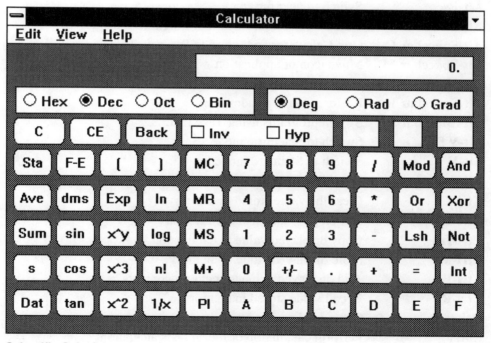

Scientific Calculator

Calculator Summary

Windows Calculator is a pop-up application that can perform simple computations as well as advanced statistical and mathematical operations.

The Calculator application window cannot be resized or maximized.

The program runs in two modes, Standard and Scientific.

Using the Clipboard, you can transfer numbers and operations between Calculator and other applications.

Calculator Keyboard Summary

Alt-E C	Copy displayed value to the Clipboard.
Alt-E P	Paste Clipboard contents into Calculator.
Alt-Esc	Switch to next program.
Alt-F4	Quit Calculator and return to Program Manager.
Alt-Spacebar C	Quit Calculator and return to Program Manager.
Alt-Spacebar M	Move icon or application window.
Alt-Spacebar N	Reduce application window to an icon.
Alt-Spacebar R	Restore icon to window.
Alt-Spacebar W	Switch programs using Task List.
Alt-V S	Switch to Scientific mode.
Alt-V T	Switch to Standard mode.
Backspace	Delete last digit of displayed number.
Ctrl-C	Clear the value stored in memory.
Ctrl-Esc	Switch programs using Task List.
Ctrl-Ins	Copy displayed value to Clipboard.
Ctrl-M	Store displayed value in memory.
Ctrl-P	Add displayed value to memory contents.
Ctrl-R	Recall value stored in memory.
Delete	Clear displayed number.
Enter	Perform calculation or repeat last calculation.
Esc	Clear current calculation.
F1	Activate Help system.

F9	Change sign of displayed number.
Left	Delete last digit of displayed number.
R	Calculate reciprocal of displayed number.
Shift-Ins	Paste Clipboard contents into program.
. or ,	Insert a decimal point.
%	Calculate percentage.
*****	Multiply.
+	Add.
-	Subtract.
/	Divide.
=	Perform calculation or repeat last calculation.
@	Compute square root of displayed number.

Calendar

Windows Calendar is a simple diary program that includes the ability to set alarms for selected appointments. You can use Calendar just as you would any other diary, although your individual entries are limited to around 80 characters apiece. The program is meant to be used not in place of a paper-based appointment book or diary but rather as an adjunct to one. The program can show you any date from January 1, 1980, all the way through to the end of the year 2099.

You can toggle the display between a monthly calendar and a daily agenda. In the daily view, you specify the time intervals between appointments: The default is hourly, but you can change the display to create entries that are 15 or 30 minutes apart if you wish. Regardless of how you set this feature, the program allows you to manually enter an appointment for any time of the day or night.

Calendar lets you set as many alarms as you like—months or even years in advance. You can tell the program to provide you with an audible or visual notice of an appointment. Because you can save the data in a diary to a disk file, you can set up any number of diaries and reload them as necessary. Except for the limitations imposed on the size of individual entries, the program is actually quite versatile.

To run the program double click on the Calendar icon in the Accessories group, or select the icon and then press **Enter**. The window contains the usual Control menu box, title bar, Minimize and Maximize buttons and menu bar. Below the menu bar is the status line, which displays the current system time and the selected date. By default, Windows Calendar starts in the Day View. The largest part of the window is the appointment area, which includes the times and descriptions of events. (Each description is limited to a single line, and only the first 32 characters or so are visible in this view.) Below the appointment area is a box called the scratch pad. Interestingly, the appointment area cannot be resized; even if you expand or maximize the application window, the list of appointments just sits in the middle of the window. A scroll bar to the right of the appointment area lets you move to events that are earlier or later than those displayed in the list.

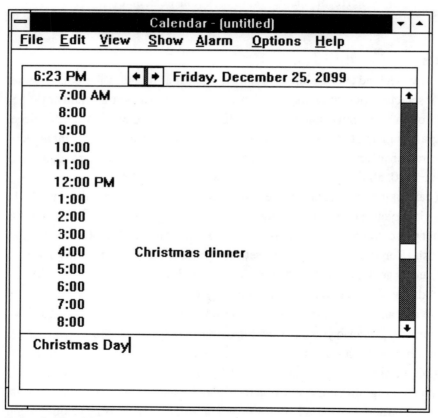

Calendar Day View

For a different perspective on your schedule, you can change the display to the Month View. When this view is selected, the appointment area is replaced by a grid containing all the dates in the current month. The status bar and scratch pad appear the same in both views. You can choose either view by clicking on **Day** or **Month** in the View menu. From the keyboard, **F8** selects the Day View, while **F9** brings up the Month View. Double clicking on the date in the status bar switches instantly between the two views.

Calendar - (untitled)						
File **Edit** **View** **Show** **Alarm** **Options** **Help**						

17:18 ← →	Friday, 25 December 2099					
December 2099						
S	M	T	W	T	F	S
		1	2	3	4	5
6	7	8	9	10	11	12
13	14	15	16	17	18	19
20	21	22	23	24	25	26
27	28	29	30	31		

Calendar Month View

Calendar Menus

The menu bar choices remain the same regardless of which Calendar view you are using. The **File** menu lets you load, save and print files. The menu contains all the expected commands, plus a few that are specific to Calendar.

New starts a new diary. If you have made changes to the current one, you will be prompted to save the changes before the new one is created.

Open lets you load a previously saved diary. The dialog box allows you to navigate through the directory structure on all available drives to find a file. Within the dialog box is a check box that lets you load the file as **Read Only**. If you make changes to a read-only file, you have to save it under a new filename.

Save is used to quickly write the current file to the last filename under which it was saved. If you issue this command with a new file, Calendar brings up the File Save As dialog box.

Save As allows you to save the current file to a new filename. A Directories list lets you choose another drive or directory, if you wish.

Print produces a hard copy of your appointment calendar. Before printing, you specify the range of dates to send to the printer.

Page Setup sets headers and footers for your printout and gives you the chance to adjust the page margins.

Printer Setup is used to select and set up your printer before printing.

Exit quits the program and returns you to the Program Manager.

The **Edit** menu includes the common Clipboard commands, plus one choice that is unique to Calendar.

Cut copies the selected text to the Clipboard and removes it from the Calendar.

Copy places the selected text in the Clipboard but leaves the Calendar entry intact.

Paste copies the Clipboard contents to the current cursor position.

Remove allows you to delete all the details for selected dates from the current Calendar.

The **View** menu lets you choose between Day and Month views.
The **Show** menu allows you to quickly move between specific dates.

Today will always bring you back to the current system date.

Previous moves back one day at a time when the Day View is active or a month at a time when the Month View is selected. **Ctrl-PgUp** is the keyboard shortcut.

Next takes you forward a day or a month at a time, depending on which view is selected. **Ctrl-PgDn** accomplishes the same effect from the keyboard.

Date switches directly to a date you specify. The command brings up a dialog box into which you can enter any date between January 1, 1980, and December 31, 2099. Dates must be entered as digits in the current date format. **F4** is the keyboard equivalent.

The **Alarm** menu contains only two commands: **Set** toggles the alarm on or off for the current time in the appointment area (**F5** toggles this setting from the keyboard); **Controls** brings up a dialog box that allows you to adjust the alarm settings.
The **Options** menu lets you customize the display.

Mark works only on the Month View. It allows you to place one or more marks next to any date you select. For example, you could use squares to indicate birthdays, brackets for travel, bullets for important appointments and so on. You can choose from five marks and use one or any combination per date. **F6** issues this command from the keyboard.

Special Time is used to add a nonstandard time to the Day View. You can configure Calendar to divide the day into 15-, 30- or 60-minute time slots; regardless of which setup you choose, you'll need to use this option if you want to add an appointment at, say, 11:50. **F7** calls up this dialog box from the keyboard.

Day Settings allows you to change the interval between appointments, the Day View starting time and the time format (12- or 24-hour).

Exercise 12.2
Pick a Date

Let's have a quick look at the different ways you can display dates and times. Run the program by selecting the icon and then pressing **Enter**, or by double clicking on the Calendar icon in the Accessories menu. You can also run the program from the Program Manager by pressing **Alt-F R** and then entering **CAL**. By default the Calendar shows today's date (assuming the system date is set correctly) in Day View, beginning at 7 AM.

 1. To see tomorrow's schedule, press **Ctrl-PgDn,** or use the menu by pressing **Alt-S N**. Pressing the key combination again lets you keep moving forward a day at a time. To return to today's appointment list, press **Ctrl-PgUp** to move back one day at a time or press **Alt-S T** to move directly to today.

2. On what day will your birthday fall in 1995? Press **Alt-V M** to switch to the Month View and find out. If you press **Ctrl-PgDn** now the display moves forward one month at a time.

3. Press **F4** (or use the menu by pressing **Alt-S D**) and the Show Date dialog box appears. Enter your birthdate and the year **1995** and the display instantly jumps there.

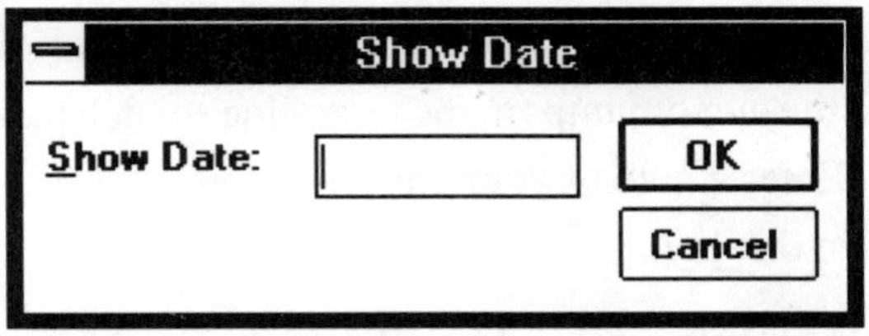

Show Date Dialog Box

4. To mark the date, press **Alt-O M** or just **F6** to bring up the Day Markings dialog box. Use the **Tab** key and then the **Spacebar** to select a mark. Pressing **Enter** closes the dialog box and applies the selected mark to the date. There are five marks to choose from:

[] draws a box around the date.

() brackets the date.

o places a bullet in the lower left corner of the date.

x places a cross in the upper left corner of the date.

_ underlines the date.

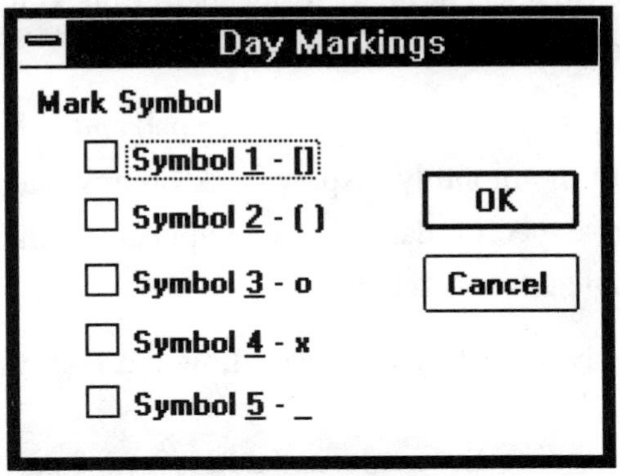

Day Markings Dialog Box

5. Since we're looking so far ahead, we want to make a note of what is special about this date. Press **Tab** and the cursor jumps to the three-line scratch pad at the bottom of the window. Enter a note of your choosing here, and then press **Tab** to return to the main display.

6. To restore today's date to the display, press **Alt-S T**.

1. Make sure the display shows the Day View. Point to the status bar and click on the arrowhead that points to the right to move forward one day. Click again to move to the day after tomorrow. To return to today's date, either click on the left arrowhead or click on **Show** in the menu bar and then click on **Today**.

2. Double click on the date in the status bar to change to the Month View. Clicking on the right arrowhead will now move through the calendar one month at a time.

3. To view a specific date, click on **Show** and then on **Date**; enter a date in the dialog box and click on OK.

4. Click on **Options** and then on **Mark** to bring up the dialog box. Click on one or more of the five check boxes to select the mark format before clicking on **OK**. The selected mark or marks appear in the date box.

5. To make a note about the selected date, click in the scratch pad and then type some text. To move back to the monthly display click on any date shown. Each note is linked with a specific date; the note appears in the scratch pad only when the associated date is selected.

6. Finally, restore the display to today's date by clicking on **Show** and **Today**.

The information you have entered, including any marks and notes, is now part of the current file and will be stored when you save the file. If you quit Calendar without saving the file, all the details will be lost.

Exercise 12.3
Alarm Calls

The Windows Calendar allows you to set one alarm for any appointment time the program can handle. Theoretically, this means you can set 1440 alarms per day— one a minute. But who needs that many? The biggest problem with this feature is that the alarm will only be active under very specific circumstances: You must be at your PC, with Windows running; the Calendar must be active, either as a window or an icon; and you can't be working in a full-screen MS-DOS program.

If you choose, you can set an audible alarm that will sound until you turn it off. With the alarm sound off, the Calendar window or icon will flash until you acknowledge the alarm. This exercise uses the mouse and keyboard in combination.

1. Before setting the alarm, change the display to show different appointment intervals. Press **Alt-O D** to bring up the Day Settings dialog box. Click on **30** and then click on **OK** to return to the Calendar. The Day View now shows appointment slots 30 minutes apart.

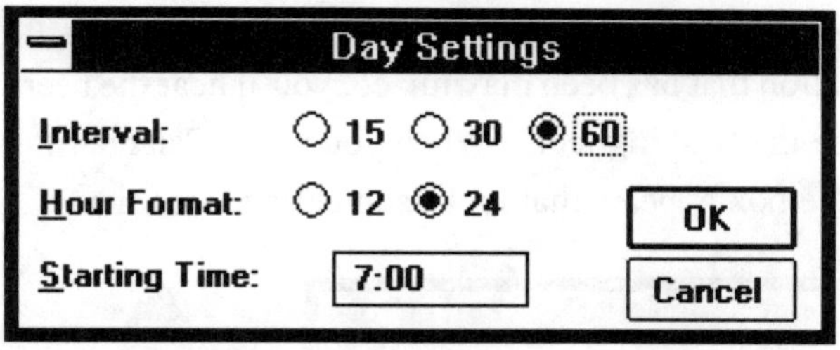

Day Settings Dialog Box

2. Set the alarm for 10:30 AM. Click anywhere to the right of **10:30 AM** and then press **F5**. An icon shaped like a bell appears to the left of the time to show that the alarm has been set. This alarm will use the default settings—audible, with no early ring.

Special Time Dialog Box

3. But what if you want to set an alarm for a time that doesn't fall neatly on the hour or half hour? You need to insert a special time. Press **F7** and a new dialog box appears. Type a new time in the box, separating the hours and minutes with a colon and using the default date format set in the Control Panel—**15:53**, say, for 24-hour format, or **3:53 PM** for 12-hour format—and then press **Enter**. Back at the Day View, the cursor will be sitting in the time slot you just created. Press **F5** to set the alarm and type THIS IS A TEST to label the appointment.

4. Reduce the Calendar to an icon by clicking on the **Minimize** button. At the set time the computer will beep four times and the icon will flash. (If you're working in another Windows application that has been maximized, you'll hear the beep, but you won't be able to see the flashing icon.) When you make Calendar the active application, a message box appears that looks something like this:

Alarm Message Box

There's no reason for the message box to be so large—it's only capable of displaying the time for the active alarm, along with a one-line message.

5. You can also set an alarm that gives you as much as 10 minutes' advance warning of an upcoming event. Follow the same procedure as in Step 3 above to set another alarm for just a few minutes from now. Then, from the Day View, press **Alt-A C** and the Alarm Controls dialog box appears.

Alarm Controls Dialog Box

6. In the text box labeled **Early Ring**, you can type any value from 0 to 10 minutes. Type **1** and click in the **Sound** check box to remove the mark. Press **Enter** to save the settings and close the dialog box. Restore the Program Manager and double click on **Clock**. Finally, reduce the Program Manager to an icon, if its window is still visible onscreen. The Clock should be the active window, sitting over but not entirely covering the Calendar.

7. Because the Calendar window is inactive, when the alarm time arrives the title bar will begin to flash and will continue to do so until you switch to the Calendar window. As soon as you do so, the alarm message box appears.

You can set alarms for any time and date that the program is capable of displaying, up to a minute before midnight on December 31, 2099. When you save the file the alarm settings are included along with the file so that when it is reloaded they can become active.

Exercise 12.4
Printing and Saving the Diary

You can produce a hard copy of your diary on any printer that is connected to your computer and that has been configured to work with Windows. There is also a range of information you can include on the printout if you wish.

1. Before you send the file to the printer press **Alt-F T** to bring up the Page Settings dialog box. This allows you to set the margins for the printed page and also determines what information will be included on the pages. In either the Header or Footer box you can include any of the following formatting codes, either singly or in combination:

&c Center the text within the margins.

&d Print the current system date.

&f Print the name of the current file—this is the default header.

&l Left justify the text.

&p Include page numbers—this is the default footer.

&r Right justify the text.

&t Include the current system time.

Any of these parameters can be combined with (or replaced by) ordinary text. For example, if your file is named **MYFILE.CAL** and you enter THIS IS **&F** in the header box, the words "This is MYFILE.CAL" will appear at the top of each page of your printout. To print with no header or footer, leave the appropriate text box blank.

```
┌──────────────────────────────────────────────────┐
│ ▭         Page Setup                               │
├──────────────────────────────────────────────────┤
│  Header:   ┌──────────────────┐   ┌───────────┐    │
│            │ &f               │   │    OK     │    │
│            └──────────────────┘   └───────────┘    │
│  Footer:   ┌──────────────────┐   ┌───────────┐    │
│            │ Page &p          │   │  Cancel   │    │
│            └──────────────────┘   └───────────┘    │
│  ┌─ Margins ──────────────────────────────────┐    │
│  │  Left:  ┌────────┐    Right:  ┌────────┐    │    │
│  │         │ .75    │            │ .75    │    │    │
│  │         └────────┘            └────────┘    │    │
│  │  Top:   ┌────────┐    Bottom: ┌────────┐    │    │
│  │         │ 1      │            │ 1      │    │    │
│  │         └────────┘            └────────┘    │    │
│  └─────────────────────────────────────────────┘   │
└──────────────────────────────────────────────────┘
```

Page Settings Dialog Box

2. Having set the page format, you can now print the file. Press **Alt-F P** to bring up the Print dialog box and specify a range of dates. To select a single date, simply leave the second text box blank.

Your printed copy will include the following: any times for which you have entered text, with alarms shown by an asterisk; any special times that you have created, even if they do not contain any detail; and any notes on the scratch pad for the days within the specified dates, even if there are no appointments that day.

```
┌──────────────────────────────────────────┐
│ ▭              Print                       │
├──────────────────────────────────────────┤
│  Print Appointments:                       │
│                                            │
│  From:  ┌──────────────┐   ┌───────────┐   │
│         │ 12/25/99     │   │    OK     │   │
│         └──────────────┘   └───────────┘   │
│  To:    ┌──────────────┐   ┌───────────┐   │
│         │              │   │  Cancel   │   │
│         └──────────────┘   └───────────┘   │
└──────────────────────────────────────────┘
```

Print Dialog Box

3. To save the file you have just created press **Alt-F A** and then enter a filename in the text box. (Use the Directories list to change the drive and directory if necessary.) Do not include an extension—Calendar will supply the default .CAL extension. Click on **OK** to write the file to disk. Close the Calendar by pressing **Alt-F4**.

Calendar Summary

Windows Calendar is a simple, page-a-day diary that can be customized to produce your own preferred time slots.

The program allows you to set alarms for any time and date between January 1, 1980, and December 31, 2099.

You may use either the Day View or the Month View and switch between the two with ease.

Calendar Keyboard Summary

Alt-A C	Set alarm options.
Alt-A S	Toggle alarm for currently selected time.
Alt-E C	Copy selected text to Clipboard.
Alt-E P	Paste Clipboard contents at current cursor position.
Alt-E R	Remove details from specific dates in current Calendar file.
Alt-E T	Copy selected text to Clipboard and delete it from the Calendar.
Alt-Esc	Switch to next program.
Alt-F A	Save the current file under a new name.
Alt-F N	Start a new file.
Alt-F O	Load a previously saved Calendar file.
Alt-F P	Print specified dates from current Calendar file.
Alt-F R	Select and/or set up a printer.
Alt-F S	Save the current file using the existing filename.
Alt-F T	Set format for printed pages.
Alt-F X	Quit Calendar and return to Program Manager.
Alt-F4	Quit Calendar and return to Program Manager.
Alt-H	Open Help menu.
Alt-O D	Change day settings.
Alt-O M	Mark a date in Month View.
Alt-O S	Insert special time into Day View.
Alt-S D	Move to a specific date.
Alt-S N	Move ahead one day.

Alt-S P	Move back one day.
Alt-S T	Jump to today's date.
Alt-Spacebar C	Quit Calendar and return to Program Manager.
Alt-Spacebar M	Move icon or application window.
Alt-Spacebar N	Reduce window to an icon.
Alt-Spacebar R	Restore window to its previous size and shape.
Alt-Spacebar S	Resize application window.
Alt-Spacebar W	Switch programs using Task List.
Alt-Spacebar X	Maximize window.
Alt-V D	Switch to Day View.
Alt-V M	Switch to Month View.
Ctrl-End	Move ahead 12 hours in Day View.
Ctrl-Esc	Switch programs using Task List.
Ctrl-Home	Return to starting time in Day View.
Ctrl-Ins	Copy selected text to Clipboard.
Ctrl-PgDn	Move ahead one next day.
Ctrl-PgUp	Move back one day.
F1	Activate Help system.
F4	Move to a specific date.
F5	Toggle alarm for currently selected time.
F6	Mark a date in Month View.
F7	Insert special time into Day View.
F8	Switch to Day View.
F9	Switch to Month View.
Shift-Delete	Copy selected text to Clipboard and delete it from the Calendar.
Shift-Ins	Paste Clipboard contents at current cursor position.

Cardfile

Windows Cardfile is a simple database that lets you record and sort data in a graphic display that resembles a stack of index cards. The number of cards you can have in any one file is limited only by available memory and disk space. However, the amount of information you can get onto each card is limited, and there is no provision for resizing the individual cards; as a result, the uses for the program are somewhat limited. Still, Cardfile is ideal for keeping track of small amounts of information. I use it to store the details of my collection of model vehicles—each card is just large enough to contain the information I want. For more complex databases I have to use something else, but for broad outlines Cardfile is ideal.

The program can also be used to dial a telephone, if it is properly configured. You can even incorporate a graphic image—from Windows Paintbrush, for example—by simply pasting it in via the Clipboard. All in all, Cardfile is one of the most useful programs that is bundled with Windows 3, although it has its limitations, and it is a shame that you cannot vary the card size.

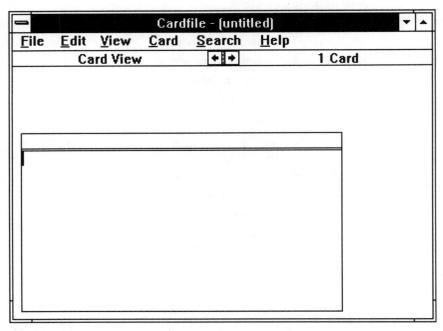

Cardfile

To run the program, double click on the Cardfile icon—it looks like a stack of index cards—or select the icon and press **Enter**.

The window layout includes the standard Control menu box, title bar, Minimize and Maximize buttons and menu bar. Immediately below the menu bar is the status line, which tells you the number of cards in the current file. It also contains a pair of scroll arrows that allow you to page through the cards one at a time. Below the status line is the portion of the window where the cards themselves are displayed. When you begin a new file, this area contains a single card.

Each card contains an index line along the top. A double line separates it from the information area below. The flashing cursor appears on the first line of the information area. You can display the Cardfile contents in either of two ways: the Cards view presents all the cards in a cascade; the List view presents the file as a list containing the index line from each card.

The cards are sorted automatically, based on the contents of the index line of each card; there is no provision to sort them on the basis of the contents of the main card. The sorting is done by character, with numbers placed first, followed by letters in normal alphabetical order, followed by symbols. Because the sorting is done one character at a time, 10 comes after 1 and before 2.

Cardfile Menus

Cardfile has a total of five menu choices, plus Help. The **File** menu is, as usual, concerned with inputting and outputting files, and contains the following commands:

New clears the current file and starts a new one. If you have modified the existing file since you last saved it, you will be asked if you want to save the current file.

Open loads a previously saved file.

Save writes the current file to disk using the name under which it was last saved.

Save As allows you to save the current file under a new name.

```
New
Open...
Save
Save As...
Print
Print All
Page Setup...
Printer Setup...
Merge...
Exit
```

File Menu

Print produces a hard copy of an individual card. This option is not available if you are using the List view.

Print All sends all of the cards in the current file to the printer.

Page Setup lets you set the margins and define a header and footer for your Cardfile printouts.

Printer Setup allows you to select and set up a printer to which the file will be sent.

Merge allows you to combine two or more files into a single file. As the files are merged, Cardfile sorts them automatically.

Exit quits Cardfile and returns you to the Program Manager.

The **Edit** menu contains the usual Clipboard commands plus a few that are unique to Cardfile.

Undo cancels the last action; **Alt-Backspace** invokes Undo as well.

Cut copies selected text to the Clipboard and then deletes it from the card.

Copy simply copies the selected text to the Clipboard but leaves it in place on the card.

Paste inserts the Clipboard contents at the current cursor position.

Index allows you to modify the index line of the current card. **F6** is the keyboard shortcut for this command.

Restore lets you cancel any changes that you have made to the card at the front of the stack and reinstate its original contents. The command will not restore a deleted card—because it is no longer at the front of the stack!

Text, the default option, switches to text mode after working with a picture.

Picture switches to picture mode so you can paste a graphic from the Clipboard into the current card or move a picture on the current card.

The **View** menu contains only two commands, **Card** and **List**. By default, Cardfile displays the file contents as a stack of cards. However, you can change the display so that it shows a list of only the index lines from the cards in the file. While you are in List view, many of the menu commands will be unavailable.

```
┌─────────────────────────────────────────────────────────────────────┐
│ ▤              Cardfile - YESTERYR.CRD                          ▼ ▲   │
├─────────────────────────────────────────────────────────────────────┤
│ File   Edit   View   Card   Search   Help                             │
├─────────────────────────────────────────────────────────────────────┤
│           List View               ◄ ▮ ►            17 Cards           │
│▓1927 Fowler Steam Wagon: Halls Promotion▓▓▓▓▓▓▓▓▓▓▓▓▓▓▓▓▓▓▓▓▓▓▓▓▓▓▓▓▓│
│To Be Got - Specials                                                   │
│To Be Got - Steam Vehicles                                             │
│To Be Got - Walker Electric Trucks                                     │
│Y08 1917 Yorkshire - William Prichard                                  │
│Y09 1924 Fowler Showman's Engine                                       │
│Y12 1829 Stephenson's Rocket                                           │
│Y18 1918 Atkinson - Bass & Co                                          │
│Y18 1918 Atkinson - Bass & Co      ****                                │
│Y18 1918 Atkinson - Blue Circle Cement                                 │
│Y21 1894 Aveling-Porter Steam Roller                                   │
│Y27 1922 Foden - Guinness                                              │
│Y27 1922 Foden - Hovis                                                 │
│Y27 1922 Foden - Joseph Rank                                           │
│Y27 1922 Foden - Tate & Lyle                                           │
│Y27 1922 Foden Steam Wagon - Spillers                                  │
│Y32 1917 Yorkshire -  Samuel Smith                                     │
└─────────────────────────────────────────────────────────────────────┘
```

List Display

The **Card** menu lets you add cards to the current stack or remove or copy the current card. It also allows you to dial a phone number directly. There are four commands in the menu:

Add inserts a card into the current stack. When you issue this command, a dialog box asks you to enter an index line for the new card. (It's OK to add a blank card.) The new card is placed at the front of the stack, and the remainder of the stack shifted around so that they follow in alphabetical order. The keyboard shortcut is **F7**.

Delete removes the current card from the stack. Once deleted, a card cannot be recovered—it is irretrievably lost.

Duplicate creates an exact copy of the current card and places it at the front of the stack. This command is extremely useful when you plan to add a group of cards that contain common information—company names or addresses, for example. Just enter the information on one card, duplicate the card as many times as necessary, and edit the copies.

Autodial allows you to dial the telephone. Cardfile looks on the current card for a number and suggests it in the Autodial dialog box. Before you use this option you must have the phone and modem connected and configured. **F5** issues the command from the keyboard.

The final menu is **Search**, which lets you find specific cards based on their index lines or search for a string of text within the cards themselves. The menu contains three commands:

Goto looks for an index line that contains a specified string of text. The command brings up a dialog box that lets you enter a word or a phrase—even a single character. After you press **Enter** or click on **OK**, the program searches through the index lines of the cards to find a match. The search routine is not case sensitive. The keyboard equivalent is **F4**.

Find is similar to **Goto**, except that it searches through the contents of the cards and ignores the index lines. This routine, too, is not case sensitive.

Find Next allows you to quickly look for the next occurrence of the string you entered in the Find dialog box. **F3** is the speediest way to issue this command.

Exercise 12.5
Creating a Stack of Cards

1. When you start the program for the first time or create a new file, Cardfile will always present you with a single blank card by default. To change the index line on this card, press **F6**. Enter a label of up to 40 characters in the Index dialog box. For the sake of this exercise, use your full name—first name and then last name—for this card. Press **Enter** to add the new label to the card.

```
┌────────────────────────────────────────────────────┐
│ ▬                       Index                        │
├────────────────────────────────────────────────────┤
│ Index Line:   │1829 Stephenson's Rocket│            │
│                                                      │
│          ┌──────────┐        ┌──────────┐           │
│          │    OK    │        │  Cancel  │           │
│          └──────────┘        └──────────┘           │
└────────────────────────────────────────────────────┘
```

Index Dialog Box

2. To add another card to the stack you can click on **Card** in the menu bar and then on **Add**, or simply press **F7**. The Add dialog box lets you create an index line for the new card. When you press **Enter** the new card is placed in the front of the stack. Go ahead and create a few cards, using any names you'd like for the index labels.

You can move through the stack of cards, regardless of how many it contains, by clicking on the arrowheads in the status line; or you can move to a specific card by clicking on the edge of the card. Let's create a template so we can store the same information about each person.

3. Go back to the card with your name on it. The cursor will be flashing on the first line of the information area below the index line. Enter the following text so that you have six lines on the card. Press **Enter** after each line.

Birthdate:

Age:

Favorite color:

Favorite flower:

Favorite food:

Nickname:

4. Now we're going to copy all of this to the second card. Point to the beginning of the first line (just before the **B**) and hold down the mouse button while drag-

ging the pointer to the end of the text. As you do so, the text in each line will be highlighted. When all six lines are selected, release the button.

5. Press **Ctrl-Ins** to copy the text into the Clipboard. Now click on the top of the second card; it will jump to the front, with the cursor on the first line. Press **Shift-Ins** and the text from the Clipboard is pasted in. The Clipboard retains its contents; for any additional cards you created, add the template copy in the same way.

6. Duplicating cards this way is fine if you are only working with a couple at a time, but there is an easier way to create two or more cards with identical information. Press **F7 Enter**. A new card appears with nothing on its index line. Paste in the Clipboard contents using **Shift-Ins**. Now click on **Card** in the menu bar and then on **Duplicate** in the pull-down menu. An exact copy of the current card will be created. Press **F6** and put another name on the index line. Click on the blank card again and make another duplicate; repeat this process until you have about ten cards—changing the index line on each so that it bears a different name. Your stack should look something like the figure on the next page.

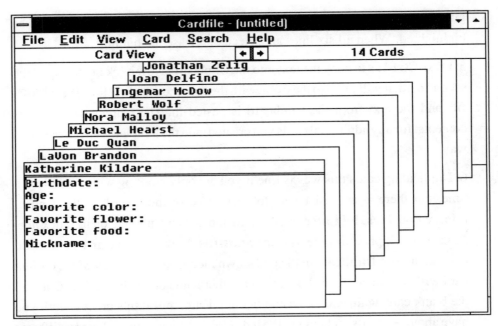

A Card Stack

7. Delete the blank card by bringing it to the front of the stack and clicking on **Card** in the menu bar, then on **Delete**. Click on **OK** in the confirming dialog box. Save the remaining cards by pressing **Alt-F A** to bring up the File Save As dialog box. Enter a filename; Cardfile automatically adds the .CRD extension. Once the file has been saved the name you gave it will appear on the title bar.

8. Fill in the relevant details on each card. Use **Ctrl-PgUp** and **Ctrl-PgDn** to move up and down the stack. To move from one line to another on a card, use the **Up** and **Down** cursor keys. (If you press **Enter**, you add a blank line at the current cursor position.) When you have entered all the details on each card, save the file again by pressing **Alt-F S**. This time no dialog box appears, because you are saving the file to the same name as before.

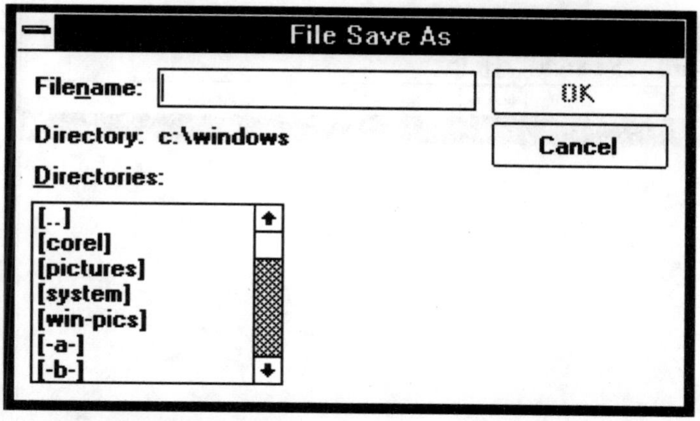

```
 ┌────────────────────────────────────────────────┐
 │ ▭                 File Save As                   │
 ├────────────────────────────────────────────────┤
 │ Filename: │                    │  ┌───────────┐ │
 │                                   │    OK     │ │
 │ Directory:  c:\windows            └───────────┘ │
 │ Directories:                      ┌───────────┐ │
 │                                   │  Cancel   │ │
 │ ┌──────────────────┐ ┌─┐         └───────────┘ │
 │ │ [..]             │ │▲│                        │
 │ │ [corel]          │ └─┘                        │
 │ │ [pictures]       │ ▓▓                         │
 │ │ [system]         │ ▓▓                         │
 │ │ [win-pics]       │ ▓▓                         │
 │ │ [-a-]            │ ┌─┐                        │
 │ │ [-b-]            │ │▼│                        │
 │ └──────────────────┘ └─┘                        │
 └────────────────────────────────────────────────┘
```

File Save As Dialog Box

9. Let's try printing the file. You can print the details in either of two ways: as a list of index lines, or as a collection of complete cards. Try doing both. Click on **View** in the menu bar and then on **List**. You should see a listing of cards like the figure shown on the next page.

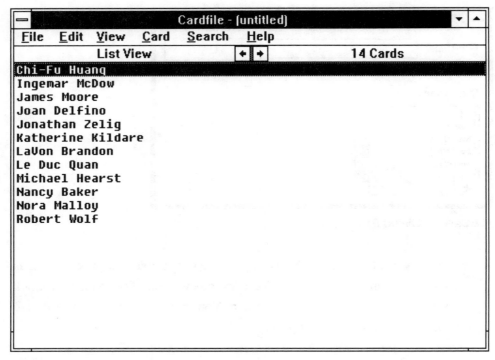

Cardfile List

10. Open the **File** menu and click on **Page Setup**. The default header is **&f**, and the default footer is **Page &p**. Click on **OK** to accept the defaults.

11. Open the **File** menu again and click on **Printer Setup**. Double click on the name of the printer you want to use to print the file. If you have only one printer installed, you can skip this step.

12. Open the **File** menu a third time and click on **Print All**. (You cannot select **Print** when the List view is active.) A message box appears while the file is being sent to the printer. Just leave it alone and it will vanish in a few seconds (the exact printing time depends on the size of your file and the speed of your printer). At the top of each page of your printout is the filename, and each page has the correct page number at the bottom.

13. Now let's print the cards themselves. Change to the Cards view by pressing **Alt-V C**, and then press **Alt-F A** to print all the cards. Use the same printer and page format as before. (If you select **Print**, only the card at the front of the stack is printed.) This time your printout will contain a number of boxes, each one representing a single card.

Depending on the page size you should get between four and six cards on a page. Even if there is enough room on the page for the cards to be printed two abreast, Cardfile will print them in a single column.

```
┌────────────────────────────────────────────────────┐
│ ▭          Page Setup                                │
├────────────────────────────────────────────────────┤
│                                                      │
│  Header:   [&f    ]            ┌──────────┐          │
│                                │    OK    │          │
│                                └──────────┘          │
│  Footer:   [Page &p    ]       ┌──────────┐          │
│                                │  Cancel  │          │
│  ┌─Margins────────────────────────────────────┐     │
│  │ Left:  [.75   ]   Right:  [.75   ]          │     │
│  │                                             │     │
│  │ Top:   [1     ]   Bottom: [1     ]          │     │
│  └─────────────────────────────────────────────┘     │
└────────────────────────────────────────────────────┘
```

Page Setup Dialog Box

Cardfile Summary

Cardfile is a simple database that stores and sorts information using graphics that resemble small index cards.

The cards are sorted automatically into alphanumeric order using the index line at the top of each card.

You can print out your file as a list of the index lines or as representations of the cards themselves.

Within its limitations, Cardfile is a handy, easy-to-use program that is ideal for managing simple lists. But it is a shame that you cannot adjust the size of the cards.

Cardfile Keyboard Summary

Alt-Backspace	Undo last text action.
Alt-C A	Add new card to stack.
Alt-C D	Delete front card in stack.
Alt-C P	Duplicate current card.
Alt-C T	Dial phone using number on card.
Alt-E C	Copy selected data to Clipboard.
Alt-E E	Switch from text mode to picture mode.
Alt-E I	Edit index line of current card.
Alt-E P	Paste Clipboard contents at cursor position.
Alt-E R	Cancel editing and restore original contents of current card.
Alt-E T	Cut selected data to Clipboard.
Alt-E U	Undo last editing action.
Alt-E X	Switch from picture mode to text mode.
Alt-Esc	Switch to next program.
Alt-F A	Save the current file under a new name.
Alt-F L	Print all cards or a list of index lines.
Alt-F M	Merge a file into the current one.
Alt-F N	Create a new cardfile.
Alt-F O	Load a previously saved file from disk.
Alt-F P	Print current card only.
Alt-F R	Select and/or set up a printer.
Alt-F S	Save file to filename shown on the title bar.
Alt-F T	Set page formats.
Alt-F X	Quit Cardfile and return to Program Manager.
Alt-F4	Quit Cardfile and return to Program Manager.
Alt-S F	Search through contents of cards for specified text.
Alt-S G	Look for matching text on index lines.
Alt-S N	Find next occurrence of text on cards.
Alt-Spacebar C	Quit Cardfile and return to Program Manager.
Alt-Spacebar M	Move icon or application window.

Alt-Spacebar N	Reduce window to an icon.
Alt-Spacebar R	Restore window to previous size and shape.
Alt-Spacebar S	Resize Cardfile application window.
Alt-Spacebar W	Switch programs using Task List.
Alt-Spacebar X	Maximize application window.
Alt-V C	Switch to Cards view.
Alt-V L	Switch to List view.
Ctrl-[letter]	Jump to first card whose index line begins with specified letter.
Ctrl-End	Bring last card in stack to front.
Ctrl-Esc	Switch programs using Task List.
Ctrl-Home	Bring first card in stack to front.
Ctrl-Ins	Copy selected data to Clipboard.
Ctrl-PgUp	Move forward one card at a time (Card view only).
Ctrl-PgDn	Move back one card at a time (Card view only).
F1	Activate Help system.
F3	Find next occurrence of text on cards.
F4	Search through contents of cards for specified text.
F5	Dial phone using number on card.
F6	Edit index line of current card.
F7	Add new card to stack.
Shift-Delete	Cut selected data to Clipboard.
Shift-Ins	Paste Clipboard contents at cursor position.

Clock

One of the simplest and most useful Windows 3 utilities is the Clock. You can choose to display the current system time in an analog or a digital clock that appears in a window. Either type of window can be resized, moved, maximized or reduced to an icon using the Control menu or direct mouse manipulation. If the Clock is reduced to an icon it still displays the time. The Clock has only one menu, which lets you toggle between the analog and digital displays.

CHAPTER 13

Games People Play

Windows 3 includes two simple but positively addictive games. The first, Reversi, is a computer version of a Japanese game called Othello; the second is Solitaire, a card game known in the U.K. as Patience. Both are good—but Solitaire is the most compulsive computer game I have ever played, and the fact that I lose more often than I win doesn't matter.

When you installed Windows, the Setup program created a separate group called Games to contain these two programs. I long ago moved them into the Accessories group and deleted the original Games group. Of course, it doesn't matter what group they are in. What really counts is how they play!

Reversi

Reversi is a fairly modern game. It was invented either in Japan or in China, and it lends itself well to being played on the computer. The game is played on a board of 64 squares, arranged in 8 rows and 8 columns; at the start of the game there are four counters, two for each player, positioned in the center of the board. The object of the game is simply to end up with more of your colored counters on the board than the computer has of its color. Your counters are red (white on a monochrome monitor), and the computer's are blue (black on a monochrome monitor).

To start the game, double click on the program icon. If you resize or maximize the program window, the game board and counters will stretch or shrink accordingly; however, because the board always has a large background, it will never completely fill the window. (Note: the numbers on the illustration below are not part of the game board; I've added them to help make the descriptions of play clearer.)

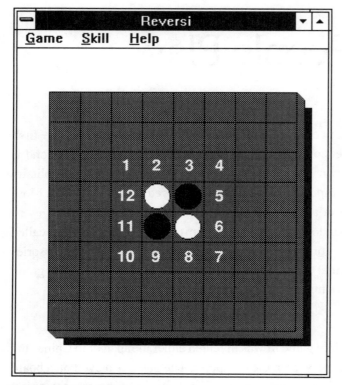

Reversi Opening Screen

You and the computer (there is no provision for playing against another person) take turns moving. Each player must make a legal move if one exists. A legal move is one where you ensnare one or more of the computer's counters between two of yours. Counters can be trapped vertically, horizontally or diagonally—or in any combination of the three. Thus, in the illustration above, the only places that red (white) can move are the squares numbered 3, 5, 9 and 11, because these are the only squares that trap the blue (black) counters. Any counter that is entrapped in this way changes to the opposite color. At the end of the game, the player with the most counters showing is the winner.

Simple? Don't you believe it! Reversi could almost have been created to run on a computer. The logic of play is purely mathematical, and computers have no equal when it comes to number crunching. The PC will beat the pants off you 99.9% of the time, because it simply doesn't make mistakes. Still, there is some fun in trying to beat the machine.

The fastest way to play the game is with the mouse. Whenever you move the cursor onto a square that represents a legal move, the cursor changes from an arrowhead to a cross. To place one of your counters on a valid square, just click the left mouse button. A counter appears, and the computer makes its move. Sometimes, especially at the Beginner and Novice levels, it seems that the computer has responded even before you have released the button!

The program provides three menus, including Help. The Help menu provides brief instructions on playing the game and nothing else—it will not provide you with any tips. The **Skills** menu is used to select a level of play; this affects how fast the computer responds when making its move. There are four levels from which to choose:

Beginner, the default, provides the simplest and fastest game.

Novice is almost as fast.

Select **Expert** and things begin to slow down. The computer takes longer to make its move.

Master is the slowest game pace. As each piece is placed, the computer takes longer and longer between moves. By the time you near the end of the game, the computer may literally be taking minutes to move.

You can change skill level as you go through the game—before every move if you like—but you invariably lose when you try this strategy.

The **Game** menu provides four commands:

Hint allows you to get a helping hand from the computer. When you select this command, the computer will position the cursor in the square that represents the best move for that position. This does not necessarily mean you will win the game—in Reversi, fortunes change with every counter placement.

Pass allows you to skip a turn. You can only choose this command on the first turn (to force the computer to move first) or when there is no legal move available for you. If you can move, you must. When you reach an impasse, you must select **Pass**; at that point, the computer gets an extra turn.

New terminates the current game and begins a new one.

Exit quits Reversi.

A tip: The computer always tries to get diagonal lines because these provide the most useful ways of trapping the opponent pieces. The four corner squares are the most valuable to any player.

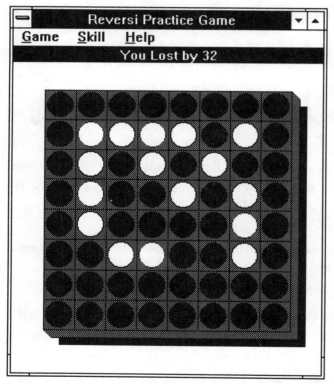

Game's End

Reversi Summary

Reversi is addictive, but the computer invariably wins—and ultimately this decreases the pleasure of the game.

To play the game, take your time, be patient and look carefully before you move.

Reversi Keyboard Summary

Alt-Esc	Switch to next program.
Alt-F4	Quit Reversi and return to Program Manager.
Alt-G H	Get a hint from the computer.
Alt-G N	Start a new game.
Alt-G P	Skip a turn.
Alt-G X	Quit Reversi and return to Program Manager.
Alt-S B	Set Beginner skill level.
Alt-S E	Set Expert skill level.
Alt-S M	Set Master skill level.
Alt-S N	Set Novice skill level.
Alt-Spacebar C	Quit Reversi and return to Program Manager.
Alt-Spacebar M	Move icon or application window.
Alt-Spacebar N	Reduce window to an icon.
Alt-Spacebar R	Restore window to its previous size and shape.
Alt-Spacebar S	Resize application window.
Alt-Spacebar W	Switch programs using Task List.
Alt-Spacebar X	Maximize window.
Ctrl-Esc	Switch programs using Task List.
Cursor keys	Move cursor in specific direction.
Enter	Place counter at cursor position.
F1	Activate Help system.
Spacebar	Place counter at cursor position.

Solitaire

Solitaire is a computer rendition of the popular card game. The basics of the game are simple: You start with a standard deck of 52 cards. When you start a new game, the cards are arranged in seven *row stacks* of one through seven cards each, with only the top card in the stack face up. The remainder of the deck is placed face down in the upper left corner. You build on the row stacks by placing cards in descending order and in alternating colors on the existing ones—for example, you can place the six of hearts or the six of diamonds onto the seven of clubs or the seven of spades. When you move a card or a group of cards from a stack, you get to turn over the face-down card that is exposed. You can move only a King to an empty position in the row stacks. Above the row stacks are spaces for four *suit stacks*. The object of the game is to assemble all the cards of the same suit into these stacks, building up from Ace to King.

To run the program, double click on the Solitaire icon in the Program Manager— it looks like a pack of cards. I suggest that you maximize the Solitaire window, because you will need a lot of space. When you resize the window the cards themselves do not change size; in a small window, you might have trouble seeing all the cards.

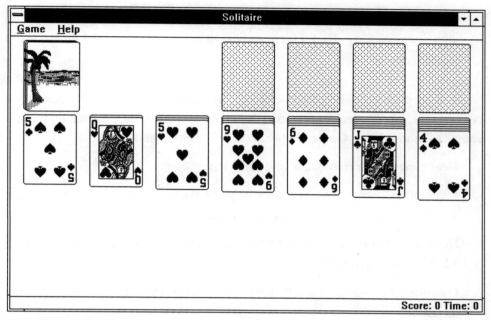

Solitaire Opening Screen

The illustrations in this chapter can't begin to do justice to Solitaire—the game depends on color to a tremendous extent, and playing on a monochrome display is simply not worth it. The Solitaire window includes the usual Control menu box, title bar, and Minimize and Maximize buttons. The playing surface consists of three areas:

In the top left-hand corner is the deck of unused cards. To play the game you draw cards from this pack, either individually or in threes.

There are seven row stacks when you deal a new game. From left to right, the first stack contains one card, the second two, and so on up to the seventh stack, which contains seven cards. The top card in each stack is face up; all the others are face down. You build the row stacks in descending order and in alternating colors.

Above the row stacks are spaces for the four suit stacks. As soon as an Ace turns face up, either on the row stacks or in the deck, you can place it on the suit stack.

313

You then build up the suit stack in the same way with the two, three, and so on, all the way to King. Each pile must consist of a single suit only; no mixing is permitted here.

The program provides only two menus. The Help menu is typically detailed—surprisingly, though, many of the details it gives you are wrong, especially when it comes to scoring! The **Game** menu contains five commands.

Deal clears the current game and starts a new one.

Undo allows you to cancel the move you have just made. If you are keeping score, using this feature will cost you points.

Deck lets you select a new pattern for the back of the cards; there are a total of 12 possible graphics.

Options brings up a dialog box that allows you to set various options for playing the game.

Exit quits the game and returns you to the Program Manager.

Playing the Game

Before we start play, let's look at some of the different ways to play. Open the **Game** menu and click on **Options**, or press **Alt-G O**, to bring up the Options dialog box. Don't change any of the options after you've started a game, or Solitaire will clear the current game and deal you a new hand.

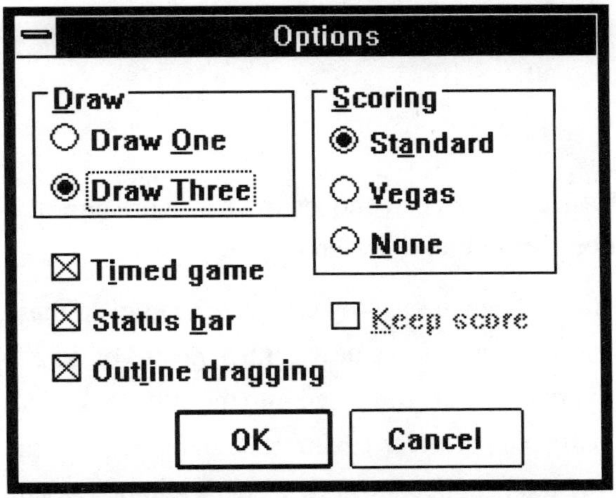

Options Dialog Box

Draw One allows you to turn over one card at a time from the unused deck and cycle through the deck an unlimited number of times. Personally, I consider this to be cheating as it makes the game too easy!

Draw Three turns over every third card. This is the default option.

Timed game means that the computer keeps track of how many seconds it takes you to complete a game. The time is displayed at the right of the status bar in the bottom of the window. If you're keeping score and you select this option, you earn a bonus based on your time.

Status bar is a toggle that turns the status bar display on or off. The default is on. Besides, you want to see your running score, don't you?

If the **Outline dragging** option is turned on, only the outline of a card appears when you move it. When you move a card over another card where it can legally be placed, the card underneath changes to inverse video. This is a very useful feature: As soon as the target card changes color, you can release the card you are moving and it will fit itself onto the stack.

Keep score lets you keep track of your game in points or in dollars (if you've selected Vegas scoring), or not at all.

Scoring

The scoring is a bit complex. Basically, you can choose to keep score or not; if you choose to keep score, you can opt for points or dollars.

Vegas is based on money. (I've never been to Las Vegas, so I don't know if these are the rules at the casinos.) Every time you start a new game it costs you $52—$1 a card. You get $5 back for every card that you place into the suit stacks. But this version is tough to win: You are only allowed to run through the cards in the deck three times. After that a large red X appears where the deck should be. The odds of completing the game this quickly must be very high, but by all means try it. It's not real money, after all!

Standard scoring awards you points for the following:

For every card you move from the deck to one of the seven row stacks, you get 5 points.

For every card that is placed onto the suit stacks, you get 10 points.

Move a card from one row stack to another and you earn 5 points.

Turn over the card that is face down on one of the row stacks, and you earn 5 points.

If you are playing a timed game and you manage to completely build the four suit piles from Ace to King, you get a huge bonus based on the elapsed time. For example, completing the game in less than 150 seconds will get you a bonus of at least 4,000 points.

On top of that, you get a wonderful display of cascading cards when you complete the game. This is the most spectacular effect I have ever seen on a standard PC monitor. The speed and clarity with which the monitor display is updated is phenomenal.

You lose points for doing any of these:

Using Undo will cost you 2 points, plus any points you earned as a result of the previous action. For instance, if you place a card on one of the row stacks you get 5 points. If you then undo it you lose 7 points—2 for using Undo and the 5 you got for placing the card in the first place. However, if you use Undo to reverse an action that cost you points, you get the points back again.

In a timed game you lose 2 points every time the clock records another 10 seconds of play.

You are allowed to turn over all the cards in the unused deck three times without incurring any penalty. But if you turn them over a fourth time you lose 20 points, and you lose another 20 points every time after that.

No matter how many points you lose you cannot end up with a negative score when using standard scoring. The highest score that I know of to date is 7,175 points, scored by my friend Pat Bitten.

Let's Play

For starters, try a **Timed Game** with **Standard Scoring** and **Outline Dragging** selected. First, change to a different deck backing. You can choose from a dozen colorful graphics.

Open the **Game** menu again and click on **Deck**, or press **Alt-G D**. The Select Card Back dialog box displays the twelve decks, with the current pattern surrounded by a black border. (The backing I've chosen, the desert island beach, is the only one that shows up with any clarity on a monochrome screen!)

Reading from left to right and top to bottom, they are:

A weave pattern in red and blue.

A weave pattern in yellow and green.

Four red and white fish against a cyan background.

Three red and white fish on a blue background.

Oak leaves and acorns on a black background.

Oak leaves and acorns on a blue background.

A cute little robot, complete with moving dial and flashing lights.

Dark red roses and leaves, extremely well drawn.

A very pretty conch shell on a multicolored background.

A dark and forbidding castle surrounded by flying bats with flapping wings.

A desert island beach with a palm tree and sun. Every so often a face appears on the sun and it sticks its tongue out at you before disappearing again!

A card shark's arm—once you begin playing, an ace pops out of his cuff now and again.

I wish I could provide an illustration for the card backs; unfortunately, most of them come out as a dark mess on a monochrome screen. Take my word for it: The color graphics on these cards are superb, and whoever designed them deserves some kind of award (the roses, in particular, are fantastic). To change to a different deck, click on the one you want and then click on **OK**. Surprisingly, you cannot select a new deck by double clicking on it, nor is there any provision for using your own graphics on the back of a deck.

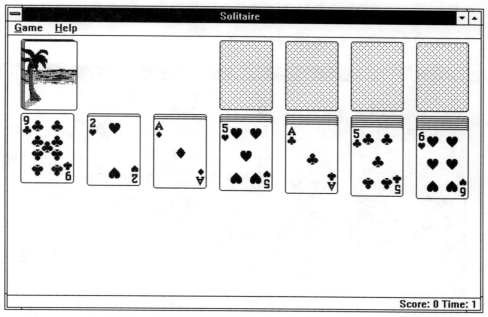

Ready to Play

With all the options set, it's finally time to play a game. Follow along in the screen shown above.

The Ace of diamonds and the Ace of clubs can be moved onto the suit stacks. If you click and drag one up to the suit stacks, the first hatched area will turn to inverse video as you near it. The easiest way to move the cards up is simply to double click on each one. Once the two aces are out of the way, click once on each of the two face-down cards to reveal them. (As it happens, both were aces, and so they were moved to the suit stacks as well; the next face-down cards were then turned over.) The five of clubs can be moved sideways onto the six of hearts, allowing us to turn over another card; click on it and we have 60 points already. With the Ace of hearts in position at the top, you can double click on the two of hearts to move it up to the suit stacks and earn another 10 points plus an additional 5 for turning up the revealed card. There are no more matches, and so you have

319

to click on the deck to turn over the third card. The cards from the deck are cascaded so you can see all three.

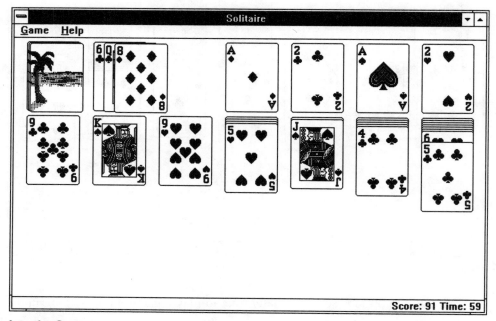

Into the Game

The eight of diamonds, the top card of the three, will go onto the nine of clubs—scoring another 5 points. (As we play, of course, the game clock keeps running and costing points. You can stop play—and the clock—at any time by reducing the Solitaire window to an icon.)

After playing a few more cards, all the cards from one row stack had been moved to other stacks, leaving a gap. This empty space can only be filled by a King, either from the deck or by moving one from another stack.

Once all the cards in the unused deck have been turned over, a green circle appears where the deck used to lie. Click on it and the deck is turned over, ready for you to draw more cards; you can combine both actions by double clicking on the circle. Keep drawing cards and placing them on the stacks, moving cards and groups of cards around the stacks until you cannot place any more cards or you win the game. As you go along, remember to add cards to the suit stacks whenever you can, either by dragging or by double clicking.

I've just played the above game out and was unable to complete it. As you can see, all the cards could not be turned over—in other words, I didn't win.

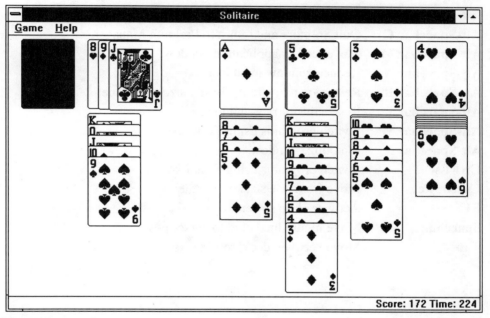

End of the Game

Solitaire Summary

Solitaire is the most compulsive and addictive game I have ever encountered on a computer. It is much better than any such program that runs under MS-DOS.

The scoring is complex and the information given in the Help menu about it is incorrect.

The graphical cascade when you win a game is one of the most spectacular screen effects Windows has to offer.

Solitaire Keyboard Summary

Alt-Esc	Switch to next program.
Alt-F4	Quit Solitaire and return to Program Manager.
Alt-G C	Select a new back for the deck.
Alt-G D	Deal a new game.
Alt-G O	Set game options.
Alt-G U	Undo last operation.
Alt-G X	Quit Solitaire and return to Program Manager.
Alt-Spacebar C	Quit Solitaire and return to Program Manager.
Alt-Spacebar M	Move icon or application window.
Alt-Spacebar N	Reduce window to an icon.
Alt-Spacebar R	Restore window to its former size and shape.
Alt-Spacebar S	Resize the current window.
Alt-Spacebar W	Switch programs using Task List.
Alt-Spacebar X	Maximize window.
Ctrl-Esc	Switch programs using Task List.
Cursor keys	Move from one stack to another.
F1	Activate Help system.
Spacebar	Move highlighted card to cursor position.
Tab	Move between deck, row stacks and suit stacks.

CHAPTER 14

Notepad

What Is It?

Notepad is a pure ASCII text editor that allows you to create and modify simple text files. It is not a word processor—nor does it pretend to be—but it is perfect for creating batch files and short notes. You can also use Notepad to create fairly long documents and then transfer the text into another program via the Clipboard. In fact, much of this chapter was created in precisely that way: I wrote the bulk of the chapter in Notepad and then pasted the resulting file directly into WordStar.

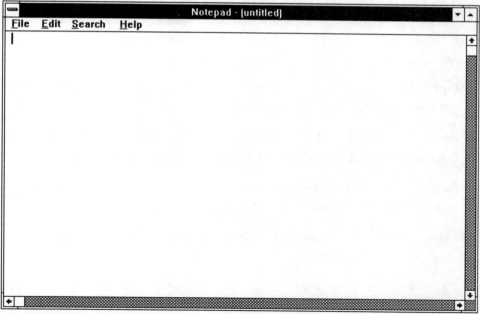

Notepad Opening Screen

I don't know of any other program, with the possible exception of Sidekick, that is as easy to use when it comes to dealing with pure ASCII files. Notepad will allow you to load a text file as large as 50 KB and create a file of between 20 and 30 KB (the maximum file size depends on the available memory in your system). As with many Windows applications, memory is the limiting factor.

To run the program, double click on the Notepad icon in the Accessories group window, or select the icon and then press **Enter**.

Along the top of the Notepad window are the usual title bar and menu bar, plus the Control menu box and Minimize and Maximize buttons; along the bottom and right side of the main editing window are scroll bars. The scroll bars are absolutely essential when working with ASCII files that can contain lines of any length; for the sake of clarity, however, you can choose to wrap long lines in a Notepad file if you wish.

The Notepad **File** menu provides the following familiar commands for working with files:

New clears the screen and starts a new document. If you have made changes to the current file, you will be asked if you want to save the changes before the new one is created.

Open allows you to load a previously saved document. The dialog box allows you to select any text file from any drive or directory.

Save writes the current file to disk using the filename in the title bar. If you use this command with a new file you will be prompted to supply a filename.

Save As allows you to save the current file to a new filename. You may specify any drive or directory along with the filename.

Print produces a hard copy of your file, using the page format established by the next command.

Page Setup lets you set the page margins and specify a header and footer for the current Notepad file. These settings are not saved with the file.

Printer Setup is used to select and, if necessary, set up a printer when printing a Notepad file.

Exit quits the program and returns you to the Program Manager.

The **Edit** menu gives you access to the Clipboard plus some other actions provided by the following commands:

Undo cancels the last editing action. **Alt-Backspace** is the keyboard equivalent.

Cut copies the selected text to the Clipboard and then deletes it from the current file.

Copy places a copy of the selected text on the Clipboard and leaves it in the current file.

Paste inserts the contents of the Clipboard at the current cursor position. You can only paste unformatted text into a Notepad file.

Delete simply clears the selected text from the screen, without affecting the contents of the Clipboard.

Select All allows you to highlight all the text in the current Notepad file, a quick and easy way to copy the current file to the Clipboard and merge it with another.

Time/Date inserts the current system time and date into the document at the current cursor position. You can issue this command with a single keystroke by pressing **F5**.

Word Wrap turns off the bottom scroll bar and wraps long lines so that any text you enter remains visible within the Notepad window, regardless of the window's size. If this option is turned off, each line will extend as far as necessary to the right—sometimes far beyond the window's borders. A new line will begin only after a hard return, created when you press **Enter**.

The **Search** menu looks for strings of text you specify. **Find** brings up a dialog box in which you enter the text to search for; **Find Next** skips the dialog box and repeats the last search (**F3** is the keyboard shortcut). You can look forward or backward in the file, and you can specify a case-sensitive search—to look for specified text using capital and lower-case letters.

To move around within a text file, you use the standard Windows key combinations. The cursor keys move the insertion point in the specified direction; **Home** and **End** take you to the beginning and end of the current line, respectively. **Ctrl-Home** and **Ctrl-End** jump directly to the beginning and end of the file.

Exercise 14.1
Using the Program

Because it produces pure ASCII files, Notepad is ideal for editing your computer's CONFIG.SYS and AUTOEXEC.BAT. Of course, your versions of these files are almost certain to be different from mine, but the principles involved in editing them are absolutely the same, regardless of the files' contents. For the sake of this exercise, we'll assume your Windows program files are in a directory called C:\WINDOWS.

When first run, the Notepad window is a bit small to work with comfortably; as the first step, let's enlarge it. Also, because the CONFIG.SYS file uses short lines we can turn on Word Wrap. Before starting this exercise, make sure the Notepad is the only application running in a window; if Program Manager is visible onscreen, reduce it to an icon.

1. Press **Alt-Spacebar W** and the Task List appears. Press **Alt-T** to select **Tile**. The window expands to fill the available space but still leaves the Program Manager icon visible at the bottom of the screen. If the Program Manager is running in a window when you select this command, the Notepad window will expand to fill the entire screen.

2. To turn on Word Wrap press **Alt-E W**. A check mark appears next to the **Word Wrap** menu choice and the bottom scroll bar vanishes.

1. Click on the Control menu box at the top left-hand corner of the window and then on **Switch To** to display the Task List. Click on the button labeled **Tile** and the Notepad window will be resized to fill the top portion of the screen while still leaving any application icons visible. If the Program Manager is running in a window when you click on this button, the Notepad will expand to fill the entire screen.

2. Click on **Edit** in the Notepad window and then on **Word Wrap**. A check mark appears next to the **Word Wrap** menu choice and the bottom scroll bar disappears.

The next step is to load your CONFIG.SYS file into the Notepad. By default, Notepad first looks in the Windows directory for files with a .TXT extension; you'll need to change directories and specify a different filename to find the file in the root of Drive C:.

 3. Press **Alt-F O** to bring up the File Open dialog box. Press **Tab** twice to move the selector (a gray dotted outline) to the Directories box. Press **Space** to highlight the [..] entry and then press **Enter**. You should now be in the root directory. Press **Alt-N** to move the highlighter back to the first text box, which contains the entry ***.TXT**. Type **CONFIG.SYS**—it will automatically replace the highlighted characters—and press **Enter** to load your CONFIG.SYS file into the Notepad.

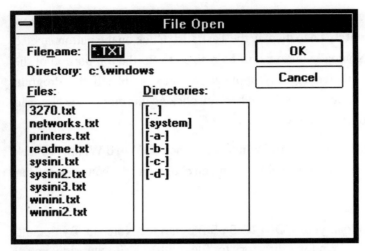

Open File Dialog Box

 3. Click on **File** in the menu bar and then click on **Open** to reveal the File Open dialog box. Double click on **[..]** in the Directories box and the program immediately logs on to the root directory of Drive C:. Double click on ***.TXT** in the Filename text box. Type **CONFIG.SYS** to replace the contents of the box and click on **OK** to load the file.

The file shown here is the one from the Laser 80386 machine, because that is the system I use most often. The black square on the last line is an end-of-file marker that Notepad doesn't know how to display. (Although Notepad is ASCII based, it can only display the original 127 ASCII characters—if your file contains characters from the Extended ASCII character set, Windows will load the file but won't correctly show these characters.) In this case the character is unnecessary, so let's get rid of it. Next, let's modify CONFIG.SYS to increase the number of buffers to 30.

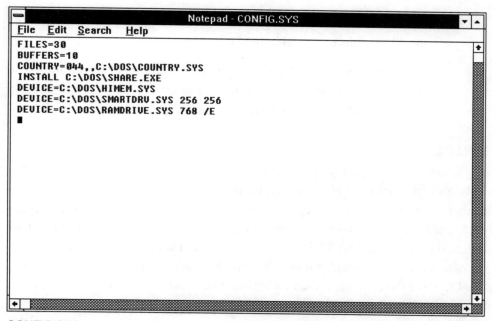

```
Notepad - CONFIG.SYS
File   Edit   Search   Help
FILES=30
BUFFERS=10
COUNTRY=044,,C:\DOS\COUNTRY.SYS
INSTALL C:\DOS\SHARE.EXE
DEVICE=C:\DOS\HIMEM.SYS
DEVICE=C:\DOS\SMARTDRV.SYS 256  256
DEVICE=C:\DOS\RAMDRIVE.SYS 768 /E
■
```

CONFIG.SYS Loaded

4. Move the cursor to the beginning of the bottom line by pressing **Ctrl-End** and then **Home**. Press **Delete** to remove the black square.

5. Press **Ctrl-Home** to send the cursor back to the beginning of the file. Press **Down** and then **End** to move to the end of the second line. Use the cursor keys and **Backspace** or **Delete** to replace **10** with **30**.

6. Now that you have changed the file, it needs to be saved. Press **Ctrl-S** and the modified file will overwrite the original. (The change won't take effect until you reboot the computer.)

4. Click on the last line of the file to move the insertion point. Use **Delete** or **Backspace** to remove the black square.

5. Double click on the **10** at the end of the second line. (In Notepad, as in most

Windows programs, double clicking on a word highlights the entire word.) Type **30** to replace the highlighted text.

6. Having changed the file, you need to save it. Click on **File** in the menu bar and then on **Save**; the modified file will overwrite the original, and the changes will take effect the next time you boot the computer.

WIN.INI

Windows uses a pair of initialization files to store information that defines the Windows environment. Windows applications—and Windows itself—use the information in these files to keep track of your system's configuration as well as preferences that you set—using Control Panel, for example. The first of these two standard files is called SYSTEM.INI; it contains all the information that Windows needs to work correctly with your specific combination of hardware. The second file, WIN.INI, for the most part contains settings that cause the Windows environment to act according to your preferences.

Windows creates and maintains both files automatically. Every time you use the Control Panel to update a printer driver, for example, Windows makes a change to the appropriate section of WIN.INI. When you use Setup to add a new hardware driver to your system, the program will modify SYSTEM.INI to reflect the change. Most Windows applications add a section to WIN.INI where essential information like default directories and color preferences is kept. One of Windows' most attractive features is that it spares you from this sort of drudgery.

Both files are stored in the Windows directory; each consists of pure ASCII text and can therefore be viewed and edited using Notepad. A word of warning: The settings in SYSTEM.INI are critical to Windows' operation. Unless you are absolutely certain that a change is necessary and the syntax is correct, you should not edit this file directly. The settings in WIN.INI are somewhat less crucial, but an editing mistake here can cause some applications to behave in unintended (and unpleasant) ways.

Let's take a look at a typical WIN.INI file—in this case, the one from the Laser 80386. Rather than make an exercise of this, I'm just going to cover the broad outlines of the file. If you want to make changes, do so just as you did with CONFIG.SYS. Any changes you make in WIN.INI will not take effect until you quit and restart Windows.

Press **Alt-F O** to bring up the File Open dialog box. Use the Directories list box to move to the Windows directory and enter **WIN.INI** in the Filename text box to load the file. Even if you have no other Windows programs installed, this is a large file.

Before you go any further, I suggest that you save a copy of WIN.INI under a new name. Even if you don't plan to make any changes, a backup copy may save you from having to reinstall Windows if the file is ever accidentally deleted or becomes corrupted. Press **Alt-F A** to bring up the File Save As dialog box. Use any filename you wish, and this time include an extension. Don't use WIN.OLD—many Windows programs routinely edit your WIN.INI file and save the old version under that name. WININI.OLD is a safe choice.

The WIN.INI file is divided into sections. Each line in the file must follow one of three formats exactly.

The first line of a section is the *section name*. It must be enclosed in brackets ([ ]), and the left bracket must be the first character in the line it occupies. Windows sets up 10 sections of its own. A Windows application (including the accessories that come with Windows 3) may add its own section to WIN.INI, using the name of the program as the section head.

Under each section name are the details stored for that section. Each line follows the format *keyname=value*. The keyname is set by Windows or the application and can consist of any number of characters. It must be followed immediately by an equals sign. The value may be a filename or directory name, a number, or a text string—the format depends on the type of information being stored.

Within WIN.INI you can add a comment—an informative note that is not acted upon—by placing a semicolon at the beginning of the line.

For purposes of illustration, I have included small samples from the full file below. Normally, the sections within WIN.INI are separated by single blank lines. Windows establishes the sections in a certain order when it first creates the file; however, this order is not essential. Let's look at each section in a typical WIN.INI file.

```
 Notepad - WIN.INI
 File   Edit   Search   Help
[windows]
load=
run=
Beep=yes
Spooler=yes
NullPort=None
device=PostScript Printer,PSCRIPT,LPT1:
BorderWidth=3
KeyboardSpeed=31
CursorBlinkRate=200
DoubleClickSpeed=500
Programs=com exe bat pif
Documents=
DeviceNotSelectedTimeout=15
TransmissionRetryTimeout=45
swapdisk=

[Desktop]
Pattern=(None)
Wallpaper=designer.bmp
TileWallpaper=1
GridGranularity=0
IconSpacing=60
```

The WIN.INI File

The first section, **[windows]**, defines some essential aspects of the Windows environment itself. Many of the changes you make in the Control Panel are reflected here.

```
[windows]
load=
run=
Beep=yes
Spooler=yes
NullPort=None
device=PostScript Printer,PSCRIPT,LPT1:
BorderWidth=3
KeyboardSpeed=31
CursorBlinkRate=200
DoubleClickSpeed=500
Programs=com exe bat pif
Documents=
DeviceNotSelectedTimeout=15
TransmissionRetryTimeout=45
```

load will start up a specified program as an icon every time you run Windows. You can include a program name or the name of a document whose extension is associated with an application. Thus, if the line reads **load=SOL** then the Solitaire program will be loaded as an icon and placed on the bottom of the screen when Windows starts up. If you enter more than one item on this line, separate the items with a space. The Program Manager is still loaded as normal. This is one of the few commands in WIN.INI that must be edited directly and cannot be set from elsewhere.

run works much like **load**, except that the application starts up in a window rather than as an icon whenever you run Windows. The Program Manager will be run first, followed by the named program or programs. You can include a list of programs or documents as long as each name is separated by a space. For example, to run Solitaire, Notepad, Calendar and Clock automatically, edit this line to read **run=SOL NOTEPAD CAL CLOCK**. This line, too, must be edited directly and cannot be set from elsewhere within Windows.

The **Beep** setting is controlled by the Sound icon in Control Panel.

Spooler stores the current Print Manager setting; **yes** means Print Manager is currently enabled.

Nullport is the name supplied in the Control Panel when a device is installed but not connected to a port. The default setting is **None**. You can edit this line directly.

device contains the name of the default printer, its driver filename, and the port to which it is connected. You should use the Printers icon in the Control Panel to change this setting.

A number of settings in this section contain numerical values that reflect selections you made using visual aids in the Control Panel. **BorderWidth** and **CursorBlinkRate** (Desktop); **MouseSpeed, MouseThreshold1, MouseThreshold2** and **DoubleClickSpeed** (Mouse); and **KeyboardSpeed** (Keyboard) fall into this category. You can change these settings directly by changing the values here, but it's much easier and safer to use the Control Panel and let Windows edit this section for you.

Programs and **Documents** tell Windows what file extensions it should represent using the appropriate File Manager icons. Extensions that are associated with an application are automatically considered documents and need not be included in this section.

DeviceNotSelectedTimeout and **TransmissionRetryTimeout** are the default settings that Windows suggests for these values when you configure a printer. You can edit these values directly. The values for specific printers are stored in the [PrinterPorts] section, not here.

The **[desktop]** section stores information about the Windows background and where windows and icons are placed. These settings are best adjusted graphically, using the Desktop icon from the Control Panel.

```
[Desktop]
Pattern=(None)
Wallpaper=designer.bmp
TileWallpaper=1
GridGranularity=0
IconSpacing=60
```

The **[extensions]** section contains the program name associated with a given document extension. This section may be as long as you like. The best way to edit it is indirectly, using the **Associate** command from the **File** menu in File Manager.

```
[Extensions]
cal=calendar.exe ^.cal
crd=cardfile.exe ^.crd
trm=terminal.exe ^.trm
txt=notepad.exe ^.txt
ini=notepad.exe ^.ini
pcx=pbrush.exe ^.pcx
bmp=PBRUSH.EXE ^.BMP
wri=write.exe ^.wri
```

The **[intl]** section contains more than 20 individual entries that control date and time display, language, currency, and other international settings. (An excerpt appears below.) These settings should only be changed using the International icon in the Control Panel. One interesting note: Windows stores a country code that is equal to the country's international telephone code.

```
[intl]
sCountry=United Kingdom
iCountry=44
iDate=1
iTime=1
sShortDate=dd/MM/yyyy
sLongDate=dddd' 'dd' 'MMMM' 'yyyy
```

The **[ports]** section contains settings for the various ports that Windows can use. It is not a list of the ports on your machine. For example, on the Laser 386 that uses this WIN.INI file, there is only one serial port, COM1, and yet the list below contains entries for a total of four. Again, it's best to use the Control Panel to tweak these settings.

```
[ports]
LPT1:=
LPT2:=
LPT3:=
COM1:=9600,n,8,1
COM2:=9600,n,8,1
COM3:=9600,n,8,1
COM4:=9600,n,8,1
EPT:=
FILE:=
```

[fonts] stores the names and descriptions of all the display fonts that are set up for use in Windows. When you delete a font in the Control Panel, its name is removed from this list. Use the Fonts icon in the Control Panel to add and remove fonts.

```
[fonts]
Symbol 8,10,12,14,18,24 (VGA res)=SYMBOLE.FON
Helv 8,10,12,14,18,24 (VGA res)=HELVE.FON
Tms Rmn 8,10,12,14,18,24 (VGA res)=TMSRE.FON
Roman (All res)=ROMAN.FON
Script (All res)=SCRIPT.FON
Modern (All res)=MODERN.FON
Courier 10,12,15 (VGA res)=COURE.FON
```

The section headed **[PrinterPorts]** lists all the printers you have installed, the ports to which they are connected, and the timeout values you selected when setting them up. The **[devices]** section duplicates this information and is only necessary so that older Windows applications can print. The only safe way to edit either of these sections is to select the Printers option in the Control Panel.

```
[PrinterPorts]
PostScript Printer=PSCRIPT,LPT1:,15,45
PCL / HP LaserJet=HPPCL,None,15,45
```

```
[devices]
PostScript Printer=PSCRIPT,LPT1:
PCL / HP LaserJet=HPPCL,None
```

The **[colors]** section (only a small portion of which is reproduced here), stores the red, green and blue values, respectively, for 19 elements of the Windows display. Most of these should only be adjusted using the Color icon in the Control Panel. If you feel adventurous, there are six settings that can only be edited directly: ButtonFace, ButtonShadow, ButtonText, GrayText, Hilight and HilightText. These are system-wide options that control the appearance of buttons and highlighted text. If you decide to tinker with any of these settings, be sure to save a backup copy of WIN.INI first, just in case!

```
[colors]
Background=128 255 255
AppWorkspace=0 255 255
Window=255 255 255
WindowText=0 0 0
Menu=255 255 0
```

In addition to the above sections, which are common to every Windows installation, there are literally dozens of additional sections on my system, each containing settings for a different Windows application. Solitaire, Paintbrush, Windows Write, Clock, PageMaker and Corel Draw, and every other Windows application has its own section in WIN.INI. Every printer installed on the system stores configuration details in a separate section as well. For example, the block shown below contains the configuration information for two printers installed on my system: the StarScript (which uses the PostScript driver) and a Hewlett-Packard LaserJet (which uses the HPPCL driver).

```
[PostScript,LPT1]
device=2
feed1=9
feed15=9
orient=1
```

```
[HPPCL,None]
paper=1
prtresfac=0
duplex=0
```

If you have made changes to the file, you will need to save it as WIN.INI, overwriting the original file, and then quit and restart Windows before your changes take effect.

Exercise 14.2
Logging Your Files

Notepad provides an easy way to add a date and time stamp to a file. Just press **F5** and the current system time and date are inserted at the cursor position. However, you can do more than just that with this facility.

1. Run the Notepad and start a new file.

2. With the cursor at the very beginning of the file type **.LOG**—you must use capital letters.

3. Save the file under any name you wish. From now on, whenever you open this file Windows will add the current system time and date to the end of the file. This feature lets you keep a running diary of activities—every time you open the file, you can add a note without having to look up and enter the date and time stamp.

Do not use this feature on any system file—CONFIG.SYS or the Windows .INI files, for example.

Summary

Notepad is a text editor that allows you to view and edit Plain ASCII files containing up to 50,000 characters or so. The maximum file size depends on the amount of free memory available on your machine.

Notepad allows you to create files that automatically log the current date and time whenever they are opened.

Windows uses two configuration files—SYSTEM.INI and WIN.INI—to keep track of important details about the Windows environment. These files can be edited directly in Notepad; however, whenever possible it's best to change these settings indirectly, using the tools in the Control Panel.

Keyboard Summary

Alt-E C	Copy selected text to Clipboard.
Alt-E D	Insert system time and date at cursor position.
Alt-E P	Paste Clipboard contents into document at cursor position.
Alt-E S	Select all the text in the current document.
Alt-E T	Cut selected text and copy to Clipboard.
Alt-E U	Undo last action.
Alt-E W	Toggle word wrap.
Alt-Esc	Switch to next program without using Task List.
Alt-F A	Save the current file to a new filename.
Alt-F N	Start a new file.
Alt-F O	Open an existing ASCII text file.
Alt-F P	Print the current document.
Alt-F R	Select or set up a printer.
Alt-F S	Save the current file to the name shown on the title bar.
Alt-F T	Set margins and define a header and footer for the printout.
Alt-F X	Quit Notepad and return to Program Manager.
Alt-F4	Quit Notepad and return to Program Manager.
Alt-S F	Search for specified text.
Alt-S N	Find next occurrence of search string.
Alt-Spacebar C	Quit Notepad and return to Program Manager.
Alt-Spacebar M	Move icon or application window.
Alt-Spacebar N	Reduce application window to an icon.
Alt-Spacebar R	Restore window to its previous size and shape.
Alt-Spacebar S	Resize applications window.
Alt-Spacebar W	Switch programs using Task List.

Alt-Spacebar X	Maximize application window.
Ctrl-Esc	Switch programs using Task List.
Ctrl-Ins	Copy selected text to Clipboard.
Delete	Delete selected text.
F1	Activate Help system.
F3	Find next occurrence of search string.
F5	Insert system time and date at cursor position.
Shift-Delete	Cut selected text and copy to Clipboard.
Shift-Ins	Paste Clipboard contents into document at cursor position.

CHAPTER 15

More Accessories

Some of the Windows 3 accessories we've looked at so far are simple tools that you'll use every time you run the program. The three advanced accessories we'll examine in this chapter are a little different. The PIF Editor, Recorder and Terminal are specialized utilities that are definitely not for everyday use. Some people, in fact, will never use any of them. But each represents a powerful way to expand the Windows environment.

PIF Editor

You can run an MS-DOS application from within Windows by setting it up as a Program Manager icon or by clicking on its filename in the File Manager. In most cases, this approach will work; sometimes, though, you need to supply additional information to help an application run reliably—what directory it should start in, how much memory it needs or what video mode it uses, for example. The PIF Editor is the program that allows you to create or modify the Program Information Files (PIFs) that contain these settings. PIFs are special files that define the various parameters that the program will use when it is run in the Windows environment.

Whenever you try to run an MS-DOS program, Windows looks for the corresponding PIF. The name of the PIF will usually match the name of the program—for example, the PIF for WordStar is named WS.PIF. If Windows cannot find the PIF for a particular program it will try to run the MS-DOS application using default settings. These may or may not work, depending on the program involved, but in general they will. You can even run a program directly by selecting its PIF, because the file contains all the vital details associated with the program.

Windows installs PIFs for some popular applications, but not every application that requires a PIF is in the list of programs that Windows looks for during Setup. Even with one of the Windows PIF files, you may find it necessary to make some changes. For example, suppose you have two configurations for a program like WordStar—one set up for a normal display as WS.EXE, the other installed as 50.EXE to use the VGA 50-line display. Because you want to be able to run both from Windows, you can load a copy of WS.PIF into the PIF Editor and change the program name from WS.EXE to 50.EXE. What if you reorganize your hard disk and change the locations of some programs? Because the PIF contains the full path details for each file, you need to edit the PIF files before you can successfully run the programs.

It is important to realize that Windows creates PIF files only for MS-DOS programs. Windows programs don't need them, because their settings are included in the WIN.INI file.

To run the PIF Editor, double click on the icon (it looks like a luggage tag with the letters PIF on it), or select the icon and press **Enter**. The PIF Editor supplies two menus, plus Help. The **File** menu allows you to create a new file or open an existing one and then save the result. The **Mode** menu allows you to switch between Standard and 386 enhanced modes, because Program Information Files contain different information, depending on which mode you're using. Let's examine the Standard mode file first.

```
┌──────────────────────────────────────────────────────────────┐
│ ▬              PIF Editor - WS.PIF                       ▼  ▲  │
├──────────────────────────────────────────────────────────────┤
│  File    Mode    Help                                          │
│                                                                │
│  Program Filename:      ┌──────────────────────────────────┐  │
│                         │C:\WS6\ws.exe                     │  │
│                         └──────────────────────────────────┘  │
│  Window Title:          ┌────────────────────────────┐        │
│                         │WordStar Professional       │        │
│                         └────────────────────────────┘        │
│  Optional Parameters:   ┌──────────────────────────────────┐  │
│                         │                                  │  │
│                         └──────────────────────────────────┘  │
│  Start-up Directory:    ┌──────────────────────────────────┐  │
│                         │C:\WS6                            │  │
│                         └──────────────────────────────────┘  │
│  Video Mode:            ○ Text    ● Graphics/Multiple Text    │
│                                                                │
│  Memory Requirements:   KB Required  ┌─────┐                   │
│                                      │384  │                   │
│                                      └─────┘                   │
│  XMS Memory:            KB Required ┌───┐    KB Limit ┌───┐    │
│                                     │0  │             │0  │    │
│                                     └───┘             └───┘    │
│  Directly Modifies:     ☐ COM1    ☐ COM3    ☐ Keyboard        │
│                         ☐ COM2    ☐ COM4                       │
│  ☐ No Screen Exchange           ☐ Prevent Program Switch       │
│  ☒ Close Window on Exit                                        │
│  Reserve Shortcut Keys: ☐ Alt+Tab   ☐ Alt+Esc   ☐ Ctrl+Esc    │
│                         ☐ PrtSc     ☐ Alt+PrtSc               │
└──────────────────────────────────────────────────────────────┘
```

PIF Editor Standard Mode

The first line contains the filename (including extension) and, if necessary, the full path of the program concerned—in this case, the filename is WS.EXE, which is stored in the \WS6 directory of Drive C:. This information is vital; if it is entered incorrectly, Windows does not know how to execute the specified program.

The next line is the title that will appear beneath the application icon (or on the title bar, if you run the MS-DOS program in a window using 386 enhanced mode) whenever you run the program. If you leave this line blank, Windows will use the program's title as the name.

The third line contains any **Optional Parameters** that you would normally use if you ran the program directly from MS-DOS. For example, when you run PC-

Outline from the system prompt you can suppress the display of the title screen by typing the program name followed by **/Q**; if you set up a Windows PIF file for PC-Outline, you could include this parameter here. Similarly, you could include a filename to be loaded into the program at startup if the program supports this feature. When there are a number of startup options and you would like Windows to prompt you to provide the parameters every time you start the application, place a question mark in this line.

If you fill in the box labeled **Start-up Directory**, Windows changes to the specified directory before running the program. Because WordStar uses a lot of overlay files, which must be available while the program is running, the sample PIF file changes to the \WS6 directory and then runs WordStar. If the application is included in your PATH, this option may not be necessary; Windows duplicates your DOS environment, including the PATH, every time you run an MS-DOS application.

The **Video Mode** tells Windows how the program uses the monitor display and thus how much memory is needed to hold the monitor image. Windows saves and restores the MS-DOS program's screen every time you switch between the MS-DOS program and Windows. The memory to hold the screen image comes out of the amount of memory allocated to the program. If you select **Text**, Windows will reserve less memory, leaving more for your application; however, if the application at some point switches to graphics mode, you will not be able to return to Windows except by quitting the application. If you're not sure how to set this option, your safest choice is **Graphics/Multiple Text**.

Memory Requirements is the absolute minimum amount of conventional memory that must be available before Windows can start the program. It is not the amount of memory that will be allocated to the program—Windows will give the program all the free memory available. If you try to start a program with less conventional memory available than is specified in this box, Windows will give you an error message and refuse to start the program. The only way you can find out how much memory a program really requires is by guessing! The documentation for most MS-DOS programs usually tells you how much total RAM you should have in your system, not how much is actually required for the application. Most non-Windows programs will run with the default setting of 128 KB.

XMS Memory refers to a special form of extended memory, based on the Lotus-Intel-Microsoft-AST Standard. There are very few MS-DOS programs that use extended memory in this fashion, and so you will rarely have to change the default settings here.

The settings in the section labeled **Directly Modifies** tell Windows that the program uses the selected element of the computer system in such a way that it cannot be shared with other programs. (This really only matters if you are running programs concurrently.) If the program takes direct control of the keyboard in this way, you will be unable to switch to Windows from the program and your only way back is to terminate the application.

If you select **No Screen Exchange** then you reduce the amount of memory required, but you will be unable to copy information from the application into the Clipboard.

Prevent Program Switch does just that—with this option selected the only way to switch back to Windows is to quit the MS-DOS application. This setting should only be checked if you absolutely need to free memory to run a program.

Close Window on Exit clears the screen when you quit the MS-DOS program. If this box is not checked, you will have to press a key to return to Windows.

Reserve Shortcut Keys is useful when certain Windows key combinations are used by the application.

```
┌─────────────────────────────────────────────────────────────────────┐
│ ─              PIF Editor - WS.PIF                            ▼  ▲    │
│  File   Mode   Help                                                   │
│  Program Filename:       C:\WS6\WS.EXE                                 │
│  Window Title:           WordStar Professional                        │
│  Optional Parameters:                                                 │
│  Start-up Directory:     C:\WS6                                       │
│  Memory Requirements:   KB Required  384    KB Desired   640          │
│  Display Usage: ◉ Full Screen        Execution:  ☐ Background         │
│                 ○ Windowed                       ☐ Exclusive          │
│  ☒ Close Window on Exit            ┌ Advanced... ┐                    │
└─────────────────────────────────────────────────────────────────────┘
```

PIF Editor Enhanced Mode

When you start an MS-DOS program under 386 enhanced mode, Windows allows you to run the program in a window and in the background. The PIF that controls the MS-DOS program must address these issues. By default, the PIF Editor starts in the mode under which you are currently running; however, you can edit a 386 enhanced PIF while running in standard mode (or vice versa) by choosing **Mode** from the menu bar and then selecting the appropriate setting. Because you have so many more options using the 386 enhanced mode PIF Editor, there are two dialog boxes. The first few lines of a 386 enhanced PIF look identical to those in a standard PIF; however, there are some crucial differences.

The **Program Filename**, **Window Title** and **Start-up Directory** are the same in both modes, as is the **Close Window on Exit** setting. However, any **Optional Parameters** you enter here will apply only when the program is running in 386 enhanced mode. This means you can specify different startup options depending on what Windows mode you are using.

Under **Memory Requirements**, you can enter **-1** in the **KB Required** box to tell Windows to give the MS-DOS program all available conventional memory. There is an extra box, **KB Desired**, next to this setting; you can limit the amount of RAM that Windows allocates to the program and save it for other applications by entering a value here. Enter **640** or **-1** to give the program all available conventional memory.

The first new option is **Display Usage**. You decide whether the MS-DOS application will start in **Full Screen** or **Windowed** mode.

Execution controls how the program will cooperate with other applications. The two options are not mutually exclusive. If you click on **Background**, the MS-DOS program is allowed to keep working even when another application is active; if this option is not checked, the application is suspended whenever you switch away from it. Selecting **Exclusive** suspends every other program while the specified application is active; this gives the maximum system resources to the program when it is running in the foreground.

That takes care of the basic options in the 386 enhanced mode PIF Editor; to view and edit the more technical settings, click on the button labeled **Advanced**.

```
┌────────────────────────────────────────────────────────────────────┐
│ ▬              Advanced Options                                       │
│ ┌─Multitasking Options────────────────────────────┐ ┌────────────┐  │
│ │ Background Priority:  ┌─────┐  Foreground Priority:│   OK       │  │
│ │                       │ 50  │           ┌─────┐    │            │  │
│ │                       └─────┘           │ 100 │    ├────────────┤  │
│ │              ☐ Detect Idle Time         └─────┘    │  Cancel    │  │
│ └─────────────────────────────────────────────────┘ └────────────┘  │
│ ┌─Memory Options──────────────────────────────────────────────────┐ │
│ │ EMS Memory:    KB Required ┌───┐   KB Limit ┌──────┐ ☐ Locked    │ │
│ │                            │ 0 │            │ 1024 │             │ │
│ │ XMS Memory:    KB Required ┌───┐   KB Limit ┌──────┐ ☐ Locked    │ │
│ │                            │ 0 │            │ 1024 │             │ │
│ │        ☒ Uses High Memory Area    ☐ Lock Application Memory      │ │
│ └─────────────────────────────────────────────────────────────────┘ │
│ ┌─Display Options─────────────────────────────────────────────────┐ │
│ │ Video Memory:   ○ Text    ○ Low Graphics   ◉ High Graphics       │ │
│ │ Monitor Ports:  ☐ Text    ☐ Low Graphics   ☐ High Graphics       │ │
│ │       ☐ Emulate Text Mode      ☐ Retain Video Memory             │ │
│ └─────────────────────────────────────────────────────────────────┘ │
│ ┌─Other Options───────────────────────────────────────────────────┐ │
│ │ ☒ Allow Fast Paste            ☐ Allow Close When Active          │ │
│ │ Reserve Shortcut Keys:  ☐ Alt+Tab  ☐ Alt+Esc    ☐ Ctrl+Esc       │ │
│ │                         ☐ PrtSc    ☐ Alt+PrtSc  ☐ Alt+Space      │ │
│ │                         ☐ Alt+Enter                              │ │
│ │ Application Shortcut Key:  ┌──────────────────────────┐          │ │
│ │                           │ None                     │          │ │
│ │                           └──────────────────────────┘          │ │
│ └─────────────────────────────────────────────────────────────────┘ │
└────────────────────────────────────────────────────────────────────┘
```

Advanced Options Dialog Box

The advanced features allow you to further customize the PIF to take advantage of the system resources and to target which resources go to what program. You should not consider changing these settings unless you have a very good understanding of how Windows uses the CPU, memory and video. Here, very briefly, is what they all mean.

The settings under **Multitasking Priority** determine how much processor time will be allocated to the program—you can set values for foreground and background operation. In each box you specify a value in the range 0 to 10,000; the default values are shown in the illustration. The values are only meaningful when compared to those of other applications running at the same time.

Memory Options control the amount of expanded (EMS) and Extended Memory Specification (XMS) memory that the program will be allowed to use. In 386 enhanced mode, Windows uses only extended memory, but it can simulate expanded memory for applications that use it. Very few applications use XMS memory, and so this setting should not need to be edited. The remaining options are technical settings that should not be adjusted unless you understand their consequences.

Display Options handle how Windows saves the application's screen display, in much the same way as it does using the standard PIF settings. The advanced options provide a greater control over video options.

Other Options let you disable specified Windows shortcut keys and allow Windows to paste text in a faster mode. If you check **Allow Close When Active**, you can shut down an MS-DOS application when it is running in a window or shrunk to an icon without having to terminate the MS-DOS program first. Don't choose this option if your application produces important work files that you'll want to save! The most useful option of all is the **Application Shortcut Key**, which lets you define a key combination that will switch directly to your MS-DOS program from anywhere within Windows.

PIF Editor Summary

The PIF Editor lets you create or modify Program Information Files (PIFs), which can then be used to run MS-DOS programs in the Windows environment.

There are two kinds of PIFs—standard and 386 enhanced. You have a different set of options available depending on which mode Windows is running in.

PIF Editor Keyboard Summary

Alt-Esc	Activate next program without using Task List.
Alt-F A	Save PIF to a new filename.
Alt-F N	Start a new Program Information File.

Alt-F O	Open a previously saved PIF.
Alt-F S	Save the PIF using the existing filename.
Alt-F X	Quit PIF Editor and return to Program Manager.
Alt-F4	Quit PIF Editor and return to Program Manager.
Alt-M 3	Switch to 386 enhanced mode PIF Editor.
Alt-M S	Switch to standard mode PIF Editor.
Alt-Spacebar C	Quit PIF Editor and return to Program Manager.
Alt-Spacebar M	Move icon or application window.
Alt-Spacebar N	Reduce window to an icon.
Alt-Spacebar R	Restore application window to its previous size and shape.
Alt-Spacebar S	Resize the current window.
Alt-Spacebar W	Switch programs using Task List.
Alt-Spacebar X	Maximize application window.
Ctrl-Esc	Switch programs using Task List.
F1	Activate Help system.

Recorder

The Recorder is brand new to Windows 3; it did not exist in previous Windows versions. The program allows you to record sequences of keystrokes and/or mouse clicks in *macros* that can be played back later. For example, suppose you want to run a program, load a specific file into that program, mark a block of data, open another program and copy the marked block into the second program. If you perform this sequence of actions often—every day, let's say—then it's worth your while to create a macro for the actions. The macro can then be run using either the menu or a combination of keystrokes, saving you time and making life much easier.

Macros are only worth creating if the sequence of actions is always going to be the same. If you want to perform the same sequence of actions as above but load a different file each time, a macro would most likely not save you any time and effort. It makes sense to use the Recorder only when the sequence of keystrokes and mouse actions is long and absolutely the same every time. One serious flaw in the Recorder is that you cannot edit a recorded macro; if you make a mistake while recording a long sequence of keystrokes and mouse clicks, or if you want to revise a macro you've already saved, your only option is to start from scratch.

To run Recorder, double click on its icon in the Program Manager—it resembles a video camera—or select the icon and press **Enter**. The Recorder window looks like those of most Windows applications, with a Control menu box, title bar, Minimize and Maximize buttons and a menu bar. Each Recorder file can contain an unlimited number of macros. When you load a Recorder file, the large space in the Recorder window will show a list of all the available macros.

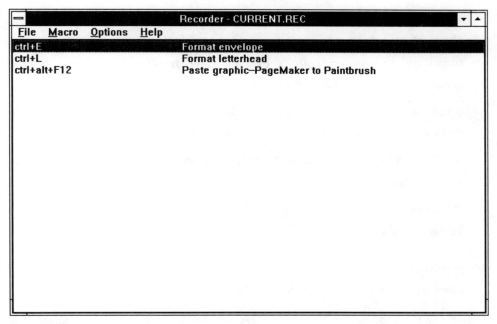

Recorder

The program provides three menus, plus Help. The **File** menu includes the usual commands—**New**, **Open**, **Save**, **Save As**, **Merge** and **Exit**. These perform the same functions as they do in other programs, so we needn't cover them here.

The **Macro** menu is the one that allows you to use macros. It contains the following commands:

Run executes the selected macro immediately.

Record lets you set some macro options and then begin recording a macro.

Delete removes the selected macro from the onscreen list.

Properties lets you change the name, description, shortcut keys or running conditions of a previously recorded macro.

The **Options** menu allows you to set which actions within the macro will be allowed. The menu contains four commands; the first three are toggles and the last brings up a dialog box.

Control+Break Checking allows you to suspend the macro if this command is turned on, which it normally is. Pressing **Ctrl-Break** or **Ctrl-C** will stop the recording or playing back of a macro.

Shortcut Keys allows you to assign a key combination to a macro so that the recorded sequence can be played back using those keys.

Minimize On Use shrinks the Recorder window to an icon every time you run a macro from it.

Preferences brings up a dialog box that allows you to set the defaults that will be presented every time you begin to record a macro.

Macro Tips

Here are some general guidelines to follow when recording macros.

1. Try to avoid using the mouse. Use keystrokes to access menu commands whenever possible. The Recorder is capable of including mouse actions in any macro you create, but it remembers the position of the mouse, not the command you were executing. For example, you might use the mouse to click on a menu while recording a macro in an application that is running maximized. If you then run the macro with the program running in a window, the menu bar is in a different position and the movement recorded in the macro will cause the mouse to point to somewhere other than the menu. This will bring up an error message and terminate the macro.

2. Work with a clear screen. Close down, or reduce to icons, any applications that will not be included in the macro.

3. Use macros only on the system they were created on. Trying to use the macro on another system—especially one with a different monitor and display adapter—will cause problems and possibly hangups.

Creating a Macro

To create a macro, start the Recorder and select **Record** from the **Macro** menu. This will bring up a dialog box that allows you to set your preferences for the macro.

Enter a name for the macro—you can use up to 40 characters, including spaces.

In the **Shortcut Key** text box, you can assign a key combination that will be used to run the macro. The keys will appear in the macro list. You do not have to use a shortcut key sequence if you would prefer to run the macro from the menu.

Macro Preferences

Playback tells the Recorder whether the macro you are creating is for a specific application or whether it can be applied to any program. You can replay the macro at the speed at which you recorded it; if you select **Fast**, the macro keystrokes will be executed as fast as the computer can operate.

Record Mouse allows you to include mouse actions in the macro.

Once you have set your preferences, select **Record** from the **Macro** menu. As long as the **Minimize On Use** option is turned on, Recorder will be reduced to an icon and will flash while it records your actions. When you have finished, click on the Recorder icon or press **Ctrl-Break** to bring up a dialog box that asks if you want to save the macro as it exists so far, continue recording or cancel the recording completely.

Select whichever option you wish. Pressing **Enter** accepts the first default choice. You can run the macro from the Recorder window or by using the hot keys you selected. The macro you just created is stored only in memory at this point; if you want to be able to use it again you must save it to a file before quitting Recorder.

Macro End Dialog Box

Recorder Summary

Recorder allows you to create macros—combinations of keystrokes and mouse actions that you can play back anytime you like.

Macros are most useful when the sequence of actions is long and absolutely the same each time.

Recorder Keyboard Summary

Alt-Esc	Activate next program without using Task List.
Alt-F A	Save the macro file to a new filename.
Alt-F M	Merge one macro file into another.
Alt-F N	Start a new Recorder file.
Alt-F O	Open a Recorder file.
Alt-F S	Save the macro file to the existing filename.
Alt-F X	Quit Recorder and return to Program Manager.
Alt-F4	Quit Recorder and return to Program Manager.
Alt-M C	Begin recording a macro.
Alt-M D	Delete a macro from the file.
Alt-M P	Show details of selected macro.
Alt-M R	Run the selected macro.
Alt-O C	Allow Ctrl-Break to interrupt macros.
Alt-O M	Minimize Recorder when playing back macros.
Alt-O P	Set new default preferences.
Alt-O S	Toggle use of shortcut keys.
Alt-Spacebar C	Quit Recorder and return to Program Manager.
Alt-Spacebar M	Move icon or application window.
Alt-Spacebar N	Reduce window to an icon.
Alt-Spacebar R	Restore window to its previous size and shape.
Alt-Spacebar S	Resize the current window.
Alt-Spacebar W	Switch programs using Task List.
Alt-Spacebar X	Maximize window.
Ctrl-Esc	Switch programs using Task List.
F1	Activate Help system.

Terminal

Terminal is a communications program that allows you to exchange information with other computer users by connecting your PC to theirs, either directly or over the telephone lines. With the help of communications software like Terminal, you can send electronic mail, dial up information services, exchange files and link up with mainframe systems. Like Windows Write, Terminal is not a full-featured or sophisticated program; if you're serious about communications, you'll want more powerful software. But for uncomplicated communications needs, Terminal will do just fine.

To use Terminal, you must have the necessary hardware. For communications over phone lines you need a modem; for direct PC-to-PC links, you need a special adapter called a null modem cable. In either case, you'll need a free serial port to make the connection and the person on the other end of the line needs similar hardware and a communications program. Once you've got that, you're all set. Boot up Windows and load the Terminal program.

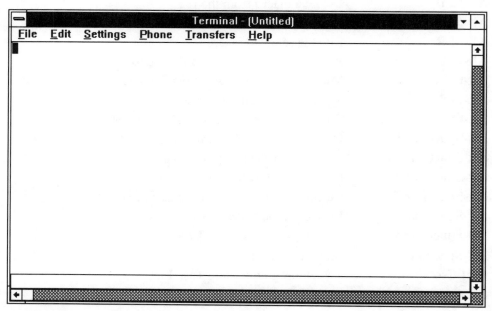

Terminal Main Screen

Window Layout

The window has the usual layout—Control menu box, title bar, Minimize and Maximize buttons and menu bar—but the bulk of the window, the *buffer area*, is blank.

We'll come to it in a minute or three. Terminal provides five menus, plus Help.

The **File** menu contains a group of familiar commands—**New, Open, Save, Save As** and **Exit,** plus **Printer Setup**—which work just as they do in other Windows applications.

The **Edit** menu provides **Copy** and **Paste**—but there is no **Cut** command. It also has the following:

> **Send** transmits the selected text to the remote computer.

> **Select All** allows you to select all the text in the buffer area in one operation.

> **Clear Buffer** deletes everything from the buffer area.

The **Settings** menu contains eleven commands. The first eight invoke dialog boxes, while the last three are toggles.

```
Phone Number...
Terminal Emulation...
Terminal Preferences...
Function Keys...
Text Transfers...
Binary Transfers...
Communications...
Modem Commands...
───────────────────
Printer Echo
Timer Mode
Show Function Keys
```

Settings Menu

Phone Number allows you to enter a number that the program will dial. You can separate the digits using hyphens or brackets—they will be ignored. However, each comma will cause a delay of two seconds during dialing. Thus, if you enter

9,,1,2125551212 the program will dial 9, wait four seconds, dial 1, wait 2 seconds, and then dial 2125551212.

Terminal Emulation allows you to select one of three terminal types. The emulation you select will affect how your computer system communicates with the remote computer.

Terminal Preferences determines how your system performs when you are connected to another computer. You can select options such as line wrap, the number of columns, the type of cursor, the font and language to be used and the number of lines for the buffer.

Function Keys allows you to define the function keys **F1** through **F8** so that they perform macro actions. You can use **Ctrl** and **Alt**, or both, in combination with the function keys for a total of 32 user-defined shortcut keys. The functions are already defined to some extent by Windows—for example, **F1** activates Help and **Alt-F4** quits an application—and so you should be careful about any redefining you do.

Text Transfers allows you to set the options to use when sending and receiving text. **Binary Transfers** lets you choose between two protocols, **XModem/CRC** and **Kermit**, to use when transferring binary files like formatted documents and programs.

Communications sets the communications parameters—baud rate, data bits, stop bits, parity, and the like. You must set these before you begin a file transfer.

Modem Commands allows you to specify the command strings that work with your modem. If your modem emulates one of several popular models, you can click on an option button to enter these settings automatically.

Printer Echo is a toggle that allows you to send any incoming information to the printer and the screen.

Timer Mode is another toggle that displays elapsed time at the lower right-hand corner of the Terminal window.

Show Function Keys displays your key mappings along the bottom of the Terminal window.

The **Phone** menu contains two commands: **Dial** transmits the last phone number you specified to the modem; **Hangup** sends the commands to disconnect from the remote system.

The **Transfers** menu controls the sending and receiving of binary and text files. During transfers, commands on this menu let you pause and resume sending or receiving.

<u>S</u>end Text File...
<u>R</u>eceive Text File...
<u>V</u>iew Text File...
Send <u>B</u>inary File...
Receive Binary <u>F</u>ile...
<u>P</u>ause
R<u>e</u>sume
S<u>t</u>op

Transfers Menu

Terminal Summary

Terminal is a communications program that allows you to link your computer with another, either over telephone lines or directly.

Before you can use the program, you must have a modem or a null modem cable connected to your system and properly configured.

Terminal Keyboard Summary

Alt-E A	Select all the text in the buffer.
Alt-E C	Copy selected text to Clipboard.
Alt-E E	Clear all buffer contents.
Alt-E N	Send selected text.
Alt-E P	Paste Clipboard contents into file.
Alt-Esc	Activate next program without using Task List.
Alt-F A	Save the current file to a new filename.
Alt-F N	Start a new file.
Alt-F O	Load a previously saved file into the buffer.
Alt-F R	Select and setup the printer to be used.
Alt-F S	Save the current file to the filename shown on the title bar.
Alt-F X	Quit Terminal and return to Program Manager.
Alt-F4	Quit Terminal and return to Program Manager.
Alt-P D	Dial programmed number.
Alt-P H	Cease dialing.
Alt-S B	Set binary transfer protocol.
Alt-S C	Set communications options.
Alt-S D	Customize modem settings.
Alt-S E	Toggle printer echo.
Alt-S K	Show function keys.
Alt-S N	Open Phone Number dialog box.
Alt-S P	Set Terminal preferences.
Alt-S T	Pop up Terminal Emulation dialog box.
Alt-S T	Toggle delayed timer activation.
Alt-S X	Set text transfer protocol.
Alt-Spacebar C	Quit Terminal and return to Program Manager.
Alt-Spacebar M	Move icon or application window.
Alt-Spacebar N	Reduce window to an icon.
Alt-Spacebar R	Restore window to its previous size and shape.
Alt-Spacebar S	Resize application window.

Alt-Spacebar W	Switch programs using Task List.
Alt-Spacebar X	Maximize window.
Alt-T B	Send binary file.
Alt-T E	Resume after pause.
Alt-T F	Receive binary file.
Alt-T O	Cancel sending or receiving.
Alt-T P	Pause sending or receiving.
Alt-T R	Receive text file.
Alt-T S	Send text file.
Alt-T V	View text file.
Ctrl-Esc	Switch programs using Task List.
Ctrl-Ins	Copy selected text to the Clipboard.
Ctrl-Shift-Ins	Send selected text.
F1	Activate Help system.
Shift-Ins	Paste Clipboard contents into file.

CHAPTER 16

Problems in Windows

What Problems?

Considering how many years Windows 3 was in development and testing, it's not surprising that there are so few real problems with the program. The program is definitely a masterpiece, and Microsoft has gone to considerable pains to make it as error free as possible. As with all major software releases, there are a few minor teething troubles, but overall the program is remarkably bug free. Most of the problems you will encounter, in fact, are not the fault of Windows at all; more often, they are hardware problems caused by BIOS faults in systems that are not fully compliant with the IBM standard. The incompatibility between large hard disks and SMARTDRV.SYS falls into this category. It hardly seems fair to lay the blame for those problems at Microsoft's door.

The major problem that you will encounter with Windows 3 is lack of memory. Although the program can use expanded memory, it is really designed to make use of as much extended memory as you can provide—and of course it needs the maximum conventional memory as well. A 386-based system with 4 MB of RAM can run Windows 3 very capably; with 8 MB, you should have no problems at all.

Earlier Versions

To use any program that was designed and written for Windows/286 or Windows/386 version 2.*xx,* you should start Windows 3 in real mode. If you load an old Windows program in standard or 386 enhanced mode, strange things can happen, especially to the screen display. When you try to use an incompatible Windows program with Windows 3, you will see a message box warning you of the consequences. All Windows 3 programs carry an identifying mark within the code that allows Windows 3 to bypass this message and start right up.

Using older Windows software in standard or 386 enhanced mode can have the following unpleasant consequences:

The screen display may become corrupted. This is the most likely and least serious problem you're likely to encounter. You may see unwanted characters along the title bar; the screen may not be properly refreshed; or the colors may be incorrect.

Without warning Windows may crash and dump you unceremoniously back at the system prompt. If this happens, you have probably encountered an interrupt clash: The two programs—your application and Windows itself—both tried to use the same system resource at the same time. Whenever this occurs, you are likely to find unassigned clusters on your hard disk. Use **CHKDSK** or a utility like Norton Disk Doctor to repair the damage. In general, this sort of problem will not harm your system irreparably.

The machine may hang completely and fail to respond to input from the keyboard. The only way out is to perform a cold boot by pressing the reset button or the on/off switch. Any work that was in progress and hadn't been saved prior to the crash is gone forever. Again, a utility like **CHKDSK** is likely to reveal a few lost clusters on your hard disk.

The moral of the story: If you use older Windows software, run Windows 3 in real mode only. A better strategy, of course, is to upgrade the application to a Windows 3 version!

MS-DOS Programs

Windows 3 handles MS-DOS programs better than any previous version of Windows, by far—but that doesn't mean you won't encounter problems. Some of the conflicts you might run into include the following:

The system may hang without warning. This happened a number of times in the course of writing this book. Using WordStar 6 from within Windows, the machine hung up completely on no less than a dozen occasions. Every time it did so, WordStar was in the process of doing a spelling check, which uses a lot of memory. Fortunately, I have learned to save my work often (especially before running the spell checker!) and so the hangup was annoying but not disastrous. The problem only occurred on the Laser 386, which leads me to suspect that the fault is hardware-related.

Many MS-DOS programs give you the capability to "shell out" to the system prompt. If you drop out to the DOS prompt from an MS-DOS application running within Windows, though, you may not be able to return to Windows. For example, on more than one occasion I switched to WordStar's DOS window while running the program under Windows 3, and then found myself unable to get back. The only answer when this occurred was to reboot the machine.

Terminate-and-stay-resident (TSR) programs—which are intended to pop up over MS-DOS programs—do not work under Windows and in fact can freeze your system. These memory-resident programs also gobble up precious RAM that Windows needs to run properly. If you have a favorite TSR program, you can probably run it in its own DOS window. If that's impossible, you'll have to decide which is more useful: Windows 3 or your TSR programs.

You may run short of memory. Some MS-DOS programs will be unable to perform certain actions—or may not load at all—if your system is short of conventional memory. And all the extended memory in the world won't help. You can try to close down any applications that you have running, either as a window or as an icon, in the hope that this will free enough RAM for your needs. If the problem persists, you can try reconfiguring your system with fewer device drivers to see if that give you enough extra memory. If those steps fail, you will have to run the program from the system prompt instead of the Windows environment.

In 386 enhanced mode only, you may find that everything onscreen suddenly vanishes. This can be caused when an MS-DOS program suddenly switches video modes but its PIF only specifies one type of display. You can fix this problem by terminating the MS-DOS program and then editing the Program Information File using the PIF Editor.

Improving Performance

There are a number of things you can do to make Windows 3 run faster and better, starting with increasing or enhancing your system resources. Most of these tips have already been covered in this book, but here is a brief summary of them and a few others.

Extra RAM

It is well worth your while to increase the amount of extended memory in your system to as much as you can afford. The extra RAM will let you load more applications and help them all run faster. If you have more than 8 MB of RAM, you might want to set up a large RAM disk for storing temporary files.

Free Memory

Disable or remove any TSR programs that you would normally use if you want to run Windows 3 for any length of time. Look carefully at your CONFIG.SYS and AUTOEXEC.BAT files and see what you can remove. If you're using the ANSI.SYS driver, for example, can you do without it? Conventional memory is the most precious resource of all when running Windows 3.

Tidy Disk

Before installing Windows 3 you should ensure that all the files on your hard disk are contiguous. A utility program like Norton Speed Disk or PC Tools Compress can reorganize your hard disk quickly and efficiently. Windows 3 is constantly loading files from disk whenever you run it; it will load files noticeably faster when the files are contiguous. You should make a habit of backing up and compressing your hard disk regularly.

Free Disk Capacity

Windows 3 will generate a number of temporary files every time it runs, not counting those files that you create yourself and then store on the disk. It is therefore in your interests to have as much free space as possible on your hard drive. Ideally, you want at least 2 MB free, although you can get by with half this amount. Archive rarely used files, delete unwanted files or remove programs and data you no longer use or need—how you free up disk space is up to you.

Swap File

In 386 enhanced mode, Windows 3 runs faster and more efficiently if you create a permanent swap file (although according to Microsoft the performance edge is very small). The swap file is not vital, because Windows can create a temporary one as necessary. The problem with a permanent swap file is that it takes up room on your disk even when Windows is not running, and disk space tends to be at a premium on any system.

By the way, don't set up a permanent swap file if you have Windows installed on a Novell NetWare file server. A minor incompatibility between Windows 3 and NetWare will cause all the network workstations to try to access the same swap file. If your system is set up in this fashion, let Windows create temporary swap files as necessary. This problem doesn't exist if you're running Windows on your local hard disk and are simply connected to a Novell network.

RAM Disks

A RAM disk is a great deal faster than even the fastest hard disk, and if you have the memory available it is worth creating one to use with Windows 3. Use the RAM disk as storage for temporary files by including the line **SET TEMP=[drive]** in your AUTOEXEC.BAT. This will greatly enhance Windows' performance. Unfortunately, such a RAM disk must be at least 2 MB in size (preferably more) to work effectively, and you still need to devote sizable amounts of memory to Windows. A RAM disk doesn't really make sense until you've upgraded your system to 8 MB or more. We're back to memory again!

Saving all your work to the RAM disk is not a wise idea under Windows, because in the event of a system crash you will lose the contents of RAM disk completely. The possibility of losing a day's work far outweighs the advantages that might be gained from using the RAM disk to store files.

Appendix
ANSI Character Set

The Windows ANSI character set is similar to but different from the IBM ASCII characters. A full list of the characters is shown on the following pages. To use any of the characters that are not available from the standard keyboard, press and hold **Alt** while typing **0** (zero), followed by the three-digit number of the character you require. You must use the numeric keypad rather than the standard number keys at the top of the keyboard. If you omit the leading 0, you will get the ASCII character for that code instead of the ANSI one. Be warned: The majority of printers do not support either the ANSI character set or the IBM extended ASCII set, and so your printed document is likely to be different from the onscreen one.

001	▮	002		003	▮	004	▮	005	▮	006	▮
007	▮	008	▮	009		010		011		012	
013		014	▮	015	▮	016	▮	017	▮	018	▮
019	▮	020	▮	021		022	▮	023	▮	024	▮
025	▮	026	▮	027	▮	028	▮	029	▮	030	▮
031		032		033	!	034	"	035	#	036	$
037	%	038	&	039	'	040	(	041	)	042	*
043	+	044	,	045	-	046	.	047	/	048	0
049	1	050	2	051	3	052	4	053	5	054	6
055	7	056	8	057	9	058	:	059	;	060	<
061	=	062	>	063	?	064	@	065	A	066	B
067	C	068	D	069	E	070	F	071	G	072	H
073	I	074	J	075	K	076	L	077	M	078	N
O79	O	080	P	081	Q	082	R	083	S	084	T
085	U	086	V	087	W	088	X	089	Y	090	Z
091	[	092	\	093	]	094	^	095	_	096	`
097	a	098	b	099	c	100	d	101	e	102	y
103	g	104	h	105	i	106	j	107	k	108	l
109	m	110	n	111	o	112	p	113	q	114	r
115	s	116	t	117	u	118	v	119	w	120	x
121	y	122	z	123	{	124			125	}	126	~

127	▮	128	▮	129	▮	130		131	▮	132	▮
133	▮	134	▮	135	▮	136	▮	137	▮	138	▮
139	▮	140	▮	141	▮	142	▮	143	▮	144	▮
145	´	146	´	147	▮	148	▮	149	▮	150	▮
151	▮	152	▮	153	▮	154	▮	155	▮	156	▮
157	▮	158	▮	159	▮	160		161	¡	162	¢
163	£	164	¤	165	¥	166	¦	167	§	168	¨
169	©	170	ª	171	«	172	¬	173		174	®
175	¯	176	°	177	±	178	²	179	³	180	´
181	µ	182		183	·	184	¸	185	¹	186	º
187	»	188	¼	189	½	190	¾	191	¿	192	À
193	Á	194	Â	195	Ã	196	Ä	197	Å	198	Æ
199	Ç	200	È	201	É	202	Ê	203	Ë	204	Ì
205	Í	206	Î	207	Ï	208	Ð	209	Ñ	210	Ò
211	Ó	212	Ô	213	Õ	214	Ö	215	×	216	
217	Ù	218	Ú	219	Û	220	Ü	221	Ý	222	Þ
223	ß	224	à	225	á	226	â	227	ã	228	ä
229	å	230	æ	231	ç	232	è	233	é	234	ê
235	ë	236	ì	237	í	238	î	239	ï	240	ð
241	ñ	242	ò	243	ê	244	ô	245	õ	246	ö
247	÷	248	ø	249	ù	250	ú	251	û	252	ü

Glossary

386 enhanced mode

　　　　See Windows modes.

Active

　　　　The selected icon or window to which the next mouse or keyboard action will apply is said to be active. When an icon has been selected its title appears in inverse video. When a window is selected, its title bar changes to the color that was defined using the Control Panel utility.

ANSI character

　　　　See Character set.

Application program

　　　　Any program that does a specific task, such as word processing. Windows applications are written to take advantage of the graphical features in the Windows environment, whereas most non-Windows applications can run under Windows but do not adhere to the Windows interface.

Application window

　　　　See Window.

Archive attribute

　　　　See Attributes.

ASCII character set

　　　　See Character set.

Associate

Windows allows you to link a file extension to a particular application. When a file extension and program name are associated in this way, the program can be invoked by double clicking on a filename bearing the extension.

Attributes

Additional information about a file's status, stored with the filename. There are four possible attributes: archive, read-only, hidden and system.

The archive attribute determines whether a file will be backed up by DOS. If the archive attribute is set, the file will be backed up by the MS-DOS BACKUP command. If the archive attribute is disabled, the file will not be backed up. The archive attribute is also used by most backup utility programs. The attribute can be changed using the MS-DOS ATTRIB command.

A read-only file cannot be modified or deleted, although it may be backed up if its archive attribute is set. The attribute can be changed using the MS-DOS ATTRIB command.

Hidden files cannot be seen, though they are still present and can be used. This attribute cannot be changed from MS-DOS; however, the Windows File Manager and a number of third-party utilities allow you to modify this attribute.

System files are special files created by DOS and essential for the functioning of the operating system. This attribute, too, can be changed by a utility program or by the Windows File Manager but not from MS-DOS.

Background

The area of the screen that appears behind an application window.

Batch file

An ASCII text file that consists of a sequence of MS-DOS commands. All batch files must have the extension .BAT and can be executed by typing the filename. MS-DOS executes the commands in a batch file just as if you had typed them from the system prompt. Batch files can be executed from within Windows like any executable program.

Binary file

A file that contains characters in computer-readable, as opposed to human-readable, form.

Bit

A contraction for binary digit—a 1 or 0. The smallest possible unit with which the computer can work.

Bitmap

A graphic image composed of a series of dots. Bitmaps are typically created in paint programs and can be imported directly into Page-Maker and other desktop publishing programs.

Boot

To load or reload the disk operating system into the computer.

Buffer

A block of computer memory that is used as temporary storage to hold data when reading from or writing to a disk. The number of buffers to be used is set in the CONFIG.SYS file and can be any value from 2 to 255. Each disk buffer takes up 512 bytes of space in the DOS environment.

Byte

Normally, a collection of 8 bits, which is the minimum space required to define a single character. Disks and memory are typically measured in bytes.

Cascade

To arrange open windows so that they overlap each other yet allow each title bar to remain visible.

CGA

See Video modes.

Character set

A collection of characters that make up a single group. The American Standard Code for Information Interchange (ASCII) character set contains 128 symbols, letters and numbers, which are common to all PCs. The American National Standards Institute (ANSI) character set, also known as the extended ASCII character set, contains an additional 128 characters.

Characters per inch

See Pitch.

Characters per second

The speed with which an impact printer can operate. Because the printer is mechanically operated, there is a limit to the number of characters that can be produced within a given time.

Check box

A small box within a dialog box that allows you to select an option.

Click

See Mouse.

Clipboard

The Windows program that allows you to transfer data from one document or program to another. The Clipboard is typically activated via an application's Edit menu.

COM port

See Port.

Command

In MS-DOS, an instruction to the operating system to carry out a specific operation or execute a program. In Windows, commands are typically included in menus.

Control menu

See Window elements.

Conventional memory

See Memory.

Coprocessor

An additional chip that can be inserted into the computer and is designed specifically to handle mathematical functions. A coprocessor is only useful with math-intensive applications like spreadsheets and drafting programs.

Copy

To duplicate a selected block of data and place it into the Clipboard, ready to be transferred to another document or application.

Cursor

The point on the screen where the keyboard or mouse interacts with an application or the Windows environment. Within Windows the cursor can appear as an arrowhead, a vertical line or another shape, depending on the application.

Cursor keys

The four arrow keys that control the movement of the cursor. One set of cursor keys is located on the numeric keypad; some keyboard models contain dedicated keys as well.

Cut

To delete a selected block of data and place a copy of it into the Clipboard.

Data file

The result of work in an application program. Any file created by that application is a data file. Within Windows, data files are also known as documents.

Default

A choice, as in a dialog box, that is selected as the first available option. In many programs the default settings can be changed.

Desktop

The Windows background, where icons and windows appear. Also, a utility program within the Control Panel that allows you to define a pattern for the background.

Dialog box

A box that allows the user to exchange information with Windows. Dialog boxes allow users to choose options, set default conditions, pick items from lists and respond to warning messages.

Directory

A group of files and subdirectories on a hard disk or a floppy disk. The hierarchical directory structure used by MS-DOS to organize files can be viewed as a Tree within the Windows File Manager.

Disk

A magnetic material used to store and retrieve data. MS-DOS and Windows read from and write to hard disk drives, floppy disk drives, network disk drives and CD-ROM drives. MS-DOS can simulate disk storage in memory using a device driver that creates a virtual disk, or RAM disk.

Disk drives

The device that reads data from and writes to a disk. By default, MS-DOS recognizes only five drives on a system unless you increase this number using the LASTDRIVE command in your CONFIG.SYS file. The first (bootable) floppy drive is defined as drive A:, and the primary partition on a hard disk is defined as drive C:.

Document window

See Window.

Double click

See Mouse.

Drag

See Mouse.

EGA

See Video modes.

EMS Memory

See Memory.

EPT Port

See Port.

Expanded Memory

See Memory.

Extended Memory

See Memory.

Extension

The three-character suffix of a filename. Normally, an extension is used to identify a type of file; for example, .DOC and .TXT are often applied to text or formatted word-processing files.

File

A collection of instructions or information that the computer can operate with. The former are known as applications or programs, while the latter are called data files or documents. An application instructs the computer to do a specific kind of work. Data files represent the work created by an application and may take one of several forms: ASCII files contain alphanumeric characters only and can be translated between applications relatively easily. Formatted text files contain ASCII data as well as control codes that can only be interpreted by the application that produced them. Graphic files generally contain no ASCII characters whatsoever and can normally be viewed only by the program that created them or by a program that can interpret the specific file format.

Filename

Under MS-DOS, a filename can include up to 8 characters, plus a period and a three-character extension. You may use any letter (A-Z) or number (0-9) plus the following symbols: $ % ' - @ { } ~ ` ! # ( ) &. Blank spaces cannot be used in a DOS filename. A number of words are reserved by MS-DOS for its own purposes and therefore cannot be used for naming files. The reserved words are aux, clock$, com, con, lpt, lst, nul and prn. Windows follows all MS-DOS filename rules.

Font

> The set of identical characters within a typeface. A font often comes in different sizes and weights—for example, italic, bold and condensed.

Footer

> Text that appears at the bottom of a printed page.

Foreground

> The active window.

Formatting

> The process of making a disk usable by a computer. During the formatting process the computer lays down a series of tracks and sectors on the disk surface.

Group

> In Program Manager, a collection of programs. Windows creates five groups during the initial Setup process. Groups can be created, deleted and changed by the user.

Header

> Text that appears at the top of a printed page.

Hidden file

> See Attributes.

Highlight

> To select an object or a block of text. In Windows, a highlighted object will be acted upon by the next command.

Icon

> A graphical representation of an element used in Windows—for example, a disk drive, a program or a document.

Inactive window

A window that is open but is not currently being used. Normally, the title bar of an inactive window is a different color than that of an active window.

Kilobyte

An amount equal to 210 (1,024) bytes, usually written as 1 KB.

List box

A dialog box containing a list of items.

Logical drive

A partition on a hard drive. Releases of MS-DOS prior to version 4.0 limited the size of a hard disk partition to 32 MB or less. Even though it is part of the same physical drive, each partition is treated as a separate logical drive and is accordingly assigned its own drive designator letter. With a hard drive of, say, 70 MB, you would divide it into three logical drives, C:, D: and E:. A number of third-party programs allow you to create large hard-disk partitions. In addition, MS-DOS 4.0 removes the need to partition a drive in this way, although a case can still be made for such subdivision. For instance, you could place all your text-based programs on one logical drive, all your graphic applications on another and all your data files on a third. This structure allows you to back up your data files without having to back up your program files at the same time.

LPT port

See Port.

Macro

A series of recorded keystrokes and mouse actions that can be played back at a later time. Windows includes an accessory called the Recorder that allows you to create macros anywhere in Windows.

Maximize button

See Window elements.

Megabyte

An amount equal to 210 (1,024) kilobytes, usually written as 1 MB.

Memory

The temporary storage area where data is held and manipulated while it is being used by the computer. Random access memory (RAM) is used to run programs and perform essential operating functions. There are several kinds of RAM available in different PCs:

Conventional memory is the first 640 KB of RAM. Ordinary MS-DOS programs can access only this block of memory.

The high memory area is the 64 KB block of RAM just above 640 KB. Windows supplies a device driver called HIMEM.SYS that allows the program to use this block of memory.

Extended memory is memory that exists over and above the 640 KB limit imposed by MS-DOS. In standard mode and 386 enhanced mode, Windows can use this memory to run applications. Windows also supports a special form of extended memory, called XMS memory, for certain MS-DOS applications.

Expanded memory (also called EMS memory) is additional memory that can be addressed through the use of a special device driver. Some MS-DOS programs, such as Lotus 1-2-3, use expanded memory. In standard or 386 enhanced mode, Windows 3 will simulate expanded memory out of extended memory. Windows can also use expanded memory directly when running in real mode.

Read-only memory (ROM) is stored on computer chips and typically contains certain unchanging routines that the computer must have to operate correctly, such as the Power-On Self-Test (POST) procedure that the PC performs every time it's started up.

Menu

A list of Windows commands. Menus can be accessed either by clicking on them or by pressing Alt and the initial letter of the menu required.

Menu bar

See Window elements.

Minimize button

See Window elements.

Mouse

A pointing device that communicates instructions to Windows. The mouse pointer is the arrow-shaped cursor that defines the area of the screen on which the mouse will act. There are four basic mouse actions:

To point to an item is to move the mouse pointer until it sits directly on the object or area you want to select.

To click is to press a mouse button (usually the left button) once and then release it. Clicking on an object typically selects an object or executes a menu command.

You double click on an object by pressing a mouse button (usually the left button) twice in rapid succession without moving the mouse in the process. Double clicking usually executes an action.

You can drag an object (such as an icon or a window) by clicking on the object and then, while still holding down the mouse button, moving it or part of it around the screen.

Network

A number of computers connected in such a way that they can share resources and information.

Parallel port

See Port.

Parameter

A condition added to a command. Parameters change the way in which the command operates.

Paste

To copy the contents of the Clipboard into another program at the current cursor position.

PIF

Acronym for Program Information File. PIFs contain essential information that Windows uses to run an MS-DOS application.

Pitch

The number of characters per inch that can be printed along one line. This method is used to measure font size, especially with dot-matrix and daisy-wheel printers. The higher the pitch value, the smaller the characters, because you are printing more characters into the same space.

Pixel

The smallest part of the screen that can be individually illuminated. Also called picture elements or pels.

Point

A unit of measurement equal to 1/72 of an inch. Used to measure font size with high-resolution output devices, such as laser printers, it refers to the height of a character block. The higher the point value, the larger the characters.

Pointer

See Mouse.

Port

A connection on the computer through which information can be sent and received.

Serial ports (also called COM ports) send information one bit at a time. Modems are commonly connected to serial ports. Windows allows up to four serial ports, COM1 through COM4.

Parallel ports send information in segments rather than one bit at a time. Printers are often connected to this type of port. Windows can address three parallel ports, LPT1 through LPT3.

An EPT port requires an add-on card to be fitted to the computer. It is used by only a very limited number of peripherals.

Print

To send data to a peripheral device that will produce a hard copy of the data—on paper or film, for example.

Print queue

A list of files that are awaiting printing. Windows includes a utility called Print Manager that intercepts print jobs and processes them in the background.

Printer

A peripheral device that produces hard copy of data.

Printer driver

A file that supplies an application program, such as Windows, with information about the printer and how to use it.

Protected mode

The operating mode of a computer that allows it to address extended memory. Available only on 80286 and later chips.

RAM

See Memory.

Read-only file

See Attributes.

Real mode

See Windows modes.

Restore button

See Window elements.

ROM

See Memory.

Root directory

The highest directory level on a disk. The root directory is created whenever you format the disk.

Scroll

To move through a list or a block of text that is larger than the current window or screen.

Scroll bars

See Window elements.

Serial port

See Port.

Standard mode

See Windows modes.

Swap file

A special file created for use only when Windows is running in 386 enhanced mode. It allows Windows to turn disk space into virtual memory, which can be used when the system runs low on actual memory. You can create a permanent swap file, which exists on your hard disk until you remove it, or you can allow Windows to create temporary swap files as necessary.

System files

See Attributes.

Text box

The area within a dialog box where you supply free-form text for Windows to work with.

Tile

To display windows in such a way that each window occupies roughly the same amount of screen area without any overlapping.

Title bar

See Window elements.

VGA

See Video modes.

Video modes

Windows supports a variety of video displays and adapter cards. The three most common color video modes are:

Color Graphics Adaptor (CGA). Thankfully, these low-quality color monitors and adapters are becoming fairly rare—they tend to be rather hard on the eyes. A CGA system can display color graphics at a resolution of 320 by 200 pixels, but you are limited to four very poor colors at one time. In monochrome mode, a CGA display can use gray scales to increase the resolution to a more acceptable 640 by 200 pixels. This configuration is popular on some laptop computers.

Enhanced Graphics Adapter (EGA). An older, but still acceptable video standard, EGA configurations allow you to display 16 colors simultaneously at a resolution of 640 by 350 pixels. Running the monitor in monochrome mode will allow you a resolution of 720 pixels by 350 and 16 gray scales.

Video Graphics Array (VGA). This is the current standard for 286 and 386 PCs. The VGA monitor will allow you to emulate EGA and CGA modes, but its standard VGA resolution is a much sharper 640 by 480 pixels using up to 16 colors. You can switch a VGA display to produce a resolution of 320 pixels by 200 and then use up to 64 colors at once. In monochrome mode you are limited to 64 gray scales. Many manufacturers now produce Super VGA boards that, when paired with a multifrequency monitor, allow you to display graphics at 1024 by 768 pixels with up to 256 simultaneous colors.

Virtual mode

The ability of an Intel 80386, 80386SX or 80486 chip to behave as if it were a number of distinct 8086 machines. In such a system, applications can run simultaneously, allowing true concurrent multitasking.

Wallpaper

A bitmap graphic used to substitute a picture for the background.

Wild-card characters

A wild card is a character that can be used to replace any other character or sequence of characters when used in conjunction with certain MS-DOS commands, such as COPY or DEL. ? can be used to replace any single character. The second wild-card character, *, can be used to replace any sequence of characters.

Window

A rectangular area of the screen that is used to contain a program or a document. An application window contains a program and can be reduced to an icon at the bottom of the screen. A document window is contained completely within an application window; some applications allow multiple document windows to be open at one time.

Window elements

Virtually all windows, application and document, contain the following common elements:

The title bar is the top line on any window. It contains the Control menu, which allows you to move, resize, close, shrink and restore the window. The title of the program and/or the current filename appear in the title bar. In the top right corner of most windows are the Minimize button and Maximize button, which allow the window to be shrunk to an icon or expanded to fill the entire screen. When the window is maximized, the Maximize button changes to a Restore button, indicated by a two-headed arrow.

The menu bar is the second line on most Windows applications. It contains a list of the available menus and their associated keywords.

When there is more data than can be displayed onscreen at any one time, scroll bars appear along the bottom and the right-hand side of a window. These bars allow you to page through the contents of the window.

Windows modes

Each time you start Windows, you have a choice of three modes in which to run. The most significant limiting factor is the processor in your system, followed closely by the amount of free memory.

Real mode is the only mode available when using Windows 3 on a computer that has less than 1 MB of free RAM. This is also the mode that provides compatibility for applications that were written for older versions of Windows.

Standard mode is the normal mode in which Windows will run. You must have at least 1 MB of free RAM and a 286 processor or higher to use this mode. In Standard mode, Windows can access extended memory directly to let you switch between Windows applications and MS-DOS programs.

386 enhanced mode allows Windows 3 to use extended memory and virtual memory to take advantage of the sophisticated memory management capabilities of the 80386 and 80386SX microprocessors. Using this mode, the program can multitask Windows and MS-DOS applications and run MS-DOS applications in a window.

Index

386 Enhanced options, 98, 146–148
in PIFs, 346–349

A

ANSI character set, 369, 376
ANSI file format, 258
ASCII character set, 369, 376
ASCII text file, 258, 326
AUTOEXEC.BAT, editing in Notepad, 326
Advanced PIF options, 348–349
Alarms, in Calendar, 281–282, 285–287
Aldus PageMaker, 65
Allen, Paul, 3
Application window, defined, 27
Application workspace, 30
Applications, 373
    defined, 11
    installing using Windows Setup, 23–25
    loading automatically, 333
    running automatically, 333
Arranging icons, using Task List, 213
Associate command, in File Manager, 167,
    184–185, 335, 374
Auto Arrange, Program Manager option, 87
Autodial, in Cardfile, 297

B

BMP files, 205, 234
Background, 375
Batch file, 375
Bitmap, 375
Boot, defined, 11, 375
Border, 28, 126
Buffer, 375
Byte, 376

C

CHKDSK, 364
CONFIG.SYS, editing in Notepad, 326
Calculator, 271–277
    and Clipboard, 274
    in Program Manager Accessories
        Group, 64
    operators, 272–273
    Scientific, 275
Calendar, 277–291
    Alarm menu, 281–282
    Day View, 278
    Edit menu, 280–281
    File menu, 280
    in Program Manager Accessories
        Group, 64
    marking dates, 281, 283–284
    Month View, 279
    print options, 288–289
    setting alarms, 285–287
Cardfile, 291–305
    adding or deleting a card, 296
    Card menu, 296–297
    duplicating a card, 296–297
    File menu, 293–295
    in Program Manager Accessories
        Group, 64
    print options, 301–303
    Search menu, 297
    View menu, 295
Cascading windows, 59–60, 376
    in File Manager, 174
    in Program Manager, 88
    using Task List, 213
Check box, defined, 32–33, 376

Clipboard, 205–211, 377
    in Program Manager Main Group, 63
    pasting to MS-DOS applications, 209–210
Clock, 64, 305
Color schemes, 103–110
Colors
    changing in Paintbrush, 224
    in WIN.INI, 337
    setting in Control Panel, 100–110
Command button, defined, 32
Confirmation options, in File Manager, 173
Control Panel, in Program Manager Main Group, 63, 97–148
Control menu, 28–29, 57–58, 89–90
Copy, defined, 11
Copy Diskette, in File Manager, 169
Copying a screen, using Clipboard, 207–209
Copying files, in File Manager, 167, 174–181
Corel Draw, 65, 217
Cursor Blink Rate, setting in Control Panel, 121, 125

D
DMDRV.BIN, incompatibility with SMARTDRV.SYS, 16–17
DOS Prompt, running in Windows, 63, 214–215
Date/Time, setting in Control Panel, 98, 145
Deleting files, in File Manager, 167, 181–182
Desktop, 378
    setting in Control Panel, 97, 120–125
Dialog box, 378
    defined, 31
    elements of, 32–33
Directory Tree, 160, 161–165, 170–172, 174, 378
    pruning and grafting directories, 191

Directory
    create in File Manager, 168
    prune and graft, 191
Disk Manager, incompatibility with SMARTDRV.SYS, 16–17
Display, adding, 150–151
Document window, defined, 27
Draw programs, defined, 217
Drawing boxes and circles, in Paintbrush, 228
Drawing lines, in Paintbrush, 225–227
Drop-down list box, defined, 33

E
Emulations, printer, 129–130, 202

F
File Attributes, 168, 185–187, 374
    changing in File Manager, 186–187
File Manager, 63, 159–194
    confirmation options, 173
    copying files, 167
    deleting files, 167
    Disk menu, 168–169
    File menu, 166–167
    moving files, 167
    Options menu, 173
    renaming files, 167
    sorting files, 172
    Tree menu, 170
    View menu, 171–172
    Window menu, 174
Filenames, legal, 380
Fonts, 381
    adding and removing via Control Panel, 111–116
    defined, 111
    in WIN.INI, 336
    raster, 113
    setting in Control Panel, 97
    vector, 113

Format Diskette, in File Manager, 169, 187–189
Function keys, redefining in Terminal, 358

G
Gates, Bill, 3
Group, 63, 381
 Accessories, 64
 adding program items, 72–79
 and .GRP files, 67
 creating, 80–85
 defined, 11–12
 deleting, 85
 deleting program items, 79–80
 Games, 65
 Main, 63
 moving program items between, 67–71
 Non-Windows Applications, 66
 Windows Applications, 65

H
HIMEM.SYS, 20
Hard disk
 compressing, 25, 366, 41
 defined, 12
 partitions, 160
Hard disks, incompatibility with SMARTDRV.SYS, 16–17
Help, 91–93
Hewlett-Packard LaserJet Series II, 127, 135, 195
Hue, 108

I
Icon, 381
 adjusting spacing, 121, 125–126
 arranging in Program Manager, 88–91
 defined, 12
 types of icons defined, 34

International options
 in WIN.INI, 335
 setting in Control Panel, 98, 138–145

K
Keyboard, 9
 installing using Windows Setup, 151–152
Keyboard speed, 98
 setting in Control Panel, 145

L
List box, defined, 33
Logging files, in Notepad, 338
Logical drive, 160, 382
Luminosity, 108

M
MS-DOS, 3
 defined, 12
 programs, defined, 12
MS-DOS Executive, 159
Macro, 350, 382
Macros, recording, 351–354
Maximize button, 30
Memory, 383–384
Memory requirements, specifying in PIFs, 344–345, 346–347
Menu
 defined, 12
 using, 34–35
Menu bar, 30
Microsoft, 3
Microsoft Word format, in Write, 258
Minimize button, 30
Minimize on Use, Program Manager option, 87–88
Mode, defined, 12

Mouse, 10, 384
    clicking, 11
    configuring in Control Panel, 97, 118–120
    double clicking, 11
    dragging, 11
    installing using Windows Setup, 152
    pointer, 30
    pointing, 10
Move, defined, 12
Moving files, in File Manager, 167
Multitasking, 147
    specifying in PIFs, 348

N
Network, 385
    configuring in Control Panel, 97, 126,
    configuring using Windows Setup, 152–153
    connect/disconnect net drive using File Manager, 169
    print queues, 201
Norton Utilities Advanced Edition, 66
Notepad, 64, 323–340
    and Clipboard, 325
    and word wrap, 325
    Edit menu, 325–326
    File menu, 324–325

O
Operators, Calculator, 272–273
Option button, defined, 33

P
PCX files, 205, 218, 234
PIF Editor, 64, 341–350
Paint programs, defined, 217
Paintbrush, 64, 120, 124, 217–250
    and Clipboard, 220, 235–236
    and text, 238–240

    changing colors, 224, 242–243
    changing file formats, 234
    cursor position, 238
    drawing boxes and circles, 228
    drawing lines, 225–227
    Edit menu, 234–235
    File menu, 229–233
    Linesize box, 219
    manipulating graphic images, 240–241, 243–246
    Options menu, 241–243
    Palette, 219
    Pick menu, 240–241
    print options, 233, 246–247
    Toolbox, 218, 220–223, 238,
    Undo, 235
    View menu, 236
Pattern, 121–124
Pitch, defined, 111
Pixel, 385
Point size, 111, 386
Ports, 131, 386
    configuring in Control Panel, 97, 116–118
PostScript printer, 195
    configuring, 135–137
Print Manager, 63, 128, 195–204
    and non-Windows applications, 196–197
    and warning messages, 200
    Options menu, 199
    View menu, 201
Print options, in Paintbrush, 233
Print queue, 197, 386
Printer buffer, 195
Printer drivers, 126–127, 387
Printer, 387
    configuring in Control Panel, 98, 126–138, 203
    emulations, 23
    installing using Windows Setup, 23

Printer problems, troubleshooting, 202

Program Information Files, 24, 385

   386 enhanced options, 346–349

   created during Windows Setup, 341

   memory requirements, 344–345

   optional parameters, 343–344

   video mode, 344

Program Manager, 45, 55–95

   adding program items, 153–156

   adding program items using File Manager, 189–190

   and application icons, 57

   File menu, 86–87

   help, 91–93

   Options menu, 87–88

   resizing windows, 58–59

   Windows menu, 88–89

Pruning and grafting, 191

R

RAM disk, 20–21, 161, 367

Recorder, 64, 350–355

   File menu, 351

   Macro menu, 351–352

   Options menu, 351

Renaming files, in File Manager, 167, 183–184

Restore button, 30

Reversi, 307–311

   Game menu, 309–310

   in Program Manager Games Group, 65

   skill levels, 309

   Skills menu, 309

S

SMARTDRV.SYS, 20

   incompatibility with certain hard disks, 16–17

SYSTEM.INI, 330

Saturation, 108

Scroll bars, 31

Search and replace, in Write, 263–265

Search command, in File Manager, 167, 179–181

Select, defined, 13

Setup, Windows, 17–25, 149–158

   adding program items, 76–79, 153–156

   and AUTOEXEC.BAT, 19

   and BUFFERS command, 21

   and CONFIG.SYS, 20–22

   changing default hardware settings, 18

   in Program Manager Main Group, 63

   installing applications, 23–25

   installing printers, 22–23

   problems with, 157

Sizing Grid, adjusting in Control Panel, 121, 126

Solitaire, 65, 312–322

   Game menu, 314

   options, 314–316

   scoring, 316–317

Sorting files, in File Manager, 172

Sound, setting in Control Panel, 98, 146

Swap files, 40–44, 367, 388

   creating, 41–44

   recommended size, 43

System message, defined, 33

T

Task List, 29, 211–214

Terminal, 64, 355–361

   File menu, 356

   Phone menu, 359

   requirements, 8

   Settings menu, 357–359

   Transfers menu, 359

Terminate-and-stay-resident programs, 365, 366

Text box, defined, 32

Tiling windows, 61–62, 388
    in File Manager, 174
    in Program Manager, 88
    using Task List, 213
Title bar, 29–30
Typeface, defined, 111

U
Undo, in Paintbrush, 235

V
Video mode, 389
    specifying in PIFs, 344

W
WIN.INI, described, 330–338
Wallpaper, 121, 124–125, 390
Warning messages, Print Manager, 200
Window elements, 390–391
Windows
    386 enhanced mode, 6–8, 22, 39–40,
        373, 391
    cursor movement and editing, 35–36
    defined, 13
    early versions, 4–5, 363
    exiting, 51–52
    improving performance, 366–368
    modes, 391
    moving a window, 46–47
    real mode, 6–8, 39, 363, 391
    reducing a window to an icon, 47–48
    requirements, 7–8, 16
    resizing windows, 48–50
    restoring a window, 50–51
    standard mode, 6–8, 22, 39, 391
    startup options, 40, 44
Windows/286, 4–5
Word Wrap, in Notepad, 325
WordStar, 66, 364–365

Write, 251–269
    adding graphics, 265
    and Clipboard, 265
    Character menu, 260
    entering and formatting text, 257
    formatting options, 252–254
    in Program Manager Accessories
        Group, 64
    keyboard shortcuts, 261–263
    print options, 265–267
    search and replace text, 263–265
    setting tabs, 255–257
    using the Ruler, 255–257, 260–261

X-Y-Z
XMS memory, 345
Zoom, in Paintbrush, 236–237

A Library of Technical References from M&T Books

NetWare User's Guide
by Edward Liebing

Endorsed by Novell, this book informs NetWare users of the services and utilities available, and how to effectively put them to use. Contained is a complete task-oriented reference that introduces users to NetWare and guides them through the basics of NetWare menu-driven utilities and command line utilities. Each utility is illustrated, thus providing a visual frame of reference. You will find general information about the utilities, then specific procedures to perform the task in mind. Utilities discussed include NetWare v2.1 through v2.15. For advanced users, a workstation troubleshooting section is included, describing the errors that occur. Two appendixes, describing briefly the services available in each NetWare menu or command line utility are also included.

Book only	Item #071-0	$24.95

Blueprint of a LAN
by Craig Chaiken

Blueprint of a LAN provides a hands-on introduction to microcomputer networks. For programmers, numerous valuable programming techniques are detailed. Network administrators will learn how to build and install LAN communication cables, configure and troubleshoot network hardware and software, and provide continuing support to users. Included are a very inexpensive zero-slot, star topology network, remote printer and file sharing, remote command execution, electronic mail, parallel processing support, high-level language support, and more. Also contained is the complete Intel 8086 assembly language source code that will help you build an inexpensive to install, local area network. An optional disk containing all source code is available.

Book & Disk (MS-DOS)	Item #066-4	$39.95
Book only	Item #052-4	$29.95

LAN Troubleshooting Handbook
by Mark A. Miller

This book is specifically for users and administrators who need to identify problems and maintain a LAN that is already installed. Topics include LAN standards, the OSI model, network documentation, LAN test equipment, cable system testing, and more. Addressed are specific issues associated with troubleshooting the four most popular LAN architectures: ARCNET, Token Ring, Ethernet, and StarLAN. Each are closely examined to pinpoint the problems unique to its design and the hardware. Handy checklists to assist in solving each architecture's unique network difficulties are also included.

Book & Disk (MS-DOS)	Item #056-7	**$39.95**
Book only	Item #054-0	**$29.95**

Building Local Area Networks with Novell's NetWare
by Patrick H. Corrigan and Aisling Guy

From the basic components to complete network installation, here is the practical guide that PC system integrators will need to build and implement PC LANs in this rapidly growing market. The specifics of building and maintaining PC LANs, including hardware configurations, software development, cabling, selection criteria, installation, and on-going management are described in a clear "how-to" manner with numerous illustrations and sample LAN management forms. *Building Local Area Networks* gives particular emphasis to Novell's NetWare, Version 2.1. Additional topics covered include the OS/2 LAN manager, Tops, Banyan VINES, internetworking, host computer gateways, and multisystem networks that link PCs, Apples, and mainframes.

Book & Disk (MS-DOS)	Item #025-7	**$39.95**
Book only	Item #010-9	**$29.95**

NetWare Supervisor's Guide
by John T. McCann, Adam T. Ruef, and Steven L. Guengerich

Written for network administrators, consultants, installers, and power users of all versions of NetWare, including NetWare 386. Where other books provide information on using NetWare at a workstation level, this definitive reference focuses on how to administer NetWare. Contained are numerous examples which include understanding and using NetWare's undocumented commands and utilities, implementing system fault tolerant LANs, refining installation parameters to improve network performance, and more.

Book only   Item #111-3   **$24.95**

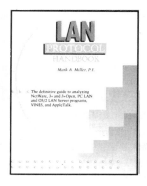

LAN Protocol Handbook
by Mark A. Miller, P.E.

Requisite reading for all network administrators and software developers needing in-depth knowledge of the internal protocols of the most popular network software. It illustrates the techniques of protocol analysis—the step-by-step process of unraveling LAN software failures. Detailed are how Ethernet, IEEE 802.3, IEEE 802.5, and ARCNET networks transmit frames of information between workstations. From that foundation, it presents LAN performnce measurements, protocol analysis methods, and protocol analyzer products. Individual chapters thoroughly discuss Novell's NetWare, 3Com's 3+ and 3+Open, IBM Token-Ring related protocols, and more!

Book only   Item 099-0   **$34.95**

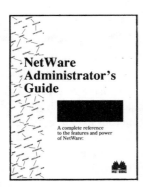

NetWare Administrator's Guide
by Russell Frye

This comprehensive guide is for all NetWare administrators responsible for the daily management of a NetWare network. Through in-depth discussions and detailed explanations, administrators will learn how to increase their network's performance and simplify file server management. All utilities available from the console are thoroughly examined. Readers will learn how to link a NetWare network to other networks, set up and manage remote access services, keep track of cabling layouts, monitor network operations, manage shared resources, and much more.

Book only   **Item #125-3**   **$34.95**

LAN Primer
An Introduction to Local Area Networks
by Greg Nunemacher

A complete introduction to local area networks (LANs), this book is a must for anyone who needs to know basic LAN principles. It includes a complete overview of LANs, clearly defining what a LAN is, the functions of a LAN, and how LANs fit into the field of telecommunications. The author discusses the specifics of building a LAN, including the required hardware and software, an overview of the types of products available, deciding what products to purchase, and assembling the pieces into a working LAN system. LAN Basics also includes case studies that illustrate how LAN principles work. Particular focus is given to ethernet and Token-Ring. Approx. 240 pp.

Book only   **Item #127-X**   **$24.95**

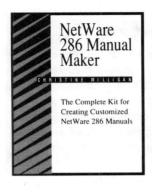

The Complete Kit for
Creating Customized
NetWare 286 Manuals

The NetWare Manual Makers
Complete Kits for Creating Customized NetWare Manuals

Developed to meet the tremendous demand for customized manuals, The NetWare Manual Makers enables the NetWare supervisor and administrator to create network training manuals specific to their individual sites. Administrators simply fill in the blanks on the template provided on disk and print the file to create customized manuals and command cards. Included are general "how-to" information on using a network, as well as fill-in-the-blank sections that help administrators explain and document procedures unique to a particular site. The disk files are provided in WordPerfect and ASCII formats. The WordPerfect file creates a manual that looks exactly like the one in the book. The ASCII file can be imported into any desktop publishing or word processing software.

The Complete Kit for
Creating Customized
NetWare 386 Manuals

The NetWare 286 Manual Maker
The Complete Kit for Creating Customized NetWare 286 Manuals
by Christine Milligan

Book/Disk	Item #119-9	$49.95

The NetWare 386 Manual Maker
The Complete Kit for Creating Customized NetWare 386 Manuals
by Christine Milligan

Book/Disk	Item #120-2	$49.95

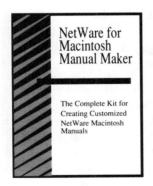

The Complete Kit for
Creating Customized
NetWare Macintosh
Manuals

The NetWare for Macintosh Manual Maker
The Complete Kit for Creating Customized NetWare for Macintosh Manuals
by Kelley J. P. Lindberg

Book/Disk	Item #130-X	$49.95

NetWare® Programmer's Guide

John T. McCann and
Steven L. Guengerich

NetWare Programmer's Guide
by John T. McCann and Steven L. Guengerich

Covered are all aspects of programming in the NetWare environment—from basic planning to complex application debugging. This book offers practical tips and tricks for creating and porting applications to NetWare. NetWare programmers developing simple applications for a single LAN or intricate programs for multi-site internetworked systems will find this book an invaluable reference to have on hand. All source code is available on disk in MS-PC/DOS format.

Book/Disk (MS-DOS)	**Item #154-7**	**$44.95**
Book only	**Item #152-0**	**$34.95**

The NetWare® Decoder:
A Dictionary of Messages and Commands

Russell Frye

The NetWare Decoder:
A Dictionary of Messages and Commands
by Russell Frye

The NetWare Decoder is a complete glossary of NetWare terms and provides network administrators and users quick and easy access to the information they need. This handy reference presents clear, easy-to-understand definitions that teach administrators and users what different network phrases and commands mean and how to use them. Numerous screen shots demonstrate the commands in use.

Book only	**Item #159-8**	**$24.95**

LAN Manager 2.0:
A Supervisor's Guide

Edward Liebing

LAN Manager 2.0: A Supervisor's Guide
by Edward Liebing

Here is a book for all supervisors, consultants, installers, and users of LAN Manager 2.0, Microsoft's powerful local area network. This book teaches readers how to approach and resolve problems faced by supervisors on a day-to-day basis. Through in-depth discussions, hands-on examples, and numerous tips and techniques, readers will learn everything they need to know to efficiently administer their LAN Manager network.

Book only:	**Item #160-1**	**$34.95**

1-800-533-4372 (in CA 1-800-356-2002)

Running WordPerfect on NetWare®

Greg McMurdie and
Joni Taylor

Running WordPerfect on Netware
by Greg McMurdie and Joni Taylor

Written by NetWare and WordPerfect experts, the book contains
practical information for both system administrators and network
WordPerfect users. Administrators will learn how to install,
maintain, and troubleshoot WordPerfect on the network. Users
will find answers to everyday questions such as how to print
over the network, how to handle error messages, and how to use
WordPerfect's tutorial on NetWare.

Book only   **Item #145-8**   **$29.95**

Graphics Programming in C
by Roger T. Stevens

All the information you need to program graphics in C, including source code, is presented. You'll find complete discussions
of ROM BIOS, VGA, EGA, and CGA inherent capabilities;
methods of displaying points on a screen; improved, faster
algorithms for drawing and filling lines, rectangles, rounded
polygons, ovals, circles, and arcs; graphic cursors; and much
more! Both Turbo C and Microsoft C are supported.

Book/Disk (MS-DOS)   **Item #019-4**   **$36.95**

Book only   **Item #018-4**   **$26.95**

Object-Oriented Programming for Presentation Manager
by William G. Wong

Written for programmers and developers interested in OS/2
Presentation Manager (PM), as well as DOS programmers who
are just beginning to explore Object-Oriented Programming
and PM. Topics include a thorough overview of Presentation
Manager and Object-Oriented Programming, Object-Oriented
Programming languages and techniques, developing Presentation Manager applications using C and OOP techniques, and
more.

Book/Disk (MS-DOS)   **Item #079-6**   **$39.95**

Book only   **Item #074-5**   **$29.95**

Fractal Programming in C
by Roger T. Stevens

If you are a programmer wanting to learn more about fractals, this book is for you. Learn how to create pictures that have both beauty and an underlying mathematical meaning. Included are over 50 black and white pictures and 32 full color fractals. All source code to reproduce these pictures is provided on disk in MS-DOS format and requires an IBM PC or clone with an EGA or VGA card, a color monitor, and a Turbo C, Quick C, or Microsoft C compiler.

Book/Disk (MS-DOS)	Item #038-9	**$36.95**
Book only	Item #037-0	**$26.95**

Fractal Programming in Turbo Pascal
by Roger T. Stevens

This book equips Turbo pascal programmers with the tools needed to program dynamic fractal curves. It is a reference that gives full attention to developing the reader's understanding of various fractal curves. More than 100 black and white and 32 full color fractals are illustrated throughout the book. All source code to reproduce the fractals is available on disk in MS/PC-DOS format. Requires a PC or clone with EGA or VGA, color monitor, and Turbo Pascal 4.0 or better.

Book/Disk (MS-DOS)	Item #107-5	**$39.95**
Book	Item #106-7	**$29.95**

Programming the 8514/A
by Jake Richter and Bud Smith

Written for programmers who want to develop software for the 8514/A, this complete reference includes information on both the 8514/A register and adapter Interface. Topics include an introduction to the 8514/A and its architecture, a discussion on programming to the applications interface specification, a complete section on programming the hardware, and more. A sample source code and programs are available on the optional disk in MS-DOS format.

Book/Disk (MS-DOS)	Item #103-2	**$39.95**
Book only	Item #086-9	**$29.95**

1-800-533-4372 (in CA 1-800-356-2002)

C++ Techniques and Applications
by Scott Robert Ladd

This book guides the professional programmer into the practical use of the C++ programming language—an object-oriented enhancement of the popular C programming language. The book contains three major sections. Part One introduces programmers to the syntax and general usage of C++ features; Part Two covers object-oriented programming goals and techniques; and Part Three focuses on the creation of applications.

Book/Disk (MS-DOS)	Item #076-1	$39.95
Book only	Item #075-3	$29.95

Fractal Programming and Ray Tracing with C++
by Roger T. Stevens

Finally, a book for C and C++ programmers who want to create complex and intriguing graphic designs. By the author of three best-selling graphics books, this new title thoroughly explains ray tracing, discussing how rays are traced, how objects are used to create ray-traced images, and how to create ray tracing programs. A complete ray tracing program, along with all of the source code is included. Contains 16 pages of full-color graphics.

Book/Disk (MS-DOS)	Item 118-0	$39.95
Book only	Item 134-2	$29.95

Advanced
Fractal
Programming
in C

Roger T. Stevens

Advanced Fractal Programming in C
by Roger T. Stevens

Programmers who enjoyed our best-selling *Fractal Programming in C* can move on to the next level of fractal programming with this book. Included are how-to instructions for creating many different types of fractal curves, including source code. Contains 16 pages of full-color fractals. All the source code to generate the fractals is available on an optional disk in MS/PC-DOS format.

Book/Disk (MS-DOS)	Item #097-4	$39.95
Book only	Item #096-6	$29.95

1-800-533-4372 (in CA 1-800-356-2002)

Using QuarkXPress
by Tim Meehan

Written in an enjoyable, easy-to-read style, this book addresses
the needs of both beginning and intermediate users. It includes
numerous illustrations and screen shots that guide readers through
comprehensive explanations of QuarkXPress, its potential and
real-world applications. Using QuarkXPress contains comprehensive explanations of the concepts, practices, and uses of
QuarkXPress with sample assignments of increasing complexity
that give readers actual hands-on experience using the program.

Book/Disk	**Item #129-6**	**$34.95**
Book only	**Item #128-8**	**$24.95**

An OPEN LOOK at UNIX
A Developer's Guide to X
by John David Miller

This is the book that explores the look and feel of the OPEN
LOOK graphical user interface, discussing its basic philiosophy,
environment, and user-interface elements. It includes a detailed
summary of the X Window System, introduces readers to object-
oriented programming, and shows how to develop commercial-
grade X applications. Dozens of OPEN LOOK program examples
are presented, along with nearly 13,000 lines of C code. All
source code is available on disk in 1.2 MB UNIX cpio format.

Book/Disk	**Item #058-3**	**$39.95**
Book only	**Item #057-5**	**$29.95**

Turbo C++ by Example
by Alex Lane

Turbo C++ by Example includes numerous code examples that
teach C programmers new to C++ how to skillfully program with
Borland's powerful Turbo C++. Detailed are key features of
Turbo C++ with code examples. Includes both Turbo Debugger
and Tools 2.0—a collection of tools used to design and debug
Turbo C++ programs, and Turbo Profiler. All listings available on
disk in MS/PC-DOS format.

Book/Disk (MS-DOS)	**Item #141-5**	**$36.95**
Book only	**Item #123-7**	**$26.95**

1-800-533-4372 (in CA 1-800-356-2002)

FoxPro: A Developer's Guide
Application Programming Techniques
by Pat Adams and Jordan Powell

Picking up where the FoxPro manual leaves off, this book shows programmers how to master the exceptional power of FoxPro. Useful tips and techniques, along with FoxPro's features, commands, and functions are all covered. Special attention is given to networking issues. Contains discussions on running FoxPro applications on both PCs and Macs that are on the same network. All source code is available on disk in MS/PC-DOS format.

Book/Disk (MS-DOS)	Item #084-2	$39.95
Book only	Item #083-4	$29.95

SQL and Relational Basics
by Fabian Pascal

SQL and Relational Basics was written to help PC users apply sound and general objectives to evaluating, selecting, and using database management systems. Misconceptions about relational data management and SQL are addressed and corrected. The book concentrates on the practical objectives of the relational approach as they pertain to the micro environment. Users will be able to design and correctly implement relational databases and applications, and work around product deficiencies to minimize future maintenance.

Book only:	Item #063-X	$28.95

A Small C Compiler, Second Edition
by James Hendrix

This is a solid resource for all programmers who want to learn to program in C. It thoroughly explains Small C's structure, syntax, and features. It succinctly covers the theory of compiler operation and design, discussing Small C's compatibility with C, explaining how to modify the compiler to generate new versions of itself, and more. A full-working Small C compiler, plus all the source code and files are provided on disk in MS/PC-DOS format.

Book/Disk (MS-DOS)	Item #124-5	$29.95

1-800-533-4372 (in CA 1-800-356-2002)

ORDER FORM

To Order: Return this form with your payment to M&T books, 501 Galveston Drive, Redwood City, CA 94063 or **call toll-free 1-800-533-4372 (in California, call 1-800-356-2002).**

ITEM #	DESCRIPTION	DISK	PRICE

Subtotal

CA residents add sales tax ＿＿%

Add $3.50 per item for shipping and handling

TOTAL

Charge my:
- ❏ **Visa**
- ❏ **MasterCard**
- ❏ **AmExpress**

- ❏ **Check enclosed, payable to M&T Books.**

CARD NO.

SIGNATURE   EXP. DATE

NAME

ADDRESS

CITY

STATE   ZIP

M&T GUARANTEE: If your are not satisfied with your order for any reason, return it to us within 25 days of receipt for a full refund. Note: Refunds on disks apply only when returned with book within guarantee period. Disks damaged in transit or defective will be promptly replaced, but cannot be exchanged for a disk from a different title.